# International Money & Debt

THE INTERNATIONAL CENTER FOR ECONOMIC GROWTH is a nonprofit research institute founded in 1985 to stimulate international discussions on economic policy, economic growth, and human development. The Center sponsors research, publications, and conferences in cooperation with an international network of correspondent institutes, which distribute publications of both the Center and other network members to policy audiences around the world. The Center's research and publications program is organized around five series: Sector Studies; Country Studies; Studies in Human Development and Social Welfare; Occasional Papers; and Reprints.

The Center is affiliated with the Institute for Contemporary Studies, and has headquarters in Panama and a home office in San Francisco, California.

For further information, please contact the International Center for Economic Growth, 243 Kearny Street, San Francisco, California, 94108, USA. Phone (415) 981-5353; Fax (415) 986-4878.

## ICEG Board of Overseers

Y. Seyyid Abdulai
*OPEC Fund for International Development, Austria*
Abdalatif Al-Hamad
*Arab Fund for Economic and Social Development, Kuwait*
Nicolás Ardito-Barletta
*Chairman, Panama*
Roy Ash
*Ash Capital Partnership, USA*
Raymond Barre
*France*
Roberto Campos
*National Senator, Brazil*
Carlos Manuel Castillo
*Costa Rica*
A. Lawrence Chickering
*International Center for Economic Growth, USA (ex officio)*
Gustavo Cisneros
*Organización Diego Cisneros, Venezuela*
Roberto Civita
*Editora Abril, Brazil*
A. W. Clausen
*BankAmerica Corp., USA*
Robert B. Hawkins, Jr.
*Institute for Contemporary Studies, USA*
Ivan Head
*International Development Research Centre (IDRC), Canada*

Woo-Choong Kim
*Daewoo Corp., Korea*
Adalbert Krieger Vasena
*Argentina*
Pedro Pablo Kuczynski
*USA*
Agustín Legorreta
*Inverlat S.A., Mexico*
Sol Linowitz
*Coudert Bros., USA*
Jorge Mejía Salazar
*Colombia*
Saburo Okita
*Institute for Domestic and International Policy Studies, Japan*
Tomás Pastoriza
*Banco de Desarrollo Dominicano, S.A., Dominican Republic*
John Petty
*Petty-FBW Associates, USA*
Donald Rumsfeld
*USA*
Stephan Schmidheiny
*Anova A.G., Switzerland*
Anthony M. Solomon
*S.G. Warburg (USA), Inc., USA*
J. J. Vallarino
*Consejo Interamericano de Comercio y Producción, Panama*
Amnuay Viravan
*Bangkok Bank Ltd., Thailand*
Paul A. Volcker
*James D. Wolfensohn, Inc., USA*

# International Money & Debt

## Challenges for the World Economy

Edited by
Rudiger Dornbusch
and Steve Marcus

An International Center for Economic Growth Publication

ICS PRESS
San Francisco, California

© 1991 International Center for Economic Growth

Printed in the United States of America. All rights reserved. No part of this book may be used or reproduced in any manner without written permission except in the case of brief quotations in critical articles and reviews.

Publication signifies that the Center believes a work to be a competent treatment worthy of public consideration. The findings, interpretations, and conclusions of a work are entirely those of the author and should not be attributed to ICEG, its affiliated organizations, its board of overseers, or organizations that support ICEG.

Inquiries, book orders, and catalog requests should be addressed to ICS Press, 243 Kearny Street, San Francisco, California 94108, USA. Telephone: (415) 981-5353; FAX: (415) 986-4878.

Distributed to the trade by
National Book Network, Lanham, Maryland.

Cover design by Lisa Tranter.

Index by Shirley Kessel.

—— Library of Congress Cataloging-in-Publication Data ——

International money and debt: challenges for the world economy / edited by Rudiger Dornbusch and Steve Marcus.
    p.   cm.
"An International Center for Economic Growth publication."
Includes bibliographical references (p.   ) and index.
ISBN 1-55815-098-6 (cloth). — ISBN 1-55815-084-6 (paper)
    1. Debts, External—Developing countries. 2. Debt relief—Developing countries. 3. Monetary policy. 4. International finance.
I. Dornbusch, Rudiger. II. Marcus, Steve.

HJ8899.I576 1991                                  90-4858
336.3'435'091724—dc20                             CIP

CONTENTS

|  |  |  |
|---|---|---|
| *List of Tables* | | vii |
| *List of Figures* | | viii |
| *Preface* | | ix |

PART ONE

CHAPTER 1 Introduction 3
Rudiger Dornbusch and Steve Marcus

PART TWO

CHAPTER 2 Recent Debt Developments 19
Stanley Fischer

CHAPTER 3 Decision Making at the Outset of the Debt Crisis: 27
Analytical and Conceptual Issues
Anne O. Krueger

CHAPTER 4 Problems of Policy Making at the Outset of the 51
Debt Crisis
Jesús Silva-Herzog

CHAPTER 5    The Colombian Debt Problem                                    61
             *Roberto Junguito*


             PART THREE

CHAPTER 6    The Changing Role of Central Banks in                         81
             International Policy Coordination
             *Alexander K. Swoboda*

CHAPTER 7    Economic Policy and Exchange Rates: Experience               101
             and Prospects
             *Wolfgang Rieke*

CHAPTER 8    Central Banks and International Cooperation                  119
             *Pierre Jacquet and Thierry de Montbrial*

CHAPTER 9    International Coordination of Economic Policies:             143
             Issues and Answers
             *Jacob A. Frenkel, Morris Goldstein,
             and Paul R. Masson*


             *Notes and References*                                       165
             *About the Contributors*                                     189
             *Index*                                                      193

LIST OF TABLES

| | | |
|---|---|---|
| Table 1.1 | Volatility | 6 |
| Table 1.2 | External Financing of Countries Experiencing Debt-Service Difficulties | 12 |
| Table 5.1 | Colombia: Basic Economic Data | 65 |
| Table 5.2 | Colombia: Balance of Payments | 66 |
| Table 5.3 | Colombia: External Debt | 73 |
| Table 6.1 | The Evolution of Current Accounts | 89 |
| Table 6.2 | Central Government Fiscal Balances | 90 |
| Table 6.3 | Long-Run Assignments | 95 |

# List of Figures

| | | |
|---|---|---|
| Figure 1.1 | United States–Germany: Variability of Real Exchange Rates | 5 |
| Figure 1.2 | U.S. Real Exchange Rate | 7 |
| Figure 1.3 | Ratio of U.S. Current Account to GNP | 8 |
| Figure 1.4 | Latin America's External Transfer | 11 |
| Figure 6.1 | Three Paths toward Current Account Equilibrium | 97 |

PREFACE

The world economy was challenged during the 1980s by the burden of debt in the developing countries and by an international monetary system characterized by highly volatile exchange rates. These challenges continue today, as the world community seeks long-term solutions to the problems of the debtor countries and as policy makers work to bring stability to the international financial market.

Since the debt crisis confronted the international consciousness in 1982, it has presented conceptual and practical difficulties for decision making. Not only the governments of the debtor countries, but the industrialized countries, too, have had to come to grips with the crisis. With the announcement of the Brady Plan in March 1989, management of international debt entered a new and hopeful phase; but the crisis is far from over. After an introduction in Part 1, current and former chief economists of the World Bank and two former finance ministers of debtor countries explore in Part 2 the policy responses that emerged during the 1980s, as well as the possible future course of international debt management.

In Part 3, eight distinguished contributors address problems of the international monetary system. They stress the need for policy coordination and examine the role of central banks in the flexible exchange rate system that prevails today. Political will and commitment will be required to establish true international coordination, in which countries undertake significant modification of their policies in recognition of economic interdependence.

Most of the essays in this book were originally prepared for a conference held in Paris on December 2 and 3, 1988, under the auspices of the Israeli International Institute for Applied Economic Policy Review. We hope they will provide important insights to aid future management of the debt crisis and development of cooperative and stabilizing international monetary policy.

Nicolás Ardito-Barletta<br>
General Director<br>
International Center for Economic Growth

Panama City, Panama
January 1991

# International
# Money & Debt

# Part One

RUDIGER DORNBUSCH
STEVE MARCUS                                         CHAPTER 1

# Introduction

World trade diplomacy, including the fate of the Uruguay Round of the General Agreement on Tariffs and Trade (GATT) and its implications for freer trade; the volatile dollar; and the debt overhang in the developing world are the three main preoccupations in international economic relations in the Western world. There is no reason to believe that these concerns will find their full solution in the near term: We are not working rapidly to establish a single world currency, and world trade is not becoming freer. Even if debt forgiveness came about, which most observers doubt, new, unsustainable debts would soon develop. Even so, there is great merit in studying these problems, probing and searching for ways to do better.

Following the Introduction, the book is organized in two more parts. In Part 2 four practitioners develop their views on the world debt problem. Anne Krueger and Stanley Fischer study world debt from the privileged vantage point of chief economist of the World Bank, a position each respectively occupied at some time during the debt crisis. Roberto Junguito and Jesús Silva-Herzog, the other authors, were directly involved in managing and negotiating the debt. Indeed, one might say

Herzog, as finance minister, fired the first shot (though he did not start the war) when he declared the Mexican moratorium in August 1982.

The discussion of world money in Part 3 brings together four essays that focus on the role of central banks in today's flexible rate system, where misalignment, halfhearted coordination, and intervention are the banks' daily bread. Here the contributions are especially interesting because they come from such different perspectives. Alexander Swoboda, writing from the Graduate Institute of International Studies, in Geneva, establishes the conceptual framework for the discussion of international money. He shows what can and cannot be done in international monetary policy—where the possibility of coordination lies and where frustration is inevitable.

Wolfgang Rieke offers his observations from the Deutsche Bundesbank, where his responsibilities for external issues give him an observation point that allows him to show us how the Bundesbank looks at the exchange rate system and how a central bank can preserve some independence in a highly interdependent and integrated international financial system.

Complementing Swoboda's and Rieke's essays is that by Pierre Jacquet and Thierry de Montbrial, who offer a French position on international money. French views on the topic, from Rueff and de Gaulle to Balladur and the present writers, always offer a very different perspective, reflecting anxiety about European independence and the need for checks on U.S. financial dominance. In the concluding chapter, Jacob Frenkel, Morris Goldstein, and Paul Masson discuss the scope, methods, and effects of international coordination of economic policy. These authors focus on the issue of how to identify gains from coordination, when the effects of policy are uncertain.

To introduce these essays, here are some broad considerations of how the dollar and debt problems appear today.

**The Dollar Problem**

The instability of financial markets is a mirror image of unstable economic policies, of policy differentials between countries, of instability in fundamentals, and of the very short horizons in asset markets. The topic is broad, ranging in interpretation from the international monetary system—fixed or flexible, with rules and coordination—to the specific level of exchange rates as they are likely to emerge from adjustments that are overdue, from trend inflation differentials, and from dynamic comparative advantage.

It is common to note the sharply increased volatility of exchange rates in the post-1973 monetary system. The variability of *real* exchange

| FIGURE 1.1 | United States–Germany: Variability of Real Exchange Rates (relative consumer prices in common currency) |

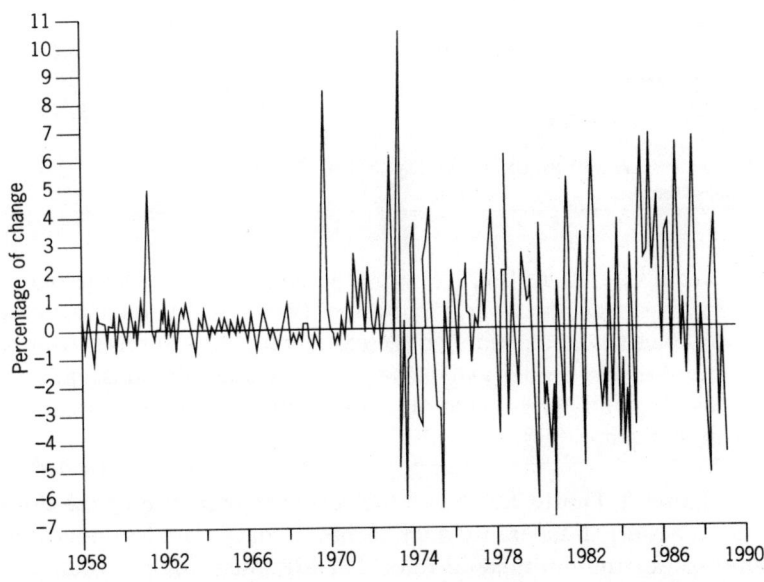

SOURCE: Author.

rates, which was practically absent under fixed rates, has become quite extraordinary, as Figure 1.1 makes clear for the U.S.-German case. Figure 1.1 shows the variability of real exchange rate changes between the United States and Germany. Under the Bretton Woods system, real exchange rates fluctuated moderately, and there were only rare spikes from adjustments in the fixed rates. Since 1973 volatility has been the rule. The discussion has not closed on the question of whether the volatility reflects increased variability of the *equilibrium* real exchange rate as a result of increased variability of underlying fundamentals or whether it simply reflects instability that is visited on foreign exchange markets by the conjunction of relatively sticky goods prices and highly volatile nominal exchange rates. There is no proof that there might not be an equilibrium model to explain these facts; but none has been offered, and the suspicion is by now pervasive that the volatility is contrived rather than of an equilibrium variety.

It is interesting to observe that the higher volatility of real exchange rates is accompanied by higher volatility of real commodity prices, but not by increased volatility of U.S. nominal short-term interest rates. This is shown in Table 1.1.

TABLE 1.1   Volatility (coefficient of variation)

|  | 1958–1971 | 1973–1989 | 1979–1989 |
|---|---|---|---|
| U.S.-German exchange rate[a] | | | |
| Real | 5.4 | 20.0 | 20.2 |
| Nominal | 4.9 | 17.1 | 19.7 |
| Real commodity prices[b] | 6.1 | 26.5 | 23.1 |
| U.S. interest rates | 37.4 | 34.1 | 31.4 |

a. Using consumer prices.
b. IMF index of non-oil commodity prices deflated by U.S. CPI.
SOURCE: Author.

It would be interesting to trace where else in the macroeconomy volatility has risen. Baxter and Stockman (1989) have claimed that other real variables have not exhibited increased variability. If this is true, we should not expect higher real exchange-rate variability on equilibrium grounds. After all, why would all the adjustment be in real prices, and none in real quantities?

**Misalignment.** Figure 1.2 shows the real exchange rate of the dollar (using the Morgan Guaranty data, including data from less-developed countries, for the multilateral rate). The argument for persistent misalignments centers on episodes such as 1980–1985 when the real value of the dollar appreciated without—at least in the end phase—any plausible basis in terms of fundamentals. The rising real value of the dollar in 1988 and 1989 was of much the same nature.

If one is to have a firm view of whether an exchange rate is or is not misaligned it is of course necessary to have *some* model of the equilibrium exchange rate. The common model uses, beyond the structural equations, the assumptions of informed, rational speculation. On this basis, whatever the market yields must be right, even if the outside (academic) observer cannot understand what possible fundamentals the market uses to warrant apparently aberrant moves. What equilibrium rates might be is wide open to discussion, but plausible limits might be set. One possible way to set limits was suggested by Krugman (1986), who used the sustainability of external deficits as a rough criterion.

Any suggestion that market rates are anything but equilibrium rates, which properly reflect fundamentals, immediately raises very serious methodological questions. It is tempting to reject the entire rational-speculation paradigm, but two difficulties emerge. First, rejection alone is not enough, since it has to be rejection in favor of an alternative paradigm, and the fact is that we do not have a better one. Second, the rational paradigm is methodologically very powerful: a good example is the peso problem, where events not observed for a

FIGURE 1.2   U.S. Real Exchange Rate (index 1980–1982 = 100)

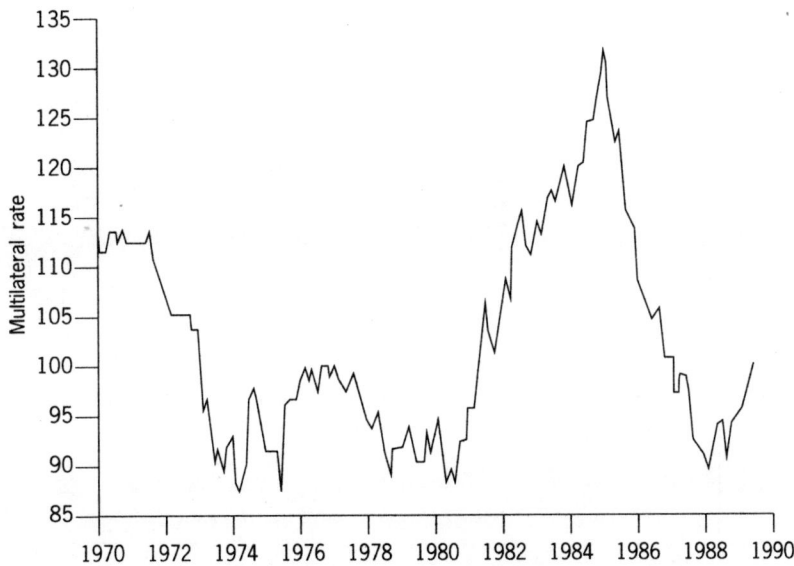

SOURCE: Morgan Guaranty Trading Company of New York.

decade in the data were nevertheless in the minds of speculators, who ultimately turned out to be rightly concerned about the possibility of peso devaluation.

Even though the rational paradigm is attractive, however, and no alternative is as yet available, there is now overwhelming evidence that the hypothesis of informed, rational speculation must be rejected. The important body of work by Frankel and Froot (1987), as well as the impressive evidence assembled by Ito (1988), simply rejects the rational paradigm as implausible.

The search is on for a better model, not only as a matter of intellectual curiosity, but for the more fundamental reason that if markets malfunction, intervention in one form or another becomes appropriate. Which form it should take depends on our understanding of how the market works. But even as the search for a better paradigm continues, it is tempting to look for immediate remedies. For some, specifically Williamson and Miller (1987), destabilizing speculation should be limited by target zones. I, as well as James Tobin, Lawrence Summers, and others, have suggested financial transactions taxes. That proposal has made few friends.

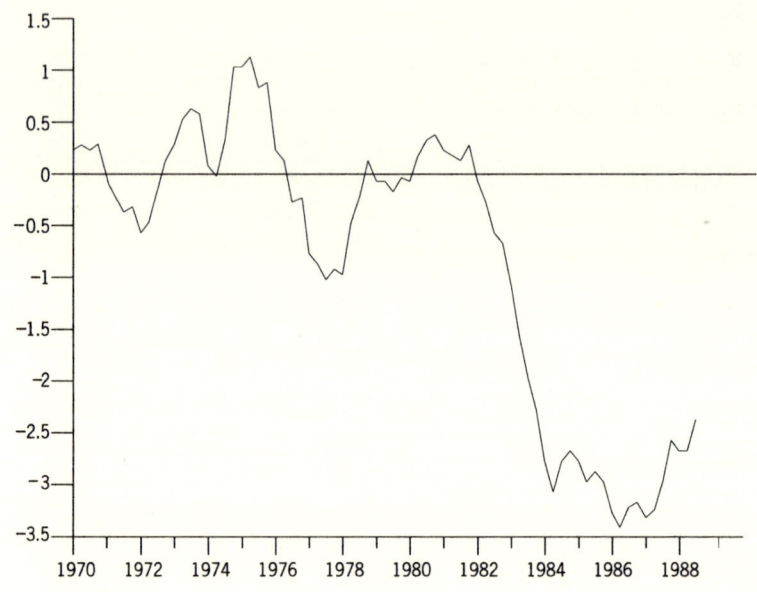

FIGURE 1.3   Ratio of U.S. Current Account to GNP

SOURCE: Author.

**Lack of an adjustment mechanism.** In the 1960s, under fixed exchange rates, the lack of a constraint on U.S. inflation policy was seen as the chief defect of flexible exchange rates. Deficit countries had to adjust because of reserve shortages; surplus countries had to adjust because of import inflation; but the United States could afford not to adjust, because it was running the system and its currency was the world's reserve asset (see Mundell 1968, 1971; Mundell and Swoboda 1968).

If flexible exchange rates were thought to resolve the adjustment problem, they certainly have failed to do so. Today the main concern of most observers is that U.S. fiscal policy is not effectively checked. The spillover effects of the fiscal stance are trade imbalances (see Figure 1.3); misalignment of real exchange rates; and, above all, the effect on real interest rates. These are widely seen as systemic problems. The reason the adjustment problem is present is that capital flows easily *over*finance trade imbalances. Capital flows dominate the movement of real exchange rates and thus create interdependence effects. This influence applies, as was well known from theory, to fiscal policy. Perhaps surprisingly, inflation or the stickiness of prices can make these statements about capital flows even more true for changes in monetary policy.

The lack of an adjustment mechanism is typically cited, not only for the United States, but also for Germany within the European Monetary System (EMS). The adjustment problem reflects the fact that economies are interdependent, whatever the exchange-rate regime may be. As long as trade imbalances are regarded as policy problems it can be acknowledged that there is an issue of coordination. One response to the coordination issue is to argue that imbalances are not a policy matter. According to this argument governments optimize fiscal policy intertemporally to achieve tax rate smoothing; under conditions of rational-expectations equilibrium economics monetary policy has no effect (except for noise and surprise); and fiscal policy likewise has no effect if households and economies are appropriately Ricardian. In such a world imbalances reflect equilibrium responses to intertemporal tastes and opportunities. There is no reason for policy to interfere with imbalances, since they are the outcome of intertemporal optimization decisions. One common rendition of this view is to argue that Japan's trade surpluses reflect predominantly demographic factors that will be self-correcting over the next half century. The alternative view is that imbalances do present a policy issue—if governments do not optimize, if money is not neutral, or if households are not exhaustively Ricardian. If any of these conditions are not met in even one country, it is enough to cause a worldwide coordination issue to arise.

From the now extensive work on coordination, it is clear that there are no easy answers. Differences in economic structure, beliefs about the model, policy objectives, even the structure of the policy coordination game, all come together, as Frankel and Rockett (1989) have shown, to keep the problem of adjustment and coordination wide open. Once again, unless there is a good model to explain what is wrong with the way the economy (including its policy makers) operates, it is difficult to determine how to do better. There is little evidence to support the equilibrium model, but it is hard to define the alternative, preferred paradigm. Without such a paradigmatic prescription, such as the one in Williamson and Miller (1987), it is hard to rationalize a plan for policy coordination. Discussion of the problem of coordination has rapidly come to the point where it must be recognized that there is certainly no easy answer.

In summary, it can be said that whatever the exchange-rate regime there is, in the words attributed to Yogi Berra, a sense of "déjà vu, all over again." Yet, the discussion of coordination is a new and potentially fruitful area of research. It highlights the principle that we ought to do better at managing the interdependent financial system, but it does not offer encouragement that the answers are easy.[1]

**The Debt Problem**

In August 1982 the debt crisis erupted when Mexico, experiencing the combined effects of imprudent borrowing and an unfavorable world macroeconomic environment, was unable to service its debt. Soon a host of countries—among them Brazil, Argentina, Bolivia, Venezuela, and the Philippines—followed suit. Today the World Bank counts seventeen countries experiencing difficulties in debt service and the list is not shrinking. Normalcy, which would require a favorable world economy and serious domestic adjustment, is simply not on the horizon.

In 1982 analysis of the debt crisis could reveal three reasons for the problems:

- excessive borrowing, with resources used to finance deficits, and consumption trade deficits at overvalued exchange rates

- overlending by banks, whose officers apparently believed that sovereign debt did not need to meet ordinary banking tests

- a sharp deterioration in the world economic environment, with a fall in commodity prices, strengthening of the dollar, record high interest rates, and a decline in demand for manufactured goods

Accepting this diagnosis made it easy to agree that muddling through was the appropriate response to the crisis. There was every expectation that the recession in the world economy would be followed by recovery, that high interest rates would decline in the aftermath of successful disinflation in the United States, and that commodity prices would show a cyclical recovery, as would exports from developing countries. On the home front, adjustment efforts in the debtor countries could not fail to improve their ability to service debts. Budget trimming and more competitive real exchange rates would enhance exports and trim imports, thus helping to close the foreign-exchange gap. If the confidence in these factors were not enough, there was an even stronger argument. If debtor countries did not make efforts to stay within the system they would lose access to the world capital market; but that would condemn their growth prospects, because, without external capital to supplement domestic saving, the outlook for capital formation would be dim.

INTRODUCTION

**The Brady Plan.** Today, eight years later, the optimism of 1982 is no longer warranted. Many of the debtor countries have undergone massive deterioration of their economies and have seen the clock turned back on social progress by a decade or more. Moreover, if the 1980s were a lost decade for these countries the 1990s are not assuredly better. It is true that there are exceptions: Chile (with the support of a repressive dictatorship) has been able to establish sound economics, though social progress has not done well; Colombia (with the help of drug money and conservative finance) has avoided high inflation and falling incomes; and Mexico (at a frightening cost in real wage cuts and output decline) has forced the budget into balance. The record of these countries, however, is countered by hyperinflation and the destruction of social stability in Argentina, in Brazil, in Peru. In much of Central and South America populism is rampant, and the ability to service debts recedes by the day.

Debt service since 1982 was achieved through a combination of involuntary lending by commercial banks, increased participation by multilateral institutions, and trade surpluses of debtor countries (see Figure 1.4). The commercial banks' increased exposure in the early phase of

FIGURE 1.4    Latin America's External Transfer (billions of U.S. dollars, 1977 prices)

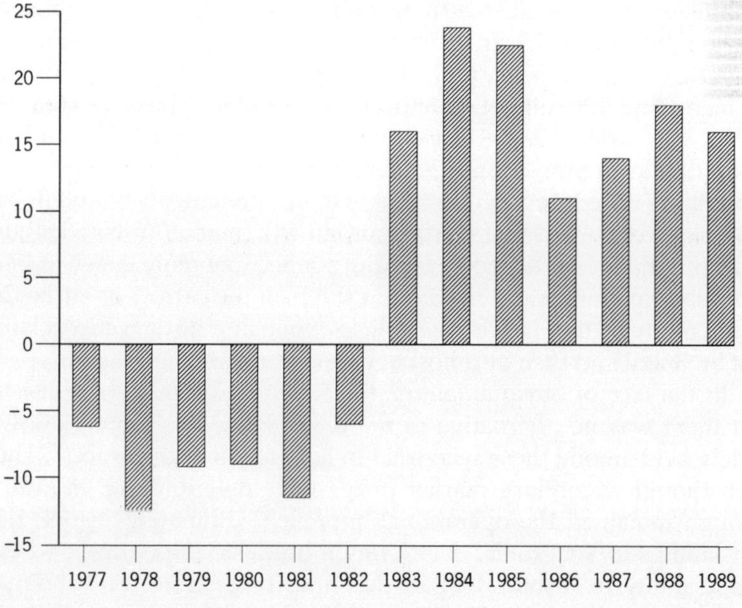

SOURCE: Author.

TABLE 1.2  External Financing of Countries Experiencing Debt-Service Difficulties
(averages of annual amounts, in billions of dollars)

|  | 1981–1982 | 1983–1988 | 1988 |
|---|---|---|---|
| Current account | −84.2 | −21.90 | −20.6 |
| Interest | −56.5 | −57.90 | −59.2 |
| Trade balance | −22.3 | 25.40 | 24.3 |
| Net external borrowing | 73.7 | 23.70 | 12.9 |
| Commercial banks | 56.8 | 0.03 | −12.4 |

SOURCE: IMF, *World Economic Outlook*, April 1989.

involuntary lending, however, has been offset by various forms of swap programs since then. As Table 1.2 strikingly shows, in the period 1983–1988 commercial banks actually did not increase their exposure.

While commercial banks withdrew (as much as they could) from lending, official agencies were increasingly drawn into the lending process. Under U.S. Treasury policy there was always a good excuse for another loan, be it to Argentina or to Brazil, even if the fundamentals of economic reform did not support the case. The World Bank estimates that the exposure of multilateral organizations alone increased from 8 percent to 16 percent of the liabilities of highly indebted countries.

It is difficult to tell at what point the expectation of an easy return to normality gave way to the realization that muddling through was not a winning strategy. A clear turning point, however, was definitely the plan announced by U.S. Treasury Secretary Baker in the fall of 1987. The Baker Plan was a response to the lack of growth in Latin America and to the increasing difficulty of structuring "new money" packages to make up for the difference between the amount of interest due and the amount that debtor countries were generating by trade surpluses. Banks were called upon to participate more spontaneously, and debtor countries were urged to undertake progrowth, market-oriented adjustment programs. Banks, however, did not become more eager to lend, and debtor countries did not find in the plan the carrots or sticks that would motivate them to change policies. Soon moratoria were declared, first by Brazil and then by a host of other countries.

In the face of obvious failure, the Reagan administration insisted that there was no alternative to the Baker Plan. The same view was widely held among those who tried to hold together the process. Thus, even though secondary market prices were deteriorating, muddling through remained the operational approach. Ultimately, it took riots and killings in Venezuela, deterioration in Mexico's political and economic ability to sustain debt service, and (possibly) second thoughts about the political implications of a stark deterioration of Latin America's prosperity to force a change in strategy. In the spring of 1989 the new secretary of the Treasury, Nicholas Brady, announced an important plan, a sharp change from the status quo. The elements of the Brady Plan were the following:

- Debt reduction was recognized as essential. The plan acknowledged that debts at existing levels could not be paid without putting social and economic stability in jeopardy. From growing out of debt, the policy shifted to getting rid of debt.

- Resources would be provided (on a case-by-case basis) to support market-based debt reduction through buy-backs or interest support. It was proposed that the multilateral institutions and Japan (not the U.S. taxpayer) would be the source.

- Multilateral institutions should begin paying for debt reduction, even if agreements with banks had not been concluded.

- Debtor countries would have to contribute to debt reduction by continued adjustment and by offering access to foreign investment, specifically in the form of debt-equity swaps and other menu items.

Initial expectations, chiefly from debtor countries and the naive, of a major debt write-off were very rapidly squashed. Support for the Brady Plan shrank as it became apparent that the plan had been ill prepared. Most foreign governments did not believe that there was a case for major public underwriting of debt reduction; and Japan, although it committed resources, did not offer enough to solve the problem. The multilaterals shrank from the opportunity to offer massive resources.

Even after the Mexico deal of 1989, the Brady Plan still has no final form. Banks are unwilling to take major write-offs without payment guarantees on the remaining loans; and debtor countries are in no better position to service debt, or buy back debt, than they have been at other times over the past few years. The U.S. Treasury has run out of bright ideas for other parties to foot the bill. Today, when a major gap in Mexico's financing requirements is unfilled, when there is strategic posturing by all parties, and when debt-service fatigue is pervasive, a 1930s-style suspension of debt service until further notice is not inconceivable and is perhaps even desirable.

If debts are to be paid, the most plausible solution continues to be the return of flight capital. Citizens of Latin American countries own substantial assets abroad—in the case of Mexico well over $50 billion and perhaps even $100 billion, if one allows for accumulated interest. If normality were achieved some of these monies would return and would provide the means for debt service. The priority for policy makers should therefore be to trigger the virtuous cycle of normality, prosperity, and stability. The current policy, even under the auspices of the Brady Plan, does not put the emphasis where it belongs. Premature debt service or buy-backs strain public finance, promote exchange rate instability in debtor countries, and thus hold off the return of flight capital.

**Economic reconstruction of Latin America.** There can be no doubt about appropriate policies—they are as old as the debt problem. Latin America must take four essential steps:

1. Tax reform is the first priority. Full and urgent attention should be given to reform of the tax system, especially of tax administration, to assure more substantial and more efficient revenue collection. In some countries governments print money outright rather than collecting income taxes; in other countries taxes are collected at extravagantly high rates from very few, while most people pay nothing. A broad-based tax system in which everybody pays (or faces jail) is likely to have moderate rates. In Latin America today, the rich pay little, and revenue comes from emergency taxation at extravagant rates on payrolls or exports. Economic development starts with serious, efficient taxation. Without a viable tax system, most Latin American countries, specifically Brazil and Argentina, have slipped back a decade or more in development. There is little doubt that the single most important issue in tax reform is an effective administration of the tax laws. Of course, that is almost countercultural in Latin America; but one must be encouraged by the progress in Spain, Italy, and now Mexico to believe that it is possible.

2. The public sector in much of Latin America should receive an emergency screening for privatization prospects. When governments are bankrupt they can hardly afford the indulgence of extremely inefficient public sectors. Simply closing many existing operations would advance the budget; selling them would provide the resources for and confidence in financial stability. There is no easy path. Inefficiency in the government sector requires spending cuts and privatization. A government might start with the telephone company and work down the list.

3. For the past few years all parties to the debt crisis have exhausted themselves, trying to find a "solution" to the debt problem. But there cannot be a solution unless debtors find a way to pay, creditors give up their claims, or taxpayers volunteer to share the burden. The extent of the pressure on Mexico and on the banks that was needed to reach an agreement in 1989 made it patently clear that neither side can or will give in and that multilateral institutions and governments are not offering enough incentives to close a deal. It is time to look for a new strategy.

External debt service must now take a back seat to economic development. The only way the large external debts can ultimately be serviced and paid is by a return of the large amount of flight capital Latin America has abroad. Luigi Einaudi, who stabilized the postwar economy in Italy, knew all about flight capital: he said of capitalists that they have the memories of elephants, the hearts of lambs, and the legs of hares. In many Latin American countries today, for every dollar of debt service a dollar leaves in capital flight; but capital is mobile, whereas labor is not. In this way the external drain sharply worsened poverty in Latin America in the 1980s. For capital to return, financial stability must come first; and stability has to be built, year after year. The best investment that creditor banks and governments can make is to foster fiscal discipline and economic growth.

Creditors need not be put off indefinitely, however. In many debtor countries it makes sense to engage them directly in the reconstruction effort. If banks were paid part of their interest in local currency, restricted to investments of the banks' choice in the debtor economy, they would be pushing investment rather than draining countries of dollars that are simply too scarce to transfer overseas. Interest recycling can be a powerful tool to bring together creditor and debtor interests in growth and stability.

4. Latin America must end its dismal neglect of education and technology. We are finding out today from Asia's supercompetitors just how critical education is in the process of economic development. By assigning low priority to education Latin America has been running down its capital—not only its physical but, far more critical, its human capital. There has also been a pervasive lack of investment in infrastructure, equipment, and technology. Latin America's investment rates in these areas are less than 20 percent of gross national product, whereas the Asian supercompetitors invest at rates above 30 percent. Both groups of countries are competing in world trade. This competition can go two ways: Better products, superior technology, market access, and finance are competitive assets. Countries short in these will have to turn to the weapon of last resort, low wages; and that is increasingly Latin America's fate.

**The lost decade.** The 1980s are seen as a lost decade for the economies of Latin America, and one fears the 1990s may go the same way. Income per capita declined more than 6.5 percent; and low investment in infrastructure, education, and productive capital cast a long shadow on Latin America's ability to make up the losses of the past decade and move ahead in the 1990s.

There is a positive counterpoint, however, in the establishment of democracy throughout Latin America. Brazil, Argentina, and Uruguay inaugurated democratic governments during the 1980s; and in Chile, the plebiscite signaled the end of Augusto Pinochet's military rule. In Mexico, the hotly contested election of 1988 made it plain that the political process in that country must become more open. Latin American democracy today stands up in the face of extraordinary challenges. In Argentina, economic distress led President Raúl Alfonsín to leave office in mid-1989, five months early, allowing the president-elect, Carlos Menem, to undertake his own program of economic reform. The transition was peaceful and democratic, without a putsch!

Democracy does not make it easier to run a tight economy. On the contrary, it encourages disorder by lending voice and power to those left out for decades. Building an economic democracy is tricky, and the temptations of populism are always present. Industrial countries' support can help Latin America build the economic foundations of stable democratic rule.

# Part Two

STANLEY FISCHER                                              CHAPTER 2

# Recent Debt Developments

In 1989, the international community turned an important corner in dealing with the debt crisis. The Brady Plan has put in place a framework for handling commercial debts, and there has also been progress in dealing with the official indebtedness of the poorest countries. We are a long way from the end of the crisis—many more problems will be encountered en route—but important progress has been achieved.

Before turning to the Brady Plan, I will review changes in the debt situation of the developing countries in 1988 and in 1989. The overall external debt of the developing countries actually declined slightly in 1988. Although that decline did not continue into 1989, total developing-country debt did not rise much in that year, either. Four factors have kept debt levels relatively constant:

*Net flows.* The most important factor in the leveling off of developing-country debt is the low level of net flows (new disbursements minus principal payments). In 1988 these net flows on long-term lending were one-third of their 1982 level.

*Dollar appreciation.* External debt is normally measured in dollars. Since the end of 1987, the dollar has held steady or appreciated against other major currencies in which developing-country external debt is denominated. The strength of the dollar has reduced the dollar value of non-dollar debt.

*Debt reduction.* An additional factor in the decline in debt levels in 1988 and 1989 was a small amount of debt reduction through buy-backs, debt swaps, and debt forgiveness. Our estimates indicate that buy-backs and swaps reduced developing country debt by $8.5 billion in 1988. Many debt swap programs slowed or stopped in 1989, so debt reduction through this channel was limited. As the new debt-reduction exercises reach the implementation stage in 1990, their effect on debt levels is likely to be far more substantial than that of previous programs.

*Debt forgiveness.* Debt forgiveness, almost entirely on concessional official development assistance (ODA) loans, totaled about $3 billion to $4 billion up to 1988. New plans for debt forgiveness by several major creditor countries can have an important impact on the debt levels of the beneficiary countries, mainly low-income African countries, but will have only a small impact on the overall external debt of developing countries. (I will return to the issues of debt reduction and debt forgiveness later.)

What do all these facts mean? Slow growth of debt could be an encouraging sign of progress in reducing the debt burden. Unfortunately that was not the case in 1988. Per capita real GNP growth in the seventeen highly indebted countries (HICs) was equal to *negative* 0.6 percent in 1988. Per capita real growth was also negative in sub-Saharan Africa, amounting to negative 0.4 percent. That region contains a large number of middle- and low-income countries with severe debt difficulties. Investment remains depressed in both groups of countries. Consequently, the leveling off of debt led to little or no improvement in the standard debt indicators.

That's the bad news. The good news is that in 1989 there was real progress in creating a framework that will enhance many severely indebted countries' prospects for growth and creditworthiness.

**Progress in Dealing with the Debt Crisis**

**The Brady Plan.** In the first six months after the Brady initiative was launched, following similar proposals from France and Japan, progress was surprisingly rapid. The World Bank and International Monetary

Fund moved quickly to put in place the operational guidelines for support of debt and debt service reduction. Since the Brady Plan was announced, the government of Japan has been generous in earmarking funds for parallel support. Altogether, an amount in excess of $30 billion is available in support of operations to reduce debt and debt service.

Two agreements involving debt relief along Brady lines, but very different in their details, have already been reached—those with Mexico and the Philippines. The tentative Mexican agreement was the first Brady agreement and represents a major success for the Brady Plan— but, more important, for Mexico and also, in the long run, I believe, for Mexico's creditors. Mexico's tentative agreement is at an advanced stage; the term sheet is in the hands of its commercial bank creditors. Subsequently, the Philippines and its creditor banks very quickly reached an agreement that will involve a significant amount of debt reduction; and that too is a success for the general Brady approach. So too is the fact that the details of these two agreements are different. Other negotiations, including those of Venezuela, Costa Rica, and Morocco, are under way. None of these negotiations is proceeding smoothly at present; but that is only to be expected, when the stakes for the creditors and the debtors are so large. The Mexican agreement was reached only with the active involvement of the U.S. government. It is possible that similar intervention will be needed to bring about agreements for other countries in which the burden is shared appropriately among the debtor country, the official creditors, and the banks.

The early results of the Mexican agreement are extremely encouraging. Our early World Bank calculations on the impact of the Brady Plan suggested that it would raise the level of GNP in the highly indebted countries (HICs) by 1 percent or less, after three years. That would have been very useful, and definite progress, but would not have represented a dramatic change in the debtors' growth prospects.

We could not factor into our calculations, however, the impact an agreement would have on confidence and on capital flight. Many analysts of the debt problem emphasized the effects of the large debt overhang on confidence and on investment. In the Mexican case, the signing of the agreement led to an immediate decline of twenty percentage points in the real interest rate, made possible in part by returning flight capital. The interest rate decline completely changes the growth prospects for Mexico. If it is maintained, the recent agreement will have a much larger impact on growth than we had earlier calculated. The point that has to be emphasized, however, is that calculations that show a large impact of the Mexican agreement on Mexico's growth prospects are based on the decline in the real interest rate that followed the agreement. That decline was in turn based on the assumption by investors that the new agreement will give Mexico financial stability for the next four to five years. It is therefore crucial to Mexican growth that the agreement be completed successfully.

What do the Mexican and Philippine agreements mean for other HICs? If other agreements provide an amount of debt relief comparable to that received by Mexico, taking into account the specific conditions of individual debtor countries, the benefits will be significant. The debt reduction could reach 10 to 20 percent of the total debt of beneficiary countries, reducing their interest burden by $4 billion to $8 billion, on the order of 0.5 to 1 percent of their GNP. That would certainly be progress. Whether more dramatic impacts on growth occur will depend on the extent to which domestic and foreign investors gain confidence in the stability of the medium-term financial outlook. Of course, not all the major debtors will be receiving Brady treatment soon—some of them still have a way to go in adopting the stabilization and adjustment programs that are a prerequisite for Brady treatment. But through the Brady Plan the international community now offers extra hope to countries that contemplate the absolute necessity of adopting new policies while fearing the short-run political costs of doing so.

The involvement of the World Bank in agreements for debt relief raises several fundamental questions. The most important is whether a development agency has any business getting involved in such financial transactions. The answer is clearly yes, for the debt crisis held back growth in the heavily indebted countries for most of the 1980s. The role the Bank is playing in the Brady Plan, attempting to reduce the impact of the overindebtedness of some of the member countries on their growth, is fully consistent with its basic developmental objectives. Indeed, more than that, I believe this is one of the most constructive measures the Bank could have taken to promote growth in many of the member countries, which could otherwise have entered the 1990s facing the grim prospect of continuing the economic decline of the 1980s. Second, is the Bank taking on risks that the commercial banks should bear? There is no question that the international financial institutions' (IFIs) share of the debt of the HICs has been rising and will continue to rise; but a limited increase in the Bank's share of the debt, *if it accompanies a reduction in the debtors' overall debt burden*, is, I believe, justifiable. The commercial banks, for their part, have to share the burden of reducing debt. They do not enjoy this process, and they would always be better off if the IFIs contributed more. Thus the pressure from the banks for more public money is entirely expected and understandable. That is not reason to think more public money should be put up, but it is reason to think that the guidelines adopted by the Bank and Fund boards to limit their involvement were essential—and that it is essential to observe them.

**Official debts.** The Brady Plan deals with commercial debt. Progress has also been made in dealing with official debts. Official creditors moved swiftly to implement the agreement reached at the 1988 Toronto summit benefiting low-income African countries. Thirteen African countries have rescheduled debt under this new set of terms. Creditors can choose from a menu of rescheduling options, comprising a significant forgiveness of the amount rescheduled, a reduction in the interest rate on the rescheduled amount, and very long-term reschedulings.[1]

By June 1989, thirteen sub-Saharan African (SSA) countries had benefited from the Toronto measures. The initial cash-flow relief from these measures is relatively small, yet the importance of the action should not be minimized. The process does slow the debt buildup, and the cash-flow reduction benefits build over time. As important, the principle of concessional rescheduling of official bilateral claims in severely indebted countries with sound adjustment programs has been established.

For poor, mainly African, countries, the forgiveness of ODA debts, mentioned earlier, has been extended. The United States began on October 1, 1989, to forgive $1 billion of loans to SSA countries. France has announced that it will forgive $2.3 billion to African countries. Germany has already cancelled DM2.6 billion of debt owed by SSA countries, and Canada has plans to write off more than C$500 million of African debt. Again, the cash-flow relief from these measures is not necessarily large. These debts carry low interest rates, and in many cases the payments coming due would have been rescheduled at concessional terms. Yet, the forgiveness has the effect of immediately and obviously reducing the debt of these countries, as well as marginally contributing to a slowing of the debt buildup.

All of the countries that received the terms agreed on at the Toronto summit and the Berlin IMF–World Bank meetings of 1988 are eligible for the Bank's Special Program of Assistance (SPA) for debt-distressed low-income African countries. Altogether, twenty-two countries are drawing on this program. The program gives these countries access to a larger share of concessional International Development Association (IDA) funds. In addition, bilateral donors have contributed $6.2 billion of concessional funds on a coordinated basis; of course, some of these funds might have been provided as aid to these countries in some other form. Bilateral donors have contributed, in varying degrees, in three ways: supplying the additional funds, enacting the Toronto-Berlin concessional reschedulings, and providing debt forgiveness. SPA countries are also eligible for the Fund's concessional Structural Adjustment Facility and Enhanced Structural Adjustment Facility, and many SPA countries have drawn or will draw on these facilities.

At their September 1989 annual meeting, the Bank's Board of Governors approved a new program under which $100 million of International Bank for Reconstruction and Development (IBRD) net income would be transferred to the IDA. The $100 million would be available to support repurchases of commercial bank debt in low-income countries (IDA-only countries), including the SPA countries. Although commercial bank debt is relatively small in most low-income countries, it often represents a disproportionately high share of debt service and can act as an impediment to access to needed trade credit, if payments are in arrears. Carefully designed repurchase programs can ensure that the burden of support is shared by all creditors.

These special programs—the Toronto-Berlin terms, further debt reduction from some of the donor countries, the Special Program of Assistance, the Bank's program for IDA debtors to commercial banks—have, in many low-income African countries, achieved a level of net resource inflows consistent with a resumption of growth; and the resources provided—highly concessional loans and fully concessional grants—fit the economic conditions of the recipient countries. Yet, adjustment is a medium-term undertaking in these low-income countries. For the programs to succeed, the extraordinary support must be maintained. The financing needs of these countries must be factored into the ninth replenishment of IDA, currently under negotiation.

These new tools for use in addressing the debt crisis are a major step forward; they have to be used to their fullest extent and as efficiently as possible. The debt crisis of the low-income African countries is far from over, however. These existing tools may need to be improved and expanded; and, in some cases, new tools may be needed.

**Other countries.** Two sets of countries have debt difficulties that fall outside the scope of the existing tools. The first is a set of severely indebted countries that fall in the lower range of the middle income category. Their debt is mainly official, so they can make only limited use of the Bank and Fund programs aimed at reducing commercial bank debt and debt service. Their income levels and, in some cases, their geographic location keep them outside of the Special Program of Assistance and ineligible for the Toronto-Berlin official rescheduling terms.[2] The success of adjustment programs in these countries can be put in jeopardy by the debt overhang. Some way of addressing their debt problems should be devised, whether through new programs or through special concessions on a case-by-case basis.

Another very small group of countries faces another sort of debt problem. These countries, including Sudan, Zambia, Liberia, and a few others, have large arrears to official multilateral creditors. Even if they adopt realistic adjustment programs, it is difficult for the Fund and the

Bank to extend the necessary external support. Not surprisingly, their adjustment efforts are discouraged by these bleak prospects. Solutions must be found to end the economic drift in these countries. At the same time, other debtor countries should take heed that neglect of debt servicing problems can cause these problems to build to an almost insurmountable barrier to sound economic growth.

**Beyond the Debt Crisis**

What comes next? Commercial bank lending on the scale of the past—certainly on the scale of the late 1970s—is inappropriate. Floating-rate sovereign lending passed all of the project risk and the interest rate risk to the borrower. In exchange, banks took on country risk at levels that turned out to be too high. A lot of attention is being given now to the fact that banks are withdrawing from the HICs. That is not a surprise, but rather an inevitable result of the simple fact that they were overextended in those countries. Of course, alternative sources of financing will be needed for the developing countries.

One alternative source of finance is official development assistance. The trends in ODA growth, in spite of the welcome generosity currently evident in Japanese development assistance, do not indicate that ODA will fill a major part of the funding needs of developing countries, beyond those of the poorest. In any case, ODA resources are not available for most middle-income developing countries.

Foreign direct investment can play a significant role, in the provision of resources in a manner that shares the risk between the host country and the source and especially because it brings with it foreign technology and management skills. The World Bank's Multilateral Investment Guarantee Agency (MIGA), which is shortly to issue its first guarantees, can help increase the flow of foreign direct investment. Further, as capital markets of developing countries deepen, and accounting and regulatory practices evolve, equity investment may play a greater role in development finance.

Creditors and developing country borrowers should consider new forms of financing as well. To be successful, these innovations should take advantage of natural risk-sharing matches between creditors and debtors. For example, commodity-price-indexed bonds may provide useful long-term hedging opportunities for commodity consumers and producers alike and may reduce the risks of debt default and renegotiation. For countries that are already creditworthy, the World Bank recently launched an experimental expanded cofinancing program designed to match developing country borrowers with appropriate lending partners. Once debtor countries return to creditworthiness, they will be eligible for support.

As financial stability and growth prospects in the debtor countries improve, some of the flight capital that has left those countries will return. Short-term hot flight capital may come back quickly, as it did in Mexico; but the bulk of what returns will come back later. We should not, however, expect all the capital invested abroad by residents of developing countries to return; nor would that be desirable, for sensible portfolio diversification implies that some assets should be held abroad.

## Summary

In 1989 there was much progress in dealing with the debt crisis, more than it would have been reasonable to anticipate in Berlin. The crisis is far from over. Recovery is, at best, getting started. Debtor countries remain vulnerable to external shocks, notably protectionism in export markets, higher real interest rates, and world recession. Some countries will take time to become eligible for the Brady Plan, and there will undoubtedly be reversals for some that have received Brady treatment. The debtor countries will have to try to avoid policy reversals. The international community must keep up the momentum, using to their fullest extent the tools we have and adding more, if they are found to be necessary. But we do seem to have changed direction, finally.

ANNE O. KRUEGER                                           CHAPTER 3

# Decision Making at the Outset of the Debt Crisis: Analytical and Conceptual Issues

To examine decision making at the outset of the debt crisis it is necessary to develop an understanding of the analytical issues surrounding debt and the relationships between "debt crises," on one hand, and "balance of payments crises," on the other. At any time, a country's level of indebtedness reflects the cumulation of that country's past borrowing and debt-servicing record. Whether debt-servicing obligations are sustainable or present significant difficulties depends in large part on the uses to which resources previously acquired through borrowing were put.

The best way to proceed is to start with the conventional wisdom on borrowing by developing countries and on the role of capital inflows in their development process. It then proves useful to trace the key characteristics of borrowing and debt as they evolved in the decade just before the outset of the debt crisis. That decade can be conveniently divided into two historical subperiods, 1973–1979 and 1980–1983. During the second of these periods the debt crisis started and was initially dealt with. The issues that arose and that are important to an understanding as perceived in 1982 and today are then discussed. Finally, some conceptual issues that underlay the organization of the multilateral institutions and that bore upon their capacity to respond are addressed.

## Conventional Wisdom about Capital Flows

**Capital flows to equalize rates of return.** From an economist's perspective, if capital flows from a region that has abundant capital and in which rates of return to capital are low to another region in which capital is scarce and rates of return are high, that capital flow can make everyone better off. In the capital-exporting country, total national income will be greater because of the higher return earned on capital abroad; in the capital-importing country, the resources financed by the capital flow can be invested in ways that will augment national product sufficiently to pay foreign owners of capital the return on their investment and still leave enough to increase domestic incomes.[1]

If, for example, construction of a railroad were financed by borrowing from abroad, the revenues from the railroad would normally be expected to finance the current payroll and other costs of operating the railroad as well as to finance depreciation and the payment of interest and principal on the debt. Assuming that the railroad became profitable, creditors would be repaid, and there would be an intramarginal gain within the country in which the railroad was built. Moreover, in an economy with satisfactory economic growth, one might expect other profitable investment opportunities to emerge as the railroad debt was being repaid. There would be additional borrowing to finance the new opportunities as long as domestic savings were less than the emerging investment opportunities at the prevailing real rate of interest. Thus, each loan would be repaid, but the volume of outstanding debt and debt servicing would increase over time (at least until domestic savings had risen sufficiently to finance desired new investment at the prevailing real rate of interest). With healthy growth, however, the ratios of debt service to exports and of debt service to GNP would level off, and rising debt-service obligations would be manageable out of rising incomes.

What could go wrong with this scenario? The same sorts of difficulties might arise in borrowing from abroad as in domestic borrowing. On one hand, the borrower might have been overly optimistic about the prospects for his project, or the economic environment might turn out to be less buoyant than he anticipated. On the other hand, the costs of debt service might be higher than expected if borrowing were undertaken at variable interest rates or if interest rates were fixed but the rate of inflation were lower than had been anticipated. In these circumstances, debtors could be faced with debt-servicing difficulties either because they misjudged the underlying economies of their investment or because an unexpected change in economic conditions produced a less profitable investment or more costly debt servicing than was expected.

When a citizen of one country borrows from a citizen of another, additional issues can arise, for, as already stated, a capital inflow represents the excess of domestic investment over domestic savings. Governments of borrowing countries can and do borrow and/or create conditions that make it attractive for their citizens to borrow. In this instance, the capital inflow may finance—directly or indirectly—governmental expenditures with low or even negative real rates of return.[2] In these circumstances, if capital inflows begin when existing debt-servicing obligations are relatively small, financing these obligations may initially be straightforward. Over time, however, mounting debt-servicing obligations can lead to difficulty. If government debt is involved, the fiscal burden of raising domestic resources with which to purchase foreign exchange may exert accelerating inflationary pressures on the economy; or the demand for foreign exchange to service debt may rise rapidly, causing difficulties with the balance of payments.[3]

**Capital flows as perceived by the architects of Bretton Woods.** This basic framework for understanding capital flows has been in the economist's tool kit for a long time and had been used to interpret capital flows from Europe to the lands of recent settlement in the nineteenth century. As we know well, however, the international financial system broke down during the 1930s and the Second World War. The planners of the Bretton Woods institutions believed that private international capital flows would not readily resume after the war. They also believed that war-devastated Europe and Japan would have high rates of return on capital relative to their domestic savings rates and that official capital flows (at market rates of interest) would therefore be desirable. To carry out this official lending, the International Bank for Reconstruction and Development (IBRD) was established. It was envisaged as an official source of long-term capital (at market rates of interest) for countries with high real rates of return on capital, when private capital markets did not provide it. In the early postwar years, the IBRD was a marginal source of capital to the war-destroyed economies, because Europe and Japan could profitably use far larger capital flows than the resources available to the IBRD could finance. American funds provided through the Marshall Plan largely eclipsed IBRD lending in the early postwar years.

As postwar recovery was achieved and rapid growth continued in Europe and Japan, the economic focus of the international community shifted to developing countries and the challenge of raising their living standards. It was natural to assume that developing countries, because of their low per capita incomes, would have low savings rates but high rates of return on capital. The underlying assumption held by most development economists was that developing countries would be unable to grow very much if their investment rates were confined to their domestic savings rates; therefore, it was concluded that foreign capital flows would be needed to supplement domestic savings. This "transfer of resources" was to permit a higher rate of investment, and therefore growth, than would otherwise be possible. For future reference, it should also be noted that it was widely assumed that sufficient transfer of resources and adequate investment rates would almost automatically ensure satisfactory rates of growth in per capita income.

Economists thought that private capital flows would not be forthcoming at early stages of development and that official capital flows would be necessary; hence, foreign aid and IBRD funding were regarded as essential for growth. It seemed possible that some countries at early stages of development would be unable to invest and earn rates of return equal to those prevailing in the long-term capital market. For this reason, economists believed that low-income countries would initially receive concessional capital flows and that as their per capita incomes rose they might become more able to borrow from official sources at market rates of interest. Finally, successfully developing countries were expected to be able, after a period of time, to rely increasingly on private international capital markets to finance the excess of investment over savings.[4]

Acting on these beliefs about development patterns, most industrial countries established foreign aid agencies; and most of the agencies extended grants or loans on highly concessional terms to developing countries. Then, in the late 1950s, the International Development Association (IDA) was formed to serve as a concessional window associated with the IBRD. IDA "credits" were long term, with long grace periods, and a "service charge" of less than 1 percent annually. The IBRD and IDA together became known as the World Bank. The Bank borrowed on the international capital market and in turn lent to those developing countries with relatively higher per capita incomes, while it extended IDA credits to low-income developing countries. In the 1950s, almost all capital flows to developing countries were official, and the great majority were concessional.

By the 1960s, several developing countries were growing very rapidly and had exceptionally high real rates of return on investment. Some of them found it in their interest to supplement domestic savings and foreign aid by borrowing from commercial banks. With their high real rates of return, they had no significant difficulties in debt servicing and achieved rates of growth previously thought unattainable. As this happened, it appeared that conventional wisdom was indeed correct: the successful developing countries were relying less and less on official capital flows, and private lenders were willing and able profitably to finance investment projects beyond those supported by domestic savings.

## Lending and Capital Flows in the 1970s

As of the early 1970s, then, conventional wisdom appeared not only to be correct but to have been an excellent forecaster of trends in international capital flows. The private, international capital market had revived beyond all expectations of the Bretton Woods founders. Although capital flowed predominantly between North America and Europe, there were increasing flows of bank lending to the successful developing economies of East Asia.

For most developing countries, savings and investment rates had risen significantly in the 1960s, although foreign aid and other official flows were still financing investment, in excess of domestic savings, of 1–2 percent of GNP. Except in sub-Saharan Africa, where concessional aid financed as much as 60 percent of domestic investment in some countries, it appeared that private capital flows would begin to supplant official flows and to augment rising domestic savings rates in more and more countries as their growth continued.

**1973–74 and its aftermath.** The tumultuous events of 1973–74 abruptly changed the international economic situation. The sparsely populated oil-exporting countries found themselves with large current account surpluses that they chose to use, at least for the first few years after 1973, to acquire short-term assets. At first, they deposited their excess receipts in the commercial banks, primarily in London and New York. Although the industrial countries incurred current account deficits in 1974, they returned to surplus positions in 1975. By contrast, many of the oil-importing developing countries did not. The commercial banks then found that they had excess liquidity and that demand for that liquidity came from one major source: the developing countries.

In one sense, the commercial banks did a very smooth job of recycling the oil revenues from the oil exporters to the oil-importing developing countries.[5] As the world economy experienced a structural shift that left an excess supply of savings in the oil-exporting countries and an excess demand for savings in the developing countries, the commercial banks had rapidly assumed their role as financial intermediary.

In another way, however, the situation was less satisfactory. Although some developing countries took immediate steps to encourage additional exports and discourage imports and thereby to restore their current accounts to levels compatible with sustained capital flows, other developing countries borrowed and did little to adjust to their altered terms of trade. The average current-account deficit of the developing countries as a group shifted from about $13 billion in 1970–1972 to $40 billion for 1975–1978.[6]

This rate of increase was unsustainable. It concealed large differences between countries. The East Asian exporters generally attempted to bring about real depreciations of their exchange rates and rapidly passed on the oil price increases to their domestic consumers. By these means, they discouraged domestic consumption as they encouraged exports, conservation, and the development of alternative energy sources. At the other extreme, some countries' governments failed to adjust the domestic price of oil at all and, instead, insulated their domestic economies from the altered terms of trade. The only immediate impacts of the oil price increase on their economies were heightened inflation and the increased current account deficit, the latter of course, financed by borrowing.

Several features of commercial banks' lending to developing countries in the 1970s should be noted:

- Most long-term lending was at fixed interest rates. Although the worldwide rate of inflation accelerated markedly in the aftermath of 1973–74, the acceleration was widely regarded as a temporary phenomenon, and the commercial banks did not immediately adjust. The result was that the rates of interest on most loans to developing countries in the 1975–1978 period were below the worldwide rate of dollar inflation; thus, the real rate of interest paid on loans was negative.

- After they discovered the reliability of the East Asian exporters as debtors, the commercial banks lent willingly to virtually all developing countries that wanted to borrow. Whether this was because the commercial bankers mistakenly regarded all developing country borrowers as being similar to the East Asian debtors, because the bankers believed that governmental guarantees (through both national governments and multilateral institutions) would assure debt servicing, or because the bankers failed to recognize the risks associated with lending on such a large scale is difficult to determine. Regardless of the reasons for it, however, the fact is that the developing countries' debts to commercial banks and their total nominal debt mounted rapidly.

- Even though total nominal debt was rising rapidly as new borrowing continued apace, most developing countries' export earnings were also growing rapidly because of worldwide inflation. Simultaneously, there was only a slow rise in the real value of debt outstanding, because of the erosion in real terms of the nominal stock of debt. There were several years in which the real value of debt outstanding actually fell, despite substantial borrowing by developing countries in those years.[7] As a result of these conditions, debt-servicing ratios rose only slightly and for many countries, they fell. For middle-income oil-importing countries, for example, the ratio of debt to exports stood at 1.11 in 1970, fell to .887 in 1974, and then rose to 1.207 by 1980. For major exporters of manufactures, the ratio fell from .915 in 1970 to .773 in 1980.[8]

- The small rise in debt-servicing ratios was the combined result of the reasonable debt-management efforts of some countries, the erosion in the real value of debt in some other countries, and the fact that some countries had experienced debt-servicing difficulties in the 1970s and were therefore constrained to reduce the amount they were borrowing. This last point bears directly on the experience of the 1980s.

By the end of the 1970s, a reasonable observer might well have concluded that many more developing countries were accessing private, international capital markets than had done so a decade earlier. The observer might further have concluded that, with occasional exceptions, most debtors had succeeded in managing their debt reasonably well. Certainly, aggregate-debt indicators did not strongly indicate any imminent difficulty. Indeed, not only did the conventional wisdom that capital flows benefited both rich and poor countries appear to be verified, but many observers attributed the growth in flows of private capital to the speed with which developing countries were becoming integrated into the world economy.

**Debt crises of the 1970s.** From their inception, the Bretton Woods institutions were expected to be the agencies that could channel capital flows for long-term development (the World Bank) and for response to short-term balance of payments difficulties (the International Monetary Fund). From 1945 to 1973, the Fund served as the international institution mediating exchange-rate and payments relationships among member countries.

Under a system of fixed exchange rates, developed countries could on occasion encounter balance of payments difficulties; if these continued for a period of time, private traders came to anticipate a change in the price of the currency of the deficit-incurring country. When they did so, they began selling that currency and buying assets denominated in foreign currencies. These speculative flows, in turn, often forced realignments of exchange rates. The IMF was charged with the responsibility of insuring that modifications in exchange rates were made only in response to longer-run, underlying changes. It was also the responsibility of the IMF to extend financing to countries whose payments difficulties were deemed to be temporary.

Even in the 1950s and 1960s, however, many developing countries attempted to contain excess demand for foreign exchange through exchange controls and restriction of imports rather than through adjustment of exchange rates. Over time, the restrictiveness of the policy regime governing trade and payments would increase as demand for foreign exchange rose more rapidly than foreign exchange earnings and as the authorities found it increasingly difficult to restrain imports to a sufficient degree.

In these circumstances, some governments would approach the International Monetary Fund and embark upon a stabilization program, agreeing to restraints upon the creation of domestic credit and receiving IMF funds to finance short-term current account deficits; at the same time, exchange rate changes were to induce increased flows of exports and of foreign exchange earnings in the longer run. It often happened, however, that the authorities, eager to maintain the exchange rate but pressed to finance imports deemed critical to development, would seek long-term loans from abroad, only to find lenders increasingly reluctant to extend further financing. When that happened, short-term finance was increasingly used, especially suppliers' credits. Often, the crisis point was reached only when debt-servicing payments became due for which no foreign exchange was available or when imports had virtually ceased.

Whereas speculative pressures on a currency were typically the factor precipitating exchange rate changes in developed economies, in a developing country, a sharp increase in indebtedness was frequently the last act of a finance minister desperate to defend the exchange rate. Parallel to that, inability to secure additional financing and to service debt was the factor which finally induced reluctant officials in developing countries to address some of their underlying economic problems in conjunction with the International Monetary Fund. As early as 1956, the International Monetary Fund dealt with an Argentine crisis in balance of payments, which was also a debt-servicing crisis. In 1958, Turkey was faced with an almost absolute cessation of imports and agreed to an IMF program.[9]

By the 1970s, many developing countries had experienced payments difficulties, followed by IMF programs. The typical policy-reform package contained several elements: ceilings on credit and possibly on other components of government monetary and expenditure policy were often negotiated; the exchange rate was usually significantly devalued; the import regime was often rationalized and, in some instances, liberalized; IMF credits—usually of three years' duration—were extended to the country; and the country's debt was very often rescheduled. Usually, the balance of payments' short-term response to policy reform was sufficient to permit repayment of IMF credits, although "stop-go" policies (alternating expansion and contraction) characterized a number of developing countries.[10]

In the middle and late 1970s, some developing countries that had earlier failed to adjust domestic economic signals after the oil price increase experienced a run-up in short-term debt and faced debt-servicing difficulty. The policy response of the international community was fairly automatic. For countries in need of immediate assistance to finance the resumption of imports—often an essential precondition to the later resumption of growth in foreign exchange earnings—interested aid donors met, usually under the leadership of the International Monetary Fund. In their meetings the donors agreed on levels of support—often including World Bank loans or IDA credits, depending on the country's per capita income level—that would be forthcoming once an IMF policy package had been negotiated. The countries' official creditors also met, to arrange debt rescheduling under the auspices of the Paris Club—the name given to the meetings because they typically were held in Paris with officials from the French Ministry of Finance serving as a secretariat.[11]

As already mentioned, however, commercial banks were not significant long-term creditors to developing countries other than the successful East Asian exporters until the 1970s. Even in 1976–1978, most developing countries' debt was to official creditors, although the fraction of new borrowing from private creditors was high. Because of this lending pattern, mechanisms by which commercial creditors might reschedule debt were unnecessary until the late 1970s. Only then did commercial obligations become a sufficiently large component of outstanding indebtedness that reschedulings began.

Starting in the late 1970s, there were a few "advisory committees" of private banks which negotiated rescheduling arrangements for debt to commercial banks once an IMF agreement was in place. The arrangements were, however, somewhat cumbersome; official debt was rescheduled under the Paris Club independently of private debt; the IMF, the World Bank, and foreign aid agencies were all party to consortium meetings to arrange for new funds; and an IMF program in any event was expected to be in place before any of these things happened. Since only a handful of reschedulings took place annually, however, the cumbersome mechanisms worked. Even in 1980, there were just three official (Liberia, Senegal, and Turkey) and three commercial (Nicaragua, Togo, and Zaire) reschedulings.

One other feature of IMF programs of the 1970s should be noted. From the inception of these programs, the assumption had been that "balance of payments" difficulties were temporary and that IMF financing was therefore needed only for a relatively short period, until a satisfactory balance of payments position was reached; hence, IMF lending was typically for a maximum of three years. Although the World Bank often lent to countries in support of their programs, these loans were generally intended to finance "projects"—particular development schemes. Even then, project financing was (and still is) mostly limited to covering the foreign exchange costs of a project. Indeed, World Bank loans were disbursed only as bills were received for expenditures incurred under a project.

## The Second Oil Price Increase and the Onset of the Debt Crisis

The second oil price increase was proportionately far smaller (50 percent contrasted with 400 percent) than the first; but its impact was almost as great, since in many oil-importing countries the share of oil in imports and in GNP was much larger in 1979–80 than it had been in 1973–74. The initial response to the second increase was not dissimilar to that in 1973–74. The worldwide inflation which had been accelerating throughout the late 1970s culminated in a worldwide recession, and most oil-importing countries experienced sharp increases in their current account deficits. These deficits were financed in part by running down reserves and in part by additional borrowing.

There were, however, dissimilarities in the underlying situation. In the industrial countries, the experience of 1973–74 convinced most leaders that traditional Keynesian techniques of demand management would simply result in inflation. The policy response was therefore to establish much tighter monetary policies than had followed the 1973–74 increase. The developing countries already had large deficits in the current account and had relatively much greater indebtedness than in 1973–74. A shift of the same magnitude in current account balances was therefore more dangerous than it had earlier been. It may also be mentioned that many developing countries had not even adjusted their economies to the altered energy prices of the 1970s, and their economies accordingly became even more maladjusted to the terms of trade confronting them than they had been in 1973–74.

To complicate matters further, the worldwide recession which followed the 1979–80 increase was not only longer and deeper than any earlier postwar recession had been; it was accompanied by a sharper and more lasting drop in real commodity prices than those of any earlier postwar recession. Moreover, the tight monetary policies of the industrial countries resulted in very high nominal rates of interest. By contrast with an average rate of interest of about 6 percent paid by Latin American countries in 1978 (with a worldwide rate of inflation of around 10 percent), the rate exceeded 14 percent by 1982. At the same time, prices received by oil-importing developing countries declined by 6 percent. This represented an increase of about 24 percent in the real rate of interest paid by developing countries that were reliant on private creditors.

Nonetheless, in 1981 and early 1982, commercial banks continued lending to developing countries, recycling oil revenues much as they had done in 1973–74. To be sure, they did so at variable interest rates, so that as outstanding debt was replaced by new borrowing, the portion of total debt at variable interest rates increased dramatically. External liabilities of developing countries, estimated to have been $610 billion at the end of 1980, rose to $702 billion by the end of 1981 and $775 billion by the end of 1982.[12] Thus, debt-servicing obligations rose because of increased debt outstanding, an increased interest rate, and a higher fraction of debt serviced at that higher interest rate.

In this climate, some countries encountered difficulties. Turkey, which had faced chronic economic difficulties after 1976, could not continue to finance imports, much less service debt, and announced a major program of economic reforms in January 1980. It was, and is, significant that the Turkish economic situation improved throughout the years 1982–1985 while other heavily indebted countries were experiencing major difficulties. Early in 1981, Brazil encountered serious economic difficulties and announced a significant economic reform program. Also in 1981, thirteen countries engaged in multilateral debt renegotiations, eight under the auspices of the Paris Club and five with private creditors. Of total rescheduled debt of $9.4 billion in 1980–81, $5.7 billion was Turkish debt—an indication of the relatively small size of other indebtedness problems. Although thirteen was a large number of countries contrasted with the average two to three reschedulings per year in the 1970s, the increase was still not perceived as anything other than a reflection of the unique situation in Turkey or a response to the declining commodity prices of the early 1980s.

The recognition that things were not normal emerged abruptly in August 1982, when the Mexican government announced that it could not continue voluntarily servicing its debt.[13] The Mexican situation differed dramatically from those leading to earlier such announcements in that the order of magnitude of the financing that would be necessary to resolve the problem was much higher than the resources commanded by the institutions that had dealt with the problem in the past. The Mexican announcement had an alarming impact also because Mexico, as an oil exporter, had been regarded as among the most creditworthy countries in the world. Had Mexico been a much smaller country or a country with a less solid reputation, the history of the debt crisis might have been far different.

The reactions to the Mexican crisis were twofold: as officials in the Mexican government, the U.S. government, and the International Monetary Fund grappled with the Mexican problem, the commercial banks reacted by reassessing their lending strategies with regard to other developing countries. That reassessment resulted in a sharp reduction in their willingness to lend; and a number of other developing countries found themselves suddenly faced with the prospect of current account deficits of 5–10 percent of GNP, and without identifiable sources of finance to meet those deficits, much less to continue servicing their debts on a voluntary basis. What was a Mexican problem in August 1982, therefore, was by mid-1983 a problem of most of the developing countries that had been borrowing from commercial banks.

## Response to the Debt Crisis

The issues that arose at the outset of the debt crisis[14] must be addressed at two levels. At one level, there were pragmatic questions surrounding the policy responses of interested parties to the Mexican, and then other countries', situation. At another level, there was the intellectual climate. Each, of course, influenced the other.

**The policy responses.** The response to the Mexican situation did much to establish a precedent that was followed by other countries when they experienced debt-servicing difficulties. In part, the response was a "logical" extension of practices of the past. In part, however, there was a situation calling for action; and those who were ready and willing to take the initiative did so.

The problem, as we have seen, centered on the magnitude of needed financing and on the fact that much of the outstanding debt was owed to commercial banks. An IMF agreement, followed by a Paris Club rescheduling, would simply not address the problem: too much of Mexico's debt was to commercial banks. For a variety of reasons, the possibility of Mexico's receiving sufficient official capital from the United States and other developed countries was not politically viable. The accusation of "bank bailout" would have been devastating.

Although the U.S. government was thus a concerned participant in discussions and an informed observer at every stage of deliberations about possible solutions, it was clear from the outset that the government either could not or would not consider taking the lead in resolving the Mexican debt problem.[15] Leadership was left to multilateral institutions. Both because the World Bank was still constrained to engage almost exclusively in project lending,[16] and because the International Monetary Fund was the institution more naturally attuned to issues involving exchange rates, macroeconomic issues, and debt rescheduling, the initiative fell to the International Monetary Fund.

The problem was, with hindsight, conceptually simple but practically exceedingly difficult. There were three components: First, Mexico had achieved its unsustainable level of debt by adopting overly expansionary monetary and fiscal policies; in particular, government expenditure programs were executed almost as if no budget constraint at all existed. Clearly, these policies would require alteration if a longer-term solution were to be found. Second, Mexico had to adjust its economy to induce more foreign-exchange earnings and to discourage imports, both to reduce the size of the current account deficit and to permit servicing of debt already outstanding. Third, since the shift in the current account could be accomplished only over time, it was clear that some new money and some rescheduling of existing debt would be essential to provide time for a program to work.[17]

Although Mexico's oil earnings were so large that the debt-service ratio was not a problem for Mexico, for other countries the expectation had to be that, were the three components put together in an appropriate package, economic growth would resume rapidly enough so that the problem of the debt would be resolved largely through growth in the denominators of debt-service ratios (exports and real GNP) and that borrowing and other capital inflows could resume, albeit at more moderate rates than those that had prevailed in 1975–1978 and 1980–1982.

The most innovative part of the response to Mexico's difficulties—and the part that captured attention—was the initiation of forced commercial bank reschedulings of outstanding private debt. In conjunction with the Mexican authorities, IMF officials, led by Managing Director Jacques de Larosière, in effect estimated the amount of new money that would be needed in support of the Mexican program. The IMF and the World Bank stood ready to lend a significant portion of that total; but they refused to do so until the advisory committee for Mexico, consisting of the large commercial bank creditors, had agreed to reschedule outstanding debt and had negotiated terms for the rollover and for new money with the Mexican authorities.

Several issues arose: First, there were at large number of smaller banks, whose consent to the agreement was essential if the large banks were not to find themselves in effect lending to repay the smaller banks; and it was extremely cumbersome to obtain the consent of these smaller banks. Second, rescheduling was, at least at first, done largely for the year in question—this left at issue the problem of what would be done in subsequent years. Third, determination of the amount of new money to support an IMF agreement-cum-rescheduling package was based almost entirely on considerations of what appeared to be feasible, which, in some instances, was arguably less than the minimum needed to permit the necessary adjustment and resource allocation without severe contraction of domestic economic activity.[18]

Once the Mexican solution was worked out, a pattern was set for other countries. On a case-by-case basis, the IMF took leadership in working out a package of policy reforms, committing some of its own resources. The policy package was often supported by lending commitments from the World Bank, the regional banks, and interested governments willing to provide foreign aid; however, these commitments did not go into effect until the commercial banks had rescheduled their outstanding obligations and provided new money for their component of the package.

During late 1982 and in 1983, a number of proposals for global solutions to the debt crisis surfaced. These proposals were based on the twin premises that developing countries' debts were so large as to be unpayable and that they were the result almost entirely of the worldwide recession and therefore had little to do with domestic economic policies within the developing countries. Within the international community, there was little support for global approaches. On one hand, there were insufficient resources in prospect for any such approach; on the other hand, some developing countries (such as those of South Asia) had avoided heavy indebtedness, and others (such as the East Asian exporters and Colombia) had become indebted but had undertaken unpopular policy measures to insure continued creditworthiness and maintenance of debt-servicing obligations. A final consideration was that there were obviously some governments whose policies were so unrealistic that support did not seem warranted, and any across-the-board scheme would have extended financing to those countries as well as to those that had adopted reasonable economic policy packages.[19]

**Understanding of the debt crisis.** When the Mexicans announced publicly that they could no longer voluntarily service their debt, the initial popular reaction was to fear an "international financial crisis."[20] It is doubtful whether this fear was well founded; but, in any event, the issues that arise for international decision making are largely centered on developing countries rather than the international financial system. For that reason, discussion here is centered on those issues.

Two interrelated questions arose at the outset of the debt crisis and appear to have underlain much of the initial reaction: First, was the inability to continue voluntary debt servicing a matter of liquidity or solvency? Second, were the debt-servicing difficulties of the developing countries due to external circumstances surrounding the worldwide recession, or were they the consequence of "overindebtedness"? Each of these issues had implications for the period of time during which, it was thought, a problem would continue to exist, and hence for the institutional responses that were forthcoming.

The liquidity-solvency distinction was well known from the literature of corporate finance. The literature stresses that there may be cash-flow problems when the underlying, long-run situation is fundamentally sound, or there may be long-run problems that are independent of the short-term situation. The issue was raised early in the debt crisis discussions. Those who focused on liquidity believed that short-term management was all that would be necessary, since, in the longer run, developing countries would be able to resume debt-servicing obligations. The distinction between liquidity and solvency is not immediately applicable to countries, for a number of reasons; but determining whether the problem was basically transitory or permanent in nature was central to conceptualization of the policy response.

Several factors suggested that developing countries' difficulties might be temporary: First, and most important, the nominal and real interest rates were high by historical standards and could reasonably be expected to drop. If one examined the interest obligations emanating from existing debt, the numbers did not appear overwhelming. Second, many observers were skeptical, even as late as 1984, that worldwide inflation had really been broken. If inflation were to resume, even with a considerable increase in nominal interest rates, it might reasonably be expected that developing countries' export earnings would grow rapidly, while the real value of the debt would be eroded. Third, even if inflation did not resume, it was reasonable to anticipate that commodity prices would rise significantly with worldwide recovery from the recession and that resumed growth of the Organization for Economic Cooperation and Development (OECD) countries and of world trade would permit a resumption of growth in the heavily indebted developing countries.[21]

The issue of whether the origins of the debt crisis were internal or external was not adequately posed early in the crisis. In fact, the question should have been, how much was the result of external, and how much of internal, factors? Many observers and commentators implicitly assumed causation by the worldwide recession. It is true that the recession had contributed greatly to the severity of the debtor countries' problems; however, an abrupt cutoff of lending, of the type experienced by those countries in 1983–84, would have resulted in major difficulties under any worldwide economic conditions. Underlying policy weaknesses had also contributed greatly to the crisis, yet there was little discussion or analysis of them. Even the International Monetary Fund, which had dealt for years with balance of payments crises and which was accustomed to imposing some degree of discipline on monetary, fiscal, trade, and exchange rate policies, negotiated for policy packages not dissimilar to those undertaken earlier.

The fact that so many developing countries encountered debt-servicing difficulties at the same time both reinforced the impression that worldwide circumstances were the chief culprit and caused observers to focus on external factors.[22] That some countries were not experiencing debt-servicing difficulties was barely noted. Possibly more surprising, the experience of Mexico, the first highly visible debtor, did not serve to call attention to the role of domestic economic policies in leading to the debt crisis.

## The Policy Response in Hindsight

As of early 1990, the problem of the heavily indebted, middle-income developing countries continues to command attention. Some countries have resumed growth and are creditworthy again, but they are few in number. More typically, domestic economic problems, debt-servicing difficulties, and slow economic growth have continued to plague the heavily indebted countries.

Since these problems persist, it may reasonably be asked what was wrong with expectations in 1983 and 1984 and what sorts of alternative policy responses or mechanisms the international community might have used to bring about a more rapid resolution of the debt problem and to permit more rapid economic growth of the developing countries. It may even be asked what sorts of mistakes continue to be made today.

**Errors in diagnosis.** With perfect hindsight, there appear to have been two related errors in diagnosis. The first error was the assumption that the debt crisis was similar in nature to earlier balance of payments crises of developing countries; the second was the assumption that the world would soon revert to the macroeconomic conditions that had prevailed in the 1970s, if not in the 1960s. The two errors were related in that the world of the 1960s and 1970s created an environment that was more permissive of economically inefficient policies.

It is not hard to find reasons why individual countries were treated as though their difficulties were similar to earlier balance of payments crises. First, the symptoms of the debt crisis and the balance of payments crises were very much the same. Second, the mechanisms and procedures for handling debt problems were in place, except for the question of the private banks; so it was logical to focus attention on finding means of dealing with debt to commercial banks. Third, had the world economic environment rapidly returned to its earlier state, the policy adjustments called for would certainly have been of lesser magnitude than they in fact were; but adjustment that sufficed in the buoyant 1960s and inflationary 1970s was insufficient in the slow-growth, low-inflation environment of the early 1980s.

That return to an inflationary environment was expected is also not surprising. The world had witnessed a rising trend rate of inflation ever since the early 1960s. There was little historical experience with efforts to reduce the inflation rate, and estimates of the costs of such efforts in terms of unemployment were necessarily conjectural. One could legitimately question whether it would be politically acceptable to incur these costs in the industrial countries. The prolonged and severe recession had a direct impact on the heavily indebted countries, but it also had a number of indirect effects. One was the rise of protectionist pressures in the developed countries, together with slower growth of trade relative to the GNPs of the OECD countries. Another was the depressed behavior of primary commodity prices long after they might normally have been expected to undergo a cyclical upturn.[23]

These optimistic assumptions led observers to underestimate the extent to which underlying economic policies were in need of change in most of the heavily indebted countries. Two years of credit ceilings and a one-time change of exchange rate were not sufficient. The underlying difficulties resulting from weak policies had built up over a substantial period of time; moreover, most of the economies of the heavily indebted countries had become used to sizable capital inflows. These new conditions called for a sustained cut in spending relative to output, together with significantly increased efficiency of that spending. Early thinking about capital flows had assumed that low ratios of investment to GNP would be the chief bottleneck to growth; yet developing countries had achieved a remarkable increase in savings and investment rates by the early 1980s, and yet growth rates had not risen. This in itself was clear evidence of increasing economic inefficiency in the uses to which new investment was put.[24]

Moreover, it was true in 1982–83 and remains true today that there is no widely accepted technique for diagnosing the nature and relative importance of policy mistakes, nor is there an easy means of estimating how much policy reform is enough. Although it is relatively simple to point to policy problems such as wasteful investment projects, lack of maintenance of transport and communications facilities, overly protective trade regimes, and suppression of producer prices in agriculture, it is not easy to estimate which policies need to be altered and by how much. Most economists would agree on the broad outlines of a prescription, but political leaders typically want to undertake the minimum that might do the job. In an uncertain world, minimum policy reform has a much higher probability of failure than more thoroughgoing changes; but without a stronger base of knowledge about policy effectiveness (and possibly even with it), there are bound to be political pressures to reduce the scope of changes.

To confound matters, there were strong imperatives from major industrial countries to resolve debt crises in particular countries.[25] In many instances, these pressures made the authorities in debtor countries less willing to consider policy reforms and resulted in lending to maintain short-run balance of payments viability in circumstances where it was apparent that the longer-run, underlying issues had not been addressed. This superficial resolution often produced a renewed crisis several years later, when all that had changed was that the country was more deeply in debt than it had been at the time of the previous crisis. For some countries, it is also true that policy reform was undertaken but that private capital flows were substantially slower to resume than had been anticipated. These events occurred far less frequently than the too-little–too-late approach to policy reform; but they happen often enough to show that the need for resources to support early stages of far-reaching reform programs was underestimated, at least by most commentators on the debt situation. Even when the magnitude of the debt-servicing obligations was recognized, the proposals were often for relief independent of policy reform efforts.

**Issues in International Decision Making**

As the preceding account suggests, there arose during the debt crisis a number of problems that were not—and some have not yet been—satisfactorily resolved. They center on key issues: (1) the role of the World Bank and the International Monetary Fund in dealing with policy issues in developing countries; (2) the need for policy reform in the debtor countries and, related to that, for willingness among the international community to abstain from assistance when reforms are not sufficiently forthcoming; (3) the relationship between private banks and official creditors and their part in developing mechanisms for rollover and rescheduling of long-term debt; (4) the link between debt-servicing prospects and the multilateral trading system; and (5) the debtor countries' needs for financing in support of their policy reform programs.

**Relationship between the World Bank and the IMF.** It will be recalled that historically the IMF dealt with balance of payments crises, whereas the World Bank concentrated on project lending. IMF lending was typically for a term of three to five years, reflecting the assumption that balance of payments difficulties would tend to be of short duration.

Even before the debt crisis, it was becoming evident to development economists everywhere that the policy environment in a particular country impacts significantly on the prospective rate of return for particular projects; however, the appeal of project financing in support of development was enormous.[26] It was only in the mid-1980s that the United States and other major industrial countries reluctantly abandoned their insistence on project financing by the World Bank. Even now, there is a strong presumption that more than two-thirds of all World Bank lending will be project-related, although the definition of "project" has become somewhat loose.

There is a range of economic policies that affect macroeconomic variables only indirectly and yet can be very important, especially in the longer-run. Some of these policies are those guiding the government investment program, current expenditures, the structure and scope of state economic enterprises, and credit availability and terms from commercial banks. Traditional IMF practice was to negotiate on credit creation and the size of overall budget deficits but to leave the cutbacks in investment programs and government expenditures and the composition of tax increases to individual governments. A difficulty with this practice was that in many countries confronting debt-crisis situations, the short-term policy responses were often the opposites of those conducive to longer-term reforms. Investment projects were halted in midstream, but expenditures on current consumption, which were less amenable to immediate cutbacks, were not touched. Import restrictions were tightened, when the dictates of long-term growth would have seen them relaxed; and exports were taxed for revenue, when they should instead have been encouraged.

In principal, the World Bank's structural adjustment programs are designed to address these issues; however, the relationship between Bank and Fund programs is inadequately understood and articulated.[27] A major question centers upon delineation of the appropriate role for each institution. This distinction is important, not so much for day-to-day operations involving individual countries, but to give the Bank and the Fund the political authority with which to carry out their tasks. It would also be highly desirable to have in place an agreement delineating each institution's role, should there arise another international financial problem of the magnitude of the debt crisis.

**Accepting the need for policy reform.** For reasons already discussed, it was natural for the international community to focus initially on assisting Mexico to meet her debt-servicing obligations. In the longer run and for most developing countries, however, the need is for a policy stance that will permit resumption of growth. Only in that environment can voluntary debt servicing and credit worthiness be reestablished while living standards rise.

Once it is accepted that significant policy reform is a prerequisite to resumed growth, it should follow that the major industrial countries will refrain from advocating support for inadequate policy packages and will be willing to witness a period of difficulty until a policy program is agreed upon with the IMF and the World Bank. To date, pressures have been placed on the international institutions to reach agreement with governments in the debtor countries regardless of the status of those countries' domestic economic policies. These pressures significantly impair the international community's ability to cope with the problems of governments that have unsustainable policies. The international institutions need strong support when they decide not to lend.

**Private banks and the need for longer-term debt rollovers.** A major institutional innovation of the debt crisis of 1982– 83 was that the Fund's managing director negotiated with private commercial banks to determine the amount of debt to be rescheduled and the amount of new money that was expected from them. Such an approach was essential at that time. As the initial crisis subsided, however, several difficulties with the mechanism for rescheduling debt to private banks became evident.[28] Rescheduling was a highly cumbersome procedure, in which the top economic officials from heavily indebted countries found themselves confronted with several hundred separate creditors. Although the private banks' advisory committees helped, the fact remained that insistence on keeping the small banks in the creditor pool meant that any single recalcitrant bank could delay an entire package.[29] Moreover, rescheduling packages were typically set up for one year or a few years. In 1984 a Multiyear Rescheduling Agreement (MYRA) for Mexico was negotiated, but there were both institutional and practical difficulties. The commercial banks wanted the IMF to provide assurances that the Mexican government was undertaking satisfactory economic policies; however, the IMF normally assumes such a task only when it has a standby agreement in place. In 1984, it was anticipated that the Mexican standby would not be renewed, and the IMF was reluctant to undertake a continuous monitoring role. Practical difficulties arose because of uncertainties about future oil prices and other variables. The 1984 MYRA in effect broke down when the oil price fell sharply in 1986.

What is needed is a rescheduling procedure in which authorities in the borrowing country can be assured of rollovers as long as they continue a reasonable economic policy. Such a conditional mechanism would provide incentives for continuing to carry out a policy package after a loan had initially been made[30] and would permit economic officials to focus on longer-term economic policies rather than on the next round of debt rescheduling.

**A missing trade-finance link.** It is unarguable that the heavily indebted developing countries as a group cannot increase their export earnings enough to resume growth and voluntary debt servicing unless the international economy, and especially world trade, grows rapidly enough to reward those whose policies are appropriate.[31] Yet, throughout the years when the industrial countries were focusing on the "problem of the debt," they were simultaneously undertaking protectionist measures that would make it more difficult to resolve debt-servicing problems. Not only was the Multifibre Arrangement, restricting imports of textiles and clothing, made more restrictive, but other so-called voluntary export restraints were imposed on developing countries, who were also accused of dumping and other unfair trade practices.

Throughout the years since 1982, economists have been unable to communicate successfully to the policy community the nature of the strong link between an open, multilateral international trading system and the developing economies' ability to grow and to resolve debt-servicing difficulties. Within the governments of most industrial countries, and among the international organizations, trade matters (including the Uruguay Round) are dealt with by officials other than those concerned with the financial or developmental aspects of the debt problem.

**Need for official resources.** In 1982–83, the IMF found itself rapidly exhausting its lending capacity. After a hard-fought battle, the United States Congress approved a quota increase for the Fund, but not without significant delays and considerable doubt as to whether the increase would be approved at all. By 1986, the Fund could no longer expand its lending; indeed, the prospect was that without a new source of finance, many heavily indebted countries would have to repay the Fund at a time when they could not do so and simultaneously finance their economies' normal needs for imports. The World Bank, too, was rapidly approaching the point where it could no longer expand its lending without a General Capital Increase. The Bank needed to receive the increase by 1987, but Congress did not pass enabling legislation until 1988. It is now a major question whether the international institutions, at their present level of funding, are equipped to deal with any significant financial emergency. Certainly the International Monetary Fund was not equipped to do so in 1982.

Among economists, there is also concern about the overall volume of resources available to developing countries. The magnitude of the current account deficits of developing countries, less interest payments, has shrunk substantially since the early 1980s. Although it may be possible for developing countries to alter their policies, service their debts, and still grow while incurring noninterest current account surpluses, they could clearly perform even more satisfactorily with more resources.

Some resources would be available if the industrial countries and international organizations could allocate support more on the basis of a recipient's economic prospects than they have been willing to do so far. There remains, however, a larger question of whether the resources committed to financing development are great enough, especially if the commercial banks do not reenter the international capital market as a source of finance.

## Conclusions

The debt crisis was much less a true crisis and much more a long-term problem than was initially supposed. When the problem burst upon international consciousness in 1982, the major issue was that the resources of the multilateral institutions were simply inadequate to the immediate task of ensuring sufficient resources for Mexico to service her debt and maintain necessary imports; the commercial creditors had to become involved. The immediate response, especially by the International Monetary Fund, was imaginative and appropriate to the immediate need. It did not provide a permanent solution, however, because the problem of the debt was less a short-term consequence of recession than a problem of domestic economic policies that were unsustainable in the long run in the harsher environment of the 1980s. The growth of the world economy has not been sufficient to offset these policy weaknesses, which have led to stagnation in many heavily indebted countries.

The world's ability to assist in restoring growth and resolving the debt crisis for the heavily indebted countries will be improved if the role of the World Bank and the IMF in policy reform can be articulated in an agreement given political support by the major industrial countries. Related to such an agreement, and perhaps even more fundamental, is that the industrial countries must recognize the need for policy reform and must support the international institutions when they refrain from lending until appropriate policy packages are in place.

The role of the commercial banks as creditors is surrounded by institutional questions, especially that of how to improve the mechanisms for rescheduling the loans of many smaller banks and provide for longer-term rescheduling subject to ascertaining that reform programs are adhered to. In this connection, it may be questioned whether the existing level of available financial support is adequate for the task.

Finally, it must be concluded that there is little, if any, prospect for resuming growth and restoring voluntary debt servicing and capital flows unless the world economy grows in the context of an open, multilateral trading system.

JESUS SILVA-HERZOG                    CHAPTER 4

# Problems of Policy Making at the Outset of the Debt Crisis

The debt crisis began on Friday, August 20, 1982, when the Mexican financial authorities announced their country's inability to continue normal payments on its public external debt to the international banking community. Nearly eight years later, the debt problem has still not been solved; and it continues to be an important element in the economic relations between creditor and debtor countries, threatening the stability of the international financial system and obstructing the development efforts of debtor countries. It remains a serious problem, affecting the lives of millions of people on our planet.

How did this situation come about? What policy discussions took place inside the Mexican government, with the financial authorities of the main industrial countries, and with the international private bankers, as the crisis developed? What kinds of internal policy decisions were made, and how were the first external negotiations carried out? The main purpose of this account is to respond to these questions. In my position as finance minister of Mexico at the outset of the crisis, I had an opportunity to play a prominent role in the events of those crucial days. In this chapter I will describe my experiences in the hope that others may learn some lessons from what happened and be prepared if they must face a similar crisis in the future.

## Origins of the Crisis

During almost four decades before the debt crisis, Mexico enjoyed rapid economic growth with internal and external monetary stability. In August 1976 the economy suffered a setback caused mainly by previous domestic expansionary policies. In that month, the Mexican peso was devalued after twenty-two years of stability. An economic adjustment program, undertaken in 1977 with the support of the International Monetary Fund, performed well during the first year but was interrupted by the discovery of important oil deposits. These discoveries brought an oil boom and led rapidly to a period of easy external borrowing. From 1978 through 1981 the Mexican economy grew at an average annual rate of 8.4 percent, in real terms. For the first time in this country's history it was possible to do everything, without looking to the financial constraints.

The value of oil exports increased in a few years from $1 billion to $16 billion. Furthermore, Mexico was specially attractive to the international banks, eager to place their excess liquid resources at profit margins above those of their domestic operations. Inflows of external credit amounted to more than $50 billion from 1977 to 1982. The enthusiastic attitude of bankers from many parts of the world made it easy for Mexico to borrow from abroad; but one of the more unfortunate consequences of this borrowing was that it allowed the government to avoid doing what was increasingly necessary, given the growing disequilibrium in the domestic economy and in its external relations.

In June 1981, confronted with the first decline in oil prices—caused by structural changes in the world market and the absence of domestic compensatory measures—the Mexican economy witnessed the beginning of an important capital flight. A climate of uncertainty and pessimism appeared, very different from the one prevailing just a few months before. Even so, expectations at that time were for higher oil prices; a number of prestigious sources were forecasting oil prices above fifty dollars a barrel. That explains the interpretation—in the end, erroneous—that the drop in the price of oil was temporary. It was not.

In 1981, the terms of trade deteriorated and international interest rates rose to levels without precedent. The Mexican peso remained overvalued, imports grew in an explosive manner, and oil exports were abruptly reduced. The cheapest thing one could buy in Mexico was the dollar. The enormous capital flight—around $9 billion in the second semester of 1981—was countered by rapid short-term foreign borrowing probably without any precedent in the world. During 1981, especially in the second half, around $23 billion were borrowed from the international markets by both the private and the public sectors, with a heavy concentration in three- or six-month maturities. The Mexican economic crisis, which exploded one year later, began in these events of 1981.

By February 1982 it had become impossible to avoid devaluation of the peso. The exchange rate movement, however, was not accompanied by other, complementary adjustment measures; for example, not long after the currency devaluation an increase in wages was announced. This was a time of uncertainty and mistrust within the society, and capital flight remained at high levels. Foreign banks began to realize the seriousness of the situation; obtaining new loans and renewing old ones became more and more difficult. As late as the end of June 1982, however, it was still possible to arrange—despite the reluctance of numerous commercial banks to participate—a jumbo loan of $2.5 billion, with relatively good terms and conditions. As a matter of fact, this loan was the last one before the crisis erupted. During the signing ceremony, confidence in the country's future was reiterated, as well as the positive attitude of the banks in contributing to the solution of the "transitory" problems that the country faced.

## Responses within the Government

Signals of the impending crisis became more and more evident, beginning in April: heavy capital flight, external disequilibrium, a growing government deficit, and upward pressures on domestic prices. Inside the government a sense of shock prevailed, as well as emotional reluctance to accept that the boom Mexico had enjoyed for four years had come to an end. After long and difficult internal negotiations between the government's economic team and elected officials, a new program of adjustment was announced at the end of April. There were to be reductions in government expenditures, increases in public revenues, and credit restrictions; however, absence of political will to carry out the program made it, in reality, a mere announcement of good intentions. The president of the republic did not accept at all the desirability of initiating talks with the IMF, although those conversations seemed every day more imminent. Intervention by the IMF was interpreted as a clear signal of failure and as an indication of serious difficulties in economic policy. That was what it had meant in the past, so the political resistance was understandable.

I and other officials who were responsible for the economic and financial management of the country knew that the explosion of the crisis was only a matter of time. At the beginning of May, we initiated discrete visits to Washington to talk with the United States financial authorities about the evolution of Mexican problems. On our side, there was a very clear understanding of the seriousness of the situation and its possible international consequences. Visits to the managing director of the International Monetary Fund, the secretary of the Treasury, the chairman of the Board of Governors of the Federal Reserve System, and a number of presidents of private banks were repeated every month. Without a doubt, this dialogue fostered a better understanding of the difficult Mexican circumstances and, at the proper time, made negotiations easier.

In the summer of 1982, the country lived in an atmosphere of uncertainty and lack of confidence. Exchange instability grew with the increasing transfers of Mexican pesos into foreign currency; every day there were long lines at the banks to buy dollars. The treasuries of the big companies, Mexican and foreign, by converting large amounts of currency, were an active and important factor in producing exchange instability. Government measures and pronouncements had no positive effect; rather, they produced negative reactions. It seemed as though all had lost their way.[1]

During June and July 1982, foreign borrowing became increasingly difficult and had ever-shorter maturities, as loans were signed to cover the borrowers' obligations to other banking institutions. Increased margins over the reference interest rate were adopted with myopia. International reserves of the Bank of Mexico were diminishing at an uninterrupted pace. Proceeds from a $700 million swap operation with the Federal Reserve were lost in a week; and during the last few weeks of July, the loss of reserves was at a level of $200 million–$300 million a day. What entered the country one day went out the following day. Confronted with a new and anguished situation, we maintained our decision to stay current in debt service. We believed we had to honor our commitments, since suspending payments could have provoked a negative reaction by the creditors and by the domestic private sector, with adverse consequences for the country. The situation was thought to be a liquidity problem, one of transitory character. It was never considered, by any one of the participants, that the problem was of a different character, with structural or more long-term elements.

In the first days of August, when a permanent reduction in international reserves was faced and when net reserves were already at a low level ($1.6 billion at the end of July compared with slightly over $5 billion in December of 1981), the decision was made to devalue the Mexican peso for the second time in six months. The positive impact of devaluation on the exchange market—again in the absence of complementary measures—was dissipated in a few days, and exchange speculation resumed. A week later, restrictions on the convertibility of bank deposits denominated in foreign currency were announced.[2] A dual system of exchange rates was established, and the exchange market was temporarily closed. At this point, financial programming of sources and uses of foreign exchange was done day by day, with frequent problems of coverage: "Tomorrow we have to pay $40 million to cover maturities due to banks X and Y; and we have only half of that amount. We need to borrow $20 million at twenty-four- or forty-eight-hour term from bank Z to cover our financial obligations. We will see, afterwards, how we solve the problem for the day after tomorrow." This was a dramatic and recurrent exercise, in which we used all available techniques on the financial menu. A few days before the crisis we placed in the London market an issue of government bonds at a very expensive cost.

**The Mexican Weekend**

On Friday, August 13, it became even clearer that we were at the point of losing all the liquid reserves of the central bank. It seemed possible that all options had been exhausted and that the only possible action was a unilateral moratorium. Hoping to find other alternatives, I placed an urgent call early in the morning to Donald Regan, secretary of the Treasury, and announced to him my immediate departure for Washington. I met early that afternoon with the secretary and his closest aides. He soon left the meeting to accompany President Reagan to Camp David; and as he said good-bye, he told me, "Hey, you really have a problem!" I responded, "No, Mr. Secretary, we both have a problem."

In a large meeting room later the same day, we began a more formal discussion that has become known as the Mexican Weekend. On the U.S. side, representatives of the State Department, National Security Council, Central Intelligence Agency, Office of Management and Budget, Energy Department, and, of course, the Federal Reserve had joined the group. On the Mexican side were the finance minister and representatives from the Bank of Mexico; the Mexican ambassador to the United States also attended. From the first moment, the participants clearly recognized the importance of the problem and its possible international consequences. We agreed on the need to design an emergency financial package to deal with what was seen as a liquidity problem. Mexico needed additional resources to cover immediate import needs and to fulfill external financial obligations, since it was crucial to be able to generate a climate of confidence within the country. Mexico's overall financial needs for the next few months were presented, discussed, and accepted. Then, gradually, in a joint effort, we designed the rescue package.

It was decided that a short-term bridge loan in the amount of $1.85 billion would be arranged from the industrial countries' central banks through the Bank for International Settlements.[3] Another element of the financial package was a special line of credit ($1 billion) from the Commodity Credit Corporation of the United States to finance food imports, mainly corn. We also arranged an "oil facility" for the same amount. It consisted essentially of prepayment by the United States, over the following twelve months, for purchases of Mexican oil for the strategic oil reserve. This operation was the most difficult and controversial of the package.

Meetings during the Mexican Weekend ended as late as four in the morning. The climate was definitely cordial, but it was tense. At my request, in view of the difficult discussions on the oil facility, President López Portillo sent the secretary of national patrimony and the general director of Pemex to join the negotiating team.

## Meeting with Private Bankers

On the morning of Saturday, the fourteenth of August, having recognized our inability to continue debt payments, I tried to get in touch with the presidents of the most important banks in the world, to let them know in advance our situation and intentions and to announce to them that I would visit New York the following Thursday. At the same time, Mexican Weekend participants were already preparing the meeting for Friday, the twentieth of August and invitations had been sent. We were able to establish contact—a difficult task on a summer weekend—with Chase Manhattan, Chemical Bank, Citibank, Morgan Guaranty Trust, Bank of Montreal, Manufacturers Hanover, Lloyds Bank, The Bank of Tokyo, Banque Nationale de Paris, and others. The banks' reactions were positive, in general, and helped to establish a constructive spirit of cooperation.

The meeting at the Treasury Department resumed Saturday afternoon and continued until very late at night. The U.S. authorities insisted on an excessive, in our view, front-end commission for the opening of the oil facility. Their position seemed to be that Mexico was in trouble and would have to pay a special price to get out of the hole. We saw their requirements as usury and their attitude as lacking the truly cooperative spirit appropriate between two neighboring countries. The size of the commission was not accepted by the Mexican group, and negotiations broke down on Sunday morning, August 15. After a conversation with the president of Mexico, we received instructions to return immediately to Mexico and to prepare the declaration of moratorium. "Let's have Rome fall into flames," said President López Portillo; perhaps the world was going to be different after such a decision. When we were ready to go to the airport, however, the U.S. Treasury Department called, accepting our position. This late acceptance did not eliminate the abusive attitude of the U.S. authorities. In this we are creditors of a debt that I hope some day will be repaid to Mexico. We went back to the negotiating table, where we agreed upon and signed a memorandum of understanding.

After a brief return to Mexico, we visited the major New York banks on Thursday, August 19. Tension predominated during the conversations, but there was also a constructive attitude toward the problem. The idea of establishing an advisory group of banks was developed gradually. It was a new situation for everyone, and we had to find the new paths.[4]

On Friday, August 20, we met at the Federal Reserve Bank of New York building, first with representatives of the fourteen banks that were to form the advisory group[5] and later with about 200 representatives of the international banking community. After a brief summary of the recent economic developments in Mexico, including the unfavorable external factors—the increase in interest rates, the drop in the volume and price of our main export products, and the interruption of credit flows—we requested a rollover of amortization payments for ninety days, beginning the following Monday, August 23. There was no other alternative; capital payments due on that day exceeded the size of our international reserves. We deliberately avoided the use of the word *moratorium*, and we assumed the compromise of remaining current in interest payments. We also announced additional domestic adjustment measures to correct the economic situation. The week before, we had used a good portion of the bridge loans to cover some arrears in interest payments so we could be completely current when we reached negotiations.

In a press conference at the end of the meeting, I thanked the banks for their understanding and acceptance of the Mexican proposal. The announcement was expected; the banks did not have an alternative. The following day, the press reported the meeting of the Mexican delegation and the banking community at the Federal Reserve Building in New York, and prices of U.S. bank stocks suffered a noticeable downturn. The debt crisis had officially begun.

**The Internal Decision Process**

During the first months of 1982, signs of the economic crisis became ever more evident. They seem especially clear now from a distance; however, the euphoria produced by the oil boom impeded officials' ability to see things realistically and objectively. As late as June of 1982, some high-level officials expected a 6 percent rate of economic growth for 1982, although some weeks earlier I had forecast zero growth for 1982. Inside the government there were conflicting positions, as in all governments.

On one side there were those—the majority—who thought that it was possible to maintain the economic expansion and resist the pressure of the financial constraints. On the other side were those who considered it necessary to initiate a profound domestic adjustment, to avoid more serious problems. The first group dominated fundamental economic decisions up to the dramatic events of June and July 1982—capital flight and loss of reserves, brought on by lack of confidence.

When the government was confronted with the permanent loss of international reserves, there was some discussion of a moratorium. There are even rumors that conversations took place with other Latin American countries to explore whether they might take unilateral or joint action; but these are only rumors. What I know, however, is that on the twelfth of August, the central bank, confronted with serious and deteriorating liquidity problems and in danger of losing all its reserves, prepared a telex to the financial community announcing a suspension of payments on the foreign debt.

In the weeks since June, I had established a special crisis group—with representatives of the Treasury, Bank of Mexico, and Nacional Financiera (the official lending institution of the Mexican federal government)—whose function was to identify, evaluate, and attend to especially difficult aspects of the developing crisis. It was within this group that the Central Bank made known its intentions. The proposed telex was considered clearly inconvenient; members of the crisis group suggested beginning formal talks with Washington, to acknowledge that the problem was not only financial but political in character. It was even suggested that there be conversations between the president of Mexico and the heads of state of the most important debtor and creditor countries. The latter conversations did not take place, but that they were suggested is a clear reflection that the problem had a political side from the beginning. Within the crisis group, the representatives of the Bank of Mexico were brought to recognize the political implications of their proposed action, and the telex was never sent. With a high sense of urgency and with previous acceptance by the main ministers of the economic cabinet, I presented the crisis group's position to the president. He gave the authorization, and a few hours later we were flying to Washington.

A suspension of payments is always an attractive alternative for debtors; but for Mexico, in those months, the alternative had some serious risks:

- Around 30 percent of the domestic consumption of corn, the basic Mexican staple, was imported from the United States.

- Mexican industry, in spite of its progress toward national integration, was still highly dependent on imports. Parts, intermediate goods, raw materials, and other basic supplies came from the outside.

- For several decades Mexico was going to require additional foreign resources to complement its domestic savings. A moratorium would have run counter to this basic and long-term need.

- In the atmosphere of uncertainty and lack of confidence prevailing inside the country, a suspension of payments would have caused the situation to deteriorate even more, probably stimulating some internal moratoria toward the domestic banks and the government and within the private sector.

- A condition of autarky—to a good extent that is what a moratorium produces—would have gone against the growing interdependence among nations, which is a clear characteristic of the recent evolution of the world economy.

Certainly, a moratorium was discussed; but it was rejected. We decided to negotiate and to avoid confrontation. After eight years, I still believe it was the right decision. To have taken the other way would have had damaging consequences for Mexico and for the world.

### The Foreign Negotiation Process

The monthly visits to the U.S. financial authorities, which began in May 1982, constituted, without any doubt, a positive element in the negotiation process, since they established an almost permanent dialogue and eliminated the surprise element in the crisis.[6] It is important to point out, however, that all through the negotiating process, the problem was identified as short term, a liquidity problem. The strategy that was followed was a direct consequence of such a diagnosis.

The U.S. Treasury Department did not recognize, at the beginning, the real importance of the problem. It was seen as a mere problem between the banks and Mexico, and U.S. officials did not grasp the possible consequences for other debtors and for the international financial system. It was not until the explosion became inevitable that they designed their strategy—basically to protect their own banking community. Their essential attitude, we can now see more clearly, was one of myopia. Why this was so is not easy to explain or understand. Too close a focus on the commissions U.S. financial institutions could earn for emergency support and on special advantages to be gained from a difficult situation is an evident element in their failure to see the wider implications of the problem.

It is necessary to recognize the crucial role played by Paul Volcker at the beginning of Mexico's debt crisis and after. Volcker clearly understood the importance of the problem, its risks, and the need to adopt new attitudes, more open than the ones presented by other U.S. agencies. Efforts to manage the debt crisis were fortunate in the leadership provided by Paul Volcker and Jacques de Larosière, managing director of the International Monetary Fund. U.S. banks followed the Federal Reserve guidelines coming out of Washington, as did the international financial institutions. The IMF later adopted an active and constructive leadership role, whereas the World Bank and the Inter-American Development Bank (IDB) were passive spectators. The same happened afterward with the other Latin American debtors.[7]

Debt negotiations have been dominated by the creditors. We have to recognize it. This dominance has been a basic characteristic of negotiations all through the years of the debt crisis. Perhaps we have reached the moment to change things, to look for better-shared leadership, with greater participation by the ones that have to pay and that have borne the heaviest part of the debt burden, and to establish leadership that is more coordinated, less isolated. This is not confrontation. It is only a new way to negotiate, and it is needed.

ROBERTO JUNGUITO                           CHAPTER 5

# The Colombian Debt Problem

Colombia is the only country among the large Latin American debtor nations to have gone through the period of the debt crisis without having to restructure its external obligations. It has been able to continue honoring on a timely basis both its principal and interest obligations, without resorting to any type of IMF support.

This chapter analyzes the characteristics of the Colombian debt problem with emphasis on the way that its economic authorities handled the economic adjustment program and its external financing strategy during the earlier phase of the debt crisis. In such a context, the chapter shows the special nature of the Colombian debt experience.

Colombia's unusually large exposure of public obligations with the multilateral institutions rather than the more common overindebtedness of the private sector with commercial banks, together with a very successful adjustment program, led it to a financing strategy oriented to regaining access to voluntary lending from commercial banks and to obtaining additional resources from the World Bank. This strategy relegated the IMF's role to the simple monitoring of Colombia's adjustment program.

With reference to economic policy, the Colombian case is especially interesting because it shows that a secret to successful adjustment is an appropriate sequencing of the adjustment measures. In fact, events in Colombia demonstrate that a strong fiscal reform and monetary discipline followed by an accelerated crawling peg devaluation is an effective way to realign the real effective exchange rate without the menace of ensuing inflation.

From the perspective of economic policy making, the Colombian experience is also revelatory because it shows the complexities and conflicts posed by adjustment programs in developing countries. It provides firsthand information on the decision-making process and illustrates the manner in which management of the debt crisis touches, and requires the reconciliation of, interests of widely diverse groups in developing and developed nations of the world.

## Domestic Concerns at the Start of the Debt Crisis

In August 1982, the debt crisis exploded when the minister of finance of Mexico informed the U.S. authorities of his country's inability to pay its external obligations. At that time, Colombia was far from being conscious of the potential magnitude of the eventual Latin American debt crisis and its economic implications. In fact, the country did not then face immediate problems in servicing its debt.

When the Mexican announcement took place, Colombia and Colombians were concentrating on their own domestic affairs, since a change of administration was to take place on August 7. Belisario Betancur, a conservative, had been elected president, in an unprecedented victory over the traditional majority liberal party. The country's attention was centered on the presidential inaugural speech and the changing priorities of the incoming administration's development strategy. It is interesting to note that the speech did not make any reference to the Mexican situation and its possible implications for the Colombian economy. Nor did it make references to the Colombian debt situation or, for that matter, to the deterioration of the economy, which, as will be shown later, was already registering a significant deficit in current account and a loss of reserves.

On the other hand, the speech did outline, in an eloquent form, new social priorities for the country. The central proposal was to develop a peace dialogue with the guerrilla movements and to reorient and increase public expenditures in far-off rural places where the guerrillas were located and where there was almost no government presence. It was argued that the peace effort implied the reduction of both the objective and the subjective motivations of violence. On the international front, it was proposed that Colombia enter the nonaligned countries movement; and it was soon apparent that the president would personally lead a Latin American movement, which was later called the Contadora Group, to promote peace in Central America.

Economics was somehow relegated to a place of secondary importance at the outset of the administration. Perhaps one could retrospectively assert that economic policy was not one of the president's preferred subjects and that the economic situation—except for the developments in the financial sector, which will be discussed later—did not seem to demand immediate drastic action. The president had been meeting throughout his campaign with a group of professional economists, many of whom were later called into the government; for example, the author of this chapter was (at first) appointed minister of agriculture. The discussions centered more on campaign issues, however, than on the formulation of an economic strategy. Moreover, it should be explained that even though there was a period of several months between the election on March 16 and the formal takeover of power on August 7, the official economic team was not named until the beginning of the administration—partly because the president chose to govern with the participation of liberals, and negotiating their roles required time. The liberal Edgar Gutierrez, a well-known economist who had been head of the Colombian Planning Board twice and a high-level official at the IBRD, was called into the Ministry of Finance.

## Economic Policies Mid-1982–1984

It has been traditional in Colombia to draft a new development plan immediately after a new administration takes office. The importance of the plan lies mainly in its explicit setting of medium-term goals and in its diagnostics and overview of the Colombian economy, rather than in the design of short-term policies, which is a principal responsibility of the minister of finance and the monetary authorities. Upon reviewing the Betancur administration's plan, titled (in translation) *Change with Equity* (República de Colombia 1983), one finds that the major concern of the government was to stimulate the growth rate.

The approach used at the beginning of the Betancur administration has been classified, in modern terminology, as nonorthodox to the extent that the slowdown of the economy was to be compensated for through deficit financing, especially in public housing, and by supporting the private-sector activity of the large manufacturing firms through monetary policy, in a typical inward-looking strategy. On the international side, commercial policy was to be addressed mainly through the use of import licenses, which had been significantly relaxed in Colombia.

Exchange rate policy was to employ the crawling peg system that the country had been following since the late 1960s, without any measures to correct significantly for the overvaluation that had been accumulating since 1975 (Lora and Ocampo 1986).

The implicit strategy was to stimulate domestic demand to overcompensate for the decline in demand for exports, a decline which had been attributed more to the slowdown of the world economy than to the currency overvaluation that had gradually developed. The administration recognized that the overall strategy implied a probable falling off of reserves, given the fiscal and current account deficits; but, for various reasons, it was believed that the reserves problem could be controlled. In the first place, raising some taxes, mainly at the level of local government, implied a reduction in transfers and in the overall public deficit; and, in 1984, a new value-added tax was approved, to replace the existing sales tax legislation. In the second place, import controls were believed to be very effective. In any case, exports were expected to show some recovery; the real exchange rate was slightly elevated, and it was thought that the world economy would soon be back on its normal path of growth. Besides, the government was confident that Colombia could resist the shock, since it had an unusually high level of reserves and had excellent standing with the international banking community. It was believed that the banks were willing to respond positively to Colombia's needs for external financing, despite the Latin American crisis. A bonus of the entire exercise would be the control of inflation, to be induced by slow growth of the monetary base, following the decrease in reserves, and by the control and administration of prices, particularly those of public utilities.

As may be gathered from Table 5.1, the economy deteriorated from mid-1982 to mid-1984. The overall deficit in the public sector was maintained at levels above 6 percent of gross domestic product (GDP). The current account deficit reached levels above 10 percent of GDP, and international reserves declined rapidly. Economic growth did not recover. Inflation was reduced; but this success was partly linked to the exceptionally good behavior of agricultural prices and, in any case, came at the risk of a balance of payments crisis arising from the increasing current account deficit and declining reserves.[1] The period also saw an increase in unemployment.

Between 1982 and 1984 external financing became especially difficult. Even though Colombia did not face a debt crisis of the magnitude observed in the other Latin American countries, the barrio, or neighborhood, effect, together with the behavior of the economy, led to a reduction in voluntary lending. Table 5.2 indicates that the capital account, which had registered over U.S. $2 billion net inflows per year just before the crisis, showed significant reductions in 1983 and 1984. This reduction

TABLE 5.1  Colombia: Basic Economic Data

| | 1980 | 1981 | 1982 | 1983 | 1984 | 1985 | 1986 | 1987 | 1988 | 1989[a] |
|---|---|---|---|---|---|---|---|---|---|---|
| Growth (%) | 4.1 | 2.3 | 0.9 | 1.6 | 3.4 | 3.1 | 5.1 | 5.4 | 3.7 | 3.0 |
| Inflation (%) | 26.0 | 26.0 | 24.0 | 17.0 | 18.0 | 22.0 | 21.0 | 24.0 | 18.0 | 26.0 |
| Budget deficit (% GDP) | 0.2 | 3.0 | 6.1 | 6.5 | 6.7 | 4.2 | -0.6 | 1.6 | 2.8 | 2.3 |
| External debt | | | | | | | | | | |
| Total ($ billions) | 6.8 | 8.5 | 10.3 | 11.4 | 12.3 | 13.8 | 15.0 | 15.6 | 16.5 | 17.2 |
| % GDP | 26.5 | 33.1 | 40.2 | 44.0 | 44.9 | 43.6 | 43.4 | 43.2 | 42.7 | 41.0 |
| Balance of payments | | | | | | | | | | |
| Current account | | | | | | | | | | |
| $ billions | 0.1 | -1.7 | -2.9 | -2.8 | -2.1 | -1.6 | 0.5 | -0.1 | -0.6 | -0.7 |
| % GDP | 0.4 | -6.7 | -11.3 | -10.8 | -7.6 | -4.9 | 1.3 | -0.3 | -1.6 | -1.7 |
| Trade balance | | | | | | | | | | |
| ($ billions) | 0.0 | -1.3 | -2.1 | -1.3 | -0.4 | 0.1 | 1.9 | 1.4 | 1.3 | 1.4 |
| Financial services | | | | | | | | | | |
| ($ billions) | -0.2 | -0.3 | -0.6 | -0.7 | -1.0 | -1.2 | -1.2 | -1.2 | -1.3 | -1.5 |
| Year-end reserve level | | | | | | | | | | |
| ($ billions) | 5.4 | 5.6 | 4.9 | 3.1 | 1.8 | 2.1 | 3.5 | 3.5 | 3.6 | 3.6 |

a. Estimated.
SOURCE: *External Financial Needs 1989–1990.*

TABLE 5.2  Colombia: Balance of Payments (millions of dollars)

| | 1980 | 1981 | 1982 | 1983 | 1984 | 1985 | 1986 | 1987 | 1988[a] | 1989[a] | 1990[a] |
|---|---|---|---|---|---|---|---|---|---|---|---|
| Current account | 104 | -1,722 | -2,885 | -2,826 | -2,088 | -1,586 | 464 | -117 | -609 | -693 | -555 |
| Trade balance | 13 | -1,313 | -2,076 | -1,317 | -404 | 109 | 1,923 | 1,417 | 1,268 | 1,393 | 1,717 |
| Exports f.o.b. | 4,296 | 3,397 | 3,282 | 3,147 | 3,623 | 3,782 | 5,332 | 5,291 | 5,667 | 6,106 | 6,799 |
| Imports f.o.b. | 4,283 | 4,730 | 5,358 | 4,464 | 4,027 | 3,673 | 3,409 | 3,874 | 4,399 | 4,713 | 5,082 |
| Total services (net) | -74 | -631 | -978 | -1,673 | -1,983 | -2,156 | -2,244 | -2,536 | -2,627 | -2,851 | -3,052 |
| Credit | 1,945 | 1,928 | 2,013 | 1,183 | 1,104 | 1,068 | 1,364 | 1,440 | 1,571 | 1,658 | 1,733 |
| Financial | 471 | 631 | 498 | 272 | 108 | 91 | 131 | 174 | 194 | 200 | 200 |
| Debit | 2,019 | 2,559 | 2,991 | 2,856 | 3,087 | 3,224 | 3,608 | 3,976 | 4,198 | 4,509 | 4,785 |
| Financial | 627 | 937 | 1,147 | 1,011 | 1,178 | 1,293 | 1,315 | 1,424 | 1,512 | 1,666 | 1,730 |
| Public | 294 | 466 | 600 | 562 | 728 | 877 | 964 | 1,169 | 1,252 | 1,360 | 1,423 |
| Private | 333 | 471 | 547 | 449 | 450 | 416 | 351 | 255 | 260 | 306 | 307 |
| Capital account | 1,138 | 1,966 | 2,183 | 1,103 | 827 | 1,871 | 1,002 | 88 | 759 | 693 | 555 |
| Total long term | 855 | 1,610 | 1,620 | 1,528 | 1,822 | 2,356 | 2,633 | 210 | 1,175 | 1,044 | 874 |
| Direct investment (net) | 51 | 226 | 337 | 514 | 561 | 1,016 | 562 | 312 | 260 | 424 | 413 |
| Public sector (net) | 747 | 979 | 953 | 941 | 1,214 | 1,147 | 1,882 | -43 | 876 | 662 | 532 |
| Disbursement | 999 | 1,247 | 1,285 | 1,342 | 1,764 | 1,793 | 2,808 | 1,202 | 2,571 | 2,690 | 2,578 |
| Amortization | 252 | 268 | 332 | 401 | 550 | 646 | 926 | 1,245 | 1,695 | 2,028 | 2,046 |
| Private sector (net) | 57 | 403 | 330 | 73 | 47 | 193 | 189 | -59 | 39 | -42 | -71 |
| Total short term | 283 | 356 | 563 | -425 | -995 | 485 | -1,631 | -122 | -416 | -351 | 319 |
| Public sector (net) | -83 | 165 | 306 | 202 | -198 | 252 | -1,025 | -182 | 152 | -45 | 40 |
| Financial sector (net) | 355 | 120 | 140 | 10 | -293 | 3 | -535 | 36 | -117 | 50 | 50 |
| Net international reserve increase | 1,242 | 244 | -702 | -1,723 | -1,261 | 285 | 1,466 | -29 | 150 | 0 | 0 |

a. Estimated.
SOURCE: Banco de la República, *Investigaciones Económicas*.

occurred especially in short-term lending to the private sector. Rather than choosing an across-the-board restructuring, the government insisted on maintaining full service of obligations.

## Fundamentals of the 1984–1985 Adjustment Program

The condition of the Colombian economy at the start of 1984 required that an economic adjustment program be designed. Adoption of a program required the support of the president and the governing party, as well as the support of the Colombian Congress, the private sector (interest groups and labor unions), the press, and the group of professional economists. The objectives of the program, spelled out in the budgetary message submitted to Congress in July 1984, included a rapid reduction in the current account and fiscal deficits—through more severe control of monetary expansion—to establish a basis for a higher sustainable growth rate, adequate control of inflation, and the prevention of a balance of payments crisis (Junguito 1986).

The new program required austerity and restrictions. On the fiscal side, it seemed necessary to increase taxes, reduce expenditures, postpone capital-intensive investments, and increase public utility tariffs. In the external sector, to boost exports without fiscal subsidies and restrict imports without the expedient of import controls, it seemed necessary to adjust the real exchange rate. To secure external financing, it was necessary to obtain the support of the commercial banks and multilateral institutions.

As it formulated the program, the Betancur administration considered it essential to show that the existing strategy was no longer viable, since the growth of the economy and control of inflation were being obtained at the expense of a reduction of international reserves. The drain produced by this strategy was capable of causing a balance of payments crisis within a few months. That danger was easily understood by the various political parties, which, in fact, were criticizing the economic policy in Congress; by the international banks, which had virtually suspended new loans, except for cofinancing arrangements; by the multilateral credit institutions, which, while disbursing loans, were simultaneously insisting on the need to reorient the economic management of the country; and by the public in general.[2]

For the sequence of events in the adjustment program, there appeared to be two options. One was to emphasize external adjustment by devaluing the exchange rate significantly, in one shot, and to follow this with fiscal adjustment. The second course, which was chosen, was to legislate tax increases and trim expenditures, then to effect a gradual but accelerated adjustment of the exchange rate through the existing crawling peg system. At the same time, the government was to enter into conversations with the international banking community and gradually adopt measures to liberalize imports.

Rather than take a series of actions based on economic theory, the government followed a course guided by political and pragmatic considerations. In the first place, it was judged that the Colombian experience with the crawling peg system, adopted in 1967, had proved to be satisfactory and that what was required was to accelerate the pace of devaluation. To start with a massive devaluation would probably have had adverse effects on expectations and may even have impeded the negotiation of tax increases in Congress. There may also have been fear of a last-minute retraction by the president, who, two decades earlier as minister of labor, had authorized unprecedented wage increases as a compensation for a massive devaluation. The economic team was also required to concentrate on the fiscal issues, because the government had to present the proposal for the 1985 budget to Congress on July 20; and the figures had to be backed up with a financing plan, including tax proposals, and with a message describing the economic program.

**Fiscal Adjustment**

The fiscal adjustment included reforms in both income and expenditures. To increase revenues, the government proposed raising a wide range of direct and indirect taxes, without paying much attention to the overall structure of the fiscal system. It was clearly understood that in the economic circumstances and in the time available, the best that could be done was to obtain approval by justifying the need for adjustment, setting up a target for the reduction of the fiscal deficit, and offering some set of optional menus. It should be added that the Colombian Congress had an excellent group of economists and experts on public finance among its members and that they had enacted fiscal legislation (on local taxes and on the approval of the VAT) during the earlier and more heterodox phase of the adjustment; but the opposition party had a majority in Congress. As expected, there were very difficult discussions on the adjustment program; however, when the failure of the previous strategy was recognized, a package that included elimination of exemptions from the VAT, an across-the-board 8 percent surcharge on imports, a 50 percent increase in the registration tax, and authorization to increase the rates of withholding for income tax was finally approved. The government was also able to obtain approval to apply a forced 8 percent five-year peso bond amounting to 20 percent of the income tax payments of corporations. Congress further authorized the administration to reform and set up open-market operations. In the decentralized sector of the economy, the government proceeded to increase public utility tariffs in a gradual manner, linked to monthly inflation.

Expenditure decisions were more widely centered on the administration. It had been estimated that, after the increases in taxes and other income, the government would still need to curtail expenditures. The principal measures adopted—after acrid debates at cabinet meetings, during which the minister of finance had to confront the opposition of his colleagues and even that of the president on certain occasions—included halting all new post assignments (except replacements), reducing general expenditure payments, and postponing large investment projects, especially in electric utilities, where a large excess capacity had developed. Undoubtedly the most important measure, however, concerned the 10 percent (with 22 percent inflation) raise in public sector wages for 1985. This significant decline in public sector real wages appeared to be necessary, despite the tax increases and other fiscal adjustment measures. The government obtained from Congress a law authorizing it to set discretionary public sector wage increases that "consulted both the defense of real income of public employees, as well as the budget resource availabilities." To meet these criteria, the president proposed a scaled wage increase that would give the lower-income employees an adjustment equivalent to inflation, but would give upper-income personnel, including the president and cabinet, no increase. After long discussions with the unions in the public sector, which involved a detailed explanation of the economic situation of the country, the need for adjustment, and the interrelations of the domestic and international sectors, the measure was adopted, without any social uprising. To the decentralized sector and the lower levels of government, the presidential instruction was to observe extreme austerity in expenditures. The minister of finance attempted to eliminate all specifically tied tax allocations (tax proceeds used exclusively to finance particular types of expenditures by government agencies). Congress allowed only some flexibility in resource allocations but stated that agencies with surplus cash flows had an obligation to subscribe to low-interest treasury bonds.

The fiscal adjustment was quite successful. Tax revenues increased more than 45 percent in 1985, while general expenditures increased 15 percent and inflation (as Table 5.1 shows) met the target of a 22 percent annual increase. Table 5.1 shows that the overall public deficit was reduced from 6.7 percent of GDP in 1984 to 4.2 percent in 1985 and that a surplus existed in 1986. Comparable IMF estimates show a reduction from 7.6 percent in 1984 to 4.9 percent in 1985, which met the goals established in the economic adjustment program.[3]

## External Adjustment

The need for external adjustment was evident from the mounting deficit in the current account and the accelerated drop in reserves. As Table 5.2 shows, from a slight surplus at the start of the decade, the current account deficit rose to a level near U.S. $2.9 billion in 1982 and U.S. $2.8 billion in 1983. The figures available in mid-1984, when the new adjustment program was initially adopted, showed that the situation was worsening.

The combination of the mounting deficit, the reduction in capital inflows caused by the Latin American debt crisis, and the developing difficulties in the Colombian economy induced a rapid erosion in international reserves, which had fallen from U.S. $5.6 billion at the end of 1981 to U.S. $3.1 billion in 1983. In fact, the situation had been aggravated to such an extent during the first half of 1984 that the decline in the first semester was more than $1 billion, and the level had fallen to less than $2 billion by July. Extrapolation of these trends revealed that unless significant adjustments were undertaken, especially since a good portion of reserves were not effectively liquid, a balance of payments crisis would develop in the first part of 1985. Recognition of the potential balance of payments crisis was not, obviously, limited to the government. In fact, it seems that members of the private sector were counting on it, if one looks at the inordinate increases in demand for import licenses and the pressure for foreign exchange in the black market.

In such circumstances, adjustment of the real exchange rate appeared to be absolutely necessary; and the choice was made, we have seen, to implement the adjustment through an accelerated form of the existing crawling peg system. Because the economic team had concentrated on the design and implementation of the fiscal adjustment, devaluation took place in the environment of an internally adjusted economy and had a much smaller impact on domestic inflation than did devaluation in other Latin American nations. The questions that remained were the speed of adjustment and the economic criteria that should determine the new real exchange-rate level. The goal established was to achieve the real exchange rate of 1975 during 1985. This historical real exchange rate was the most competitive level reached in the previous several decades and occurred in a period when the current account was in equilibrium. In fact, the economic team found no model that could provide any better criteria. That the team's plan sought to distribute the real adjustment uniformly through the course of the year implied that the nominal devaluation would be dependent on the course of local inflation and the fluctuation of foreign currencies. As had been the norm in Colombia, the exchange rate policy was decided upon in a meeting of the minister of finance, the governor of the Banco de la República, and the president. The scheme could not have been more successful. Acceleration of the devaluation rate went largely unnoticed during the initial months, because people were accustomed to looking at the yearly rate, and the system seemed familiar. By the end of the year, the target had been met. The yearly nominal devaluation amounted to 51.2 percent, whereas inflation reached 22.5 percent.

The strategy for imports was to follow a path of gradual liberalization parallel to the exchange rate adjustment. The use of a crawling peg system did not permit a one-shot suspension of licensing systems. Rather, the foreign exchange budget was increased monthly throughout the year, and the baskets of goods which were previously prohibited or subject to license requirements were gradually transferred to the free import list. Furthermore, import tariffs were raised, both by a 15 percent surcharge in late 1984 and, in a more significant way, by approval of the extra 8 percent ad valorem import tax in 1985. The success of the import policy was assured by a World Bank trade-policy sector loan to finance imports of raw materials for export activities and by a reduction in oil imports. These developments were linked to the external finance strategy which is discussed later in this chapter. In any case, the fact is that imports were significantly reduced in 1984 and 1985, without a setback in output growth. On the contrary, as Table 5.1 shows, the growth rate in those two years improved compared to the rate in the previous three years.

An important element in the Colombian case during the early phase of the debt crisis was undoubtedly the behavior of the coffee sector. The international price of coffee remained quite stable during the first half of the 1980s and increased significantly in 1986 as a result of a Brazilian drought that damaged the coffee crop. This mini-bonanza strengthened the favorable impact of the adjustment program on the balance of payments. Of the policy measures affecting coffee and adopted during the adjustment period, the only one worth pointing out was the increase of the retention duty on coffee, in step with the exchange rate adjustment. The purpose of the increase was to capitalize the Coffee Fund and transfer resources to the public sector, where they could contribute to reduction of the public sector's deficit.

The policy for nontraditional manufacturing and agricultural exports was to stimulate them through the exchange rate, while reducing the level of fiscal subsidies. Finally, it ought to be noted that mineral exports (oil and coal) helped significantly to reduce the current deficit and that this success was possible because of the external resources from commercial banks that were in turn obtained as a result of the economic program.

Table 5.2 summarizes the results of the trade and exchange rate policies. Through increased exports and reduced imports the trade balance became positive in 1985, and the current account deficit was also significantly reduced. The current deficit declined from levels near

U.S. $3 billion in 1982 and 1983 to about U.S. $1.6 billion in 1985, and it became a surplus in 1986.

**External Finance Strategy**

To understand Colombia's external financing strategy during the adjustment years early in the debt crisis and, particularly, the government's negotiations with the multilateral institutions and the commercial banks in 1984 and 1985, it is important to look not only at the economic situation of Colombia compared with the other large Latin American nations but also at the size and structure of its external debt. As Table 5.3 shows, the external debt was largely public and was largely medium and long term. A larger-than-usual proportion of the debt was owed to multilaterals, and debt service ratios were lower than in the highly indebted Latin American countries. Such conditions explain Colombia's efforts throughout the debt crisis to distinguish itself from the rest of the continent and its permanent but almost fruitless efforts to obtain significant volumes of voluntary lending.

Despite the fiscal problems and balance of payments difficulties the country encountered during the crisis, Colombia insisted on its strategy of fully servicing its interest and amortizations. At the political level, the less radical and even moderating position of Colombia surfaced very clearly at the meeting of the Cartagena Group, which brought together in late June, for the first time, all foreign affairs ministers and finance ministers of Latin America to discuss the debt crisis. At this meeting, President Betancur, acting as host, played a key role in establishing the Latin nations' middle-of-the-road stand on the debt issue (Presidencia de la República de Colombia 1984).

The strategy that led to a series of externally financed jumbo loans without a restructuring of the public debt was not explicitly defined, however, until late 1984, after meetings were held with the multilateral institutions, the commercial banks, and the U.S. government on the occasion of the IMF-IBRD meetings in Washington. At those meetings, it became absolutely clear to the minister of finance that in view of the Latin American situation and the deterioration of the Colombian economy, it would be impossible to insist on obtaining small, syndicated, project loans, as the fruitless attempts by the previous minister of finance had already shown. It seemed necessary to pursue a semivoluntary jumbo loan, but this would involve demonstrating that Colombia had put adjustment measures into place and that such policies would be effective in correcting the disequilibria in the public and external sectors.

At this point, two policy issues are worth pointing out. One is the Colombian arguments for not restructuring obligations; the second is

TABLE 5.3   Colombia: External Debt

| | 1980 | 1981 | 1982 | 1983 | 1984 | 1985 | 1986 | 1987 | 1988[a] | 1989[a] | 1990[a] |
|---|---|---|---|---|---|---|---|---|---|---|---|
| Total external debt ($ millions) | 6,805 | 8,518 | 10,269 | 11,408 | 12,265 | 13,834 | 14,963 | 15,639 | 16,499 | 17,169 | 17,680 |
| Medium and long term | 4,694 | 6,034 | 7,270 | 8,236 | 9,527 | 11,008 | 13,353 | 13,975 | 14,890 | 15,510 | 15,971 |
| Public | 4,179 | 5,168 | 6,078 | 6,958 | 8,090 | 9,432 | 11,512 | 12,183 | 13,098 | 13,798 | 14,368 |
| Private | 515 | 866 | 1,192 | 1,278 | 1,437 | 1,576 | 1,599 | 1,550 | 1,589 | 1,547 | 1,476 |
| Financial system | | | | | | | 242 | 242 | 203 | 165 | 127 |
| Short term | 2,111 | 2,484 | 2,999 | 3,172 | 2,738 | 2,826 | 1,610 | 1,664 | 1,609 | 1,659 | 1,709 |
| Public | 348 | 476 | 741 | 854 | 654 | 987 | 228 | 105 | 167 | 167 | 167 |
| Private | 390 | 514 | 621 | 474 | 439 | 444 | 523 | 664 | 664 | 679 | 694 |
| Financial system | 1,373 | 1,494 | 1,637 | 1,844 | 1,645 | 1,395 | 859 | 895 | 778 | 813 | 848 |
| Flows ($ millions) | | | | | | | | | | | |
| Disbursements | 1,069 | 1,937 | 1,713 | 1,650 | 2,064 | 2,020 | 3,002 | 1,282 | 2,753 | 2,810 | 2,728 |
| Public | 1,078 | 1,299 | 1,291 | 1,342 | 1,764 | 1,794 | 2,807 | 1,202 | 2,571 | 2,690 | 2,578 |
| Private | 51 | 638 | 422 | 308 | 300 | 326 | 195 | 80 | 182 | 120 | 150 |
| Amortizations | 333 | 378 | 430 | 636 | 704 | 750 | 1,084 | 1,383 | 1,838 | 2,187 | 2,262 |
| Public | 258 | 266 | 336 | 415 | 562 | 654 | 936 | 1,255 | 1,695 | 2,025 | 2,041 |
| Private | 75 | 112 | 94 | 221 | 142 | 96 | 148 | 128 | 143 | 162 | 221 |
| Interest payments | 627 | 937 | 1,147 | 1,011 | 1,178 | 1,234 | 1,283 | 1,428 | 1,511 | 1,666 | 1,730 |
| Public | 284 | 402 | 600 | 565 | 620 | 795 | 969 | 1,173 | 1,251 | 1,360 | 1,423 |
| Private | 343 | 535 | 547 | 446 | 558 | 439 | 314 | 255 | 260 | 306 | 307 |
| Ratios (%) | | | | | | | | | | | |
| Interest/current account receipts | 9.8 | 16.8 | 20.9 | 22.4 | 22.1 | 22.4 | 17.5 | 18.4 | 18.9 | 19.5 | 18.5 |
| Total service/current account receipts | 13.8 | 36.7 | 28.6 | 36.4 | 36.0 | 36.5 | 32.0 | 36.2 | 41.8 | 45.1 | 42.7 |

NOTE: Blank cell = no medium- and long-term financial system debt in that year.
a. Estimated.
SOURCE: Banco de la República, National Planning Department.

the country's position on the IMF and, particularly, on the need to enter into a standby agreement.

One can identify historical, political, and economic reasons for Colombia's reluctance to restructure public debt obligations. Historically, ever since the nineteenth-century debt crisis, Colombia had been less prompt than other Latin American countries to take radical measures toward external creditors (Junguito 1988). Politically, the restructuring of public debt appeared to the governing party to be a clear sign of failure in its economic management. At the same time, it appeared to be an easy way to give the liberal opposition reason to continue criticizing the government for irresponsible policies on public expenditures. Economically, it was clear that the size and structure of the Colombian debt allowed the country to service its obligations and that the real bottleneck in the country was the fiscal deficit. It had been suggested that the key elements in reducing the deficit were financing the completion of the coal and oil projects in association with Exxon and Occidental and complementary support by the commercial banks for investment projects of the central government.

The challenge, then, was to obtain the commercial banks' support with a minimum of conditionality. In fact, a great fear in the Colombian government was that the banks and institutions might insist on entering into a standby agreement with the IMF. In recent Colombian history, a demonstration of economic autonomy under the Liberal president Lleras Restrepo had led to a classic confrontation with the IMF in 1967 and ultimately to the installation of a conservative president who led a peace dialogue with the leftist guerrillas at home and, abroad, attempted to solve Central American problems without the involvement of the United States. Many believed that dealing with the IMF would lead to nothing less than political chaos.

On his return from Washington, the minister of finance delivered to the president an economic memorandum reporting that all parties involved in the conversations in Washington—the IMF; the IBRD; the U.S. government through authorities of the Federal Reserve and the Treasury Department; and, not least of all, the major creditors among the commercial banks—insisted on the standby not so much for economic reasons as for a guarantee that the adjustment measures were effectively placed. The Colombian economic team's demand to have the World Bank and the Fund substitute joint monitoring of the Colombian program for a standby could succeed only if the government showed that it was rapidly undertaking the adjustments. In the minister's mind, the memorandum represented a more-than-clear account of the conversations, as well as a tool to convince the administration, the Congress, and the decision makers of the country that the economic situation was difficult, that the adjustment program had to be adopted completely, and that the country could not obtain the foreign loans without the program (Ministerio de Hacienda y Crédito Público 1984).

After the memorandum was given to the president it was presented to the Council of Ministers. With the president's approval, it was discussed and confidentially handed to the key political figures of the country. Its unauthorized publication in the Colombian press naturally shook the country, and the economic team had a hard time explaining the situation to Congress. The memorandum did serve the purpose of facilitating approval of tax reform and permitting the administration to cut public expenditures, adjust public utility and gasoline prices, and implement wage policies. Above all it created an impression that austerity was needed and that the program had to be implemented if the country wished to obtain resources without the IMF standby.[4]

The economic team of the country met formally with selected commercial banks for the first time in December 1984 to present its economic program and its requirements for external financing. The team insisted that monitoring be done by a joint group of the IMF and the IBRD. Colombia had a long-standing relationship with the IBRD, which was its largest creditor. Moreover, far from fearing double conditionality, the Colombian economic team believed that the IBRD, given its good knowledge of the Colombian economy, could provide countervailing power to the IMF's proposals.

The banks agreed to form a consultative group, which found the economic program adequate in principle but, on a majority and divided vote, insisted on the formal engagement of a standby. When the IBRD, in a second meeting in February, clearly supported the Colombian program and its achievements, the major conditions for a loan of U.S. $1 billion were agreed upon, and the banks relaxed their insistence on the standby.[5] In April 1985, the IMF issued a positive, confidential Article IV consultation report on Colombia, which reviewed the economic policies and the general performance of the economy and which was unexpectedly published in the Colombian press.[6] Later that month, the U.S. Federal Reserve chairman, Paul Volcker, who had been meeting with the Colombian economic team, suggested a concrete joint monitoring scheme that would link disbursements to the performance of the economy, without a standby. His proposal was satisfactory to the Colombian team and contributed significantly to the final solution.[7] The last step was to persuade the director of the Fund that the monitoring scheme was viable. This President Betancur accomplished during his visit to Washington, thanks to the support of the American government. This support in turn was partially based on Mr. Volcker's understanding of the Colombian case, as well as on President Reagan's support of the Colombian authorities' fight against drug production and trafficking.

With IMF agreement, the negotiations advanced rapidly. By the time of the June meetings with the banks, the loan conditions—whereby Colombia was granted a billion-dollar jumbo loan to the public sector, with financial conditions similar to those in the new-money component of the restructuring packages of the larger Latin American debtor nations—had been fully approved.[8] The participation of banks was only semivoluntary. The matter of private-sector debt was also largely settled by then. The size of this debt was modest; and the more heavily indebted enterprises had already bilaterally restructured their obligations to the commercial banks, making use of a facility extended by the monetary authorities. This bilateral restructuring implied that the private debt would not be nationalized.

**Growth and Stabilization: Goals and Reality**

A description of the decision-making process during the 1984 and 1985 Colombian adjustment program must include discussion of how well the country met the growth and stabilization goals that were set up. One of the great debates in Latin America has been about the difficulties of maintaining adequate growth rates despite the stabilization efforts of the adjustment programs. In Colombia, as Table 5.1 shows, the growth rate of the economy increased from around 1 percent in the two years before the program began to over 3 percent during the adjustment years; and the basis was solidly established for maintaining annual rates at or above 3 percent in the following years.

Table 5.1 reveals that in 1985 the goal of a 22 percent ceiling on inflation was effectively met, even though climatic conditions caused an unexpected surge in food prices in the first semester. This level of success in price stabilization is especially significant when one recalls that devaluation of the nominal exchange rate was on the order of 51 percent in 1985.

It can be asserted, in summary, that the Colombian adjustment program met its growth and stabilization objectives and that the success of the program may be attributed to control of fiscal and external disequilibria. Because the country met all the quantitative goals of its economic programs, the monitoring plan did not interfere with disbursement of the external loan. In meeting all criteria of the monitoring plan, the Colombian experience provided the model for the Baker initiative. The positive results of its adjustment program and of its strategy for debt management permitted Colombia to negotiate a new billion-dollar loan, the Concorde, in 1987 without submitting to any kind of formal monitoring. At the same time, however, despite the success of its economic performance and its compliance with all the service of its external debt, the country was not able to obtain fully voluntary lending from foreign commercial banks. At the time of writing, it has even been difficult for Colombia to obtain a $1.8 billion loan from commercial banks to complement its external financing for 1989–1990.[9]

## Final Comments

The Colombian debt experience analyzed in this chapter offers several important lessons that are worth pointing out. The first and clearest of these is that a prudent debt strategy centered on longer-term loans and softer interest rates, such as those extended by multinational agencies and used by Colombia, facilitates debt servicing and prevents the bunching of amortizations faced by other Latin American countries.

The second distinguishing aspect of the Colombian debt handling is the nature of its adjustment program. The Colombian case clearly shows that the sequencing of the adjustment measures has a lot to do with the success of the program. Adopting the fiscal adjustment and tightening the monetary expansion before starting an accelerated crawl of the exchange rate permitted Colombia to adjust the real exchange rate in a significant manner without the resulting inflationary pressures so common in the adjustment programs of other Latin American nations.

Besides, the scope of the decision-making process described in this chapter, involving the Colombian adjustment program, shows that debt management in Latin America extends far beyond economic theory and economic management to highly sensitive political, social, and international issues. In fact, international debt negotiations directly involve not only the most important actors in the world economic arena, such as ministers of finance, governors of central banks, presidents and directors of multilateral institutions, economic advisers, prominent academicians, and, naturally, world bankers but also the political, social, and even religious representatives of developed and developing countries. Presidents, prime ministers, national assemblies, political parties, pressure groups, labor unions, the church, the press, and the man on the street can all affect complex adjustment decisions.

# Part Three

ALEXANDER K. SWOBODA                          CHAPTER 6

# The Changing Role of Central Banks in International Policy Coordination

The necessary role of central banks in international policy coordination appears, at first sight, relatively straightforward: Tell me how much exchange rate flexibility you have, and I will tell you how much policy cooperation you need from your central bank—and perhaps also how much cooperation you already have. When exchange rates are fixed, monetary policy needs to be tightly coordinated to sustain the existing set of parities; when exchange rates float, no coordination of international macroeconomic policy or, even more certainly, of monetary policy is required. Or so the answer went until some fifteen years ago. Since then, both the record of interdependence and analysis of its implications for policy coordination suggest that the conventional wisdom is not entirely correct.

The brunt of the argument in this chapter is that the old answer remains valid as a long-run proposition, although a case for some form of monetary cooperation, even under floating exchange rates, can be made for the short run. Why central banks have recently been called on to play such an important role in the coordination of international policy is, first, I will argue, that they control the only instrument of macroeconomic policy that retains some flexibility and for that reason are asked to pursue any policy objective that catches the fancy of the political authorities and, second, that the role of exchange rates and monetary policy in current account adjustment is all too often misunderstood. Monetary policy is then cast in the wrong role; and coordination of fiscal policies, the crucial element of international economic cooperation in today's circumstances, receives lip service only. One can only fear that this misuse of monetary policy will perpetuate current international economic imbalances longer than necessary.

The chapter is divided into four main parts. The first is a brief discussion of the nature of the policy coordination that was required by the institutions of the international monetary system, as they evolved after 1958, and the form such coordination actually took. In the second part I consider current international macroeconomic imbalances and their origins. The discussion of origins leads us, in a third section, to a simple analysis of the use of monetary and fiscal policy under alternative exchange-rate regimes. That examination, in turn, leads to an appraisal of a few active proposals for reform of the international monetary system or, more modestly, for improved international coordination of macroeconomic policies. I also offer a few suggestions of my own.

## International Coordination of Monetary Policy since 1959

December 1958 marked the return to nonresident convertibility of the main industrialized countries' currencies and the beginning of the heyday of the Bretton Woods system. What role did central banks play, in practice as well as in theory, in the process of international policy coordination as it evolved in that system?

The vision of coordination that underlay the design of the IMF system can be summarized as one of rules for ordinary times and discretion for extraordinary ones, with the national exercise of discretion for extraordinary ones, with the national exercise of discretion to be tempered by the Bretton Woods institutions. The role of the central bank was expected to be a simple one: Follow a monetary policy compatible with maintenance of the existing parity (or, equivalently, with balance of payments equilibrium) over the medium run; should maintenance prove impossible because of the existence of a fundamental disequilibrium, devalue or revalue as needed, but only with the approval of the Fund. In a properly designed system of fixed exchange rates there is very little need for explicit coordination of monetary policies; these are automatically coordinated as central banks strive to maintain the parity of their currency or, put another way, as they let the requirements of balance-of-payments equilibrium govern the course of their policies.

Technically, the task of the central banker is straightforward; the difficulty, of course, is to secure a credible commitment by all major central banks to abide by the rules and to defend the announced parities. There must also be agreement on an anchor for the system as a whole; or, if you prefer, there must be some accepted way of controlling the growth and composition of the supply of international reserves. This is where the Bretton Woods system was rather loose in its design. The Articles of Agreement were compatible with a variety of mechanisms to control the growth of international reserves. In theory the system could have worked like a textbook gold standard, with periodic revaluations of the metal in terms of all currencies; it could have functioned like a gold exchange standard, with the emphasis on either the gold or the exchange factor; or it could have relied more than it actually did on IMF credit as a substitute for or complement to owned reserves. Clearly, however, cooperation in creating international reserves is something that neither falls easily into the category of policy coordination nor is normally within the purview of central banks acting on their own initiative.

As it turned out, the Bretton Woods system evolved fairly rapidly toward a de facto, and eventually de jure, dollar standard. There was also a great deal of explicit cooperation among central banks, beyond the collaboration required by the Fund's charter. The London gold pool, the General Agreement to Borrow (GAB), work within the Group of Ten, the regular meetings of the Bank for International Settlements, the creation of a swap network with the Federal Reserve, and the regular meetings of Working Party 3 (WP3) at the Organization for Economic Cooperation and Development (OECD) are all instances of such cooperation. It is, however, interesting to note that these cooperative efforts, with the possible exception of the work of WP3, were very different from what we have in mind when we speak of policy coordination today.

The policy coordination of the time did not seek to any significant extent to affect the course of macroeconomic activity in the IMF or the industrialized world as a whole; nor did it seek to minimize, in a discretionary manner, the external spillovers from changes in national macroeconomic policies; nor, finally, did it view current account imbalances as systematic problems that required policy coordination for their resolution. Rather, the various forms of cooperation named in the preceding paragraph were undertaken to cope with a number of inherent problems of the Bretton Woods system or to help overcome occasional national problems.

The gold pool, for instance, was designed to help deal with the tensions that arose over the composition of international liquidity. The GAB was established to help supplement the insufficient resources of the Fund in view of the increasing mobility of capital and to do so in a manner that reflected the rising economic power of Europe, Canada, and Japan better than did the distribution of voting power within the IMF. The swap network served the same purpose and also helped mitigate the increasing problems of confidence facing the U.S. dollar. The swap network, together with central bank cooperation arranged at the regular (or, occasionally, emergency) meetings of the BIS, served not only to lessen systemic tensions but also to help deal with balance of payments crises (for example, Italy's in the early 1960s and the United Kingdom's several times during the Bretton Woods period). In many ways, the 1960s were the heyday of international cooperation among central banks. In that decade there emerged a club of central bankers whose mission seemed to be, in their own eyes, to defend members from the attacks of speculators. The modus operandi was to put together emergency credit packages and the mark of success the maintenance of existing parities. By that criterion, the cooperation was quite successful: the period 1959–1970 witnessed only a few, even if occasionally dramatic, changes in the parities of major currencies.

The cooperative effort succeeded, I believe, partly because of the relative simplicity of the task at hand and partly because of the political capital invested in the symbol of fixity. The task was simple in the sense that having as the main objective the defense of parity focuses the mind, and the monetary policy it creates, wonderfully. Even a simple task, however, may be difficult to accomplish if it requires forgoing the use of monetary policy for other purposes and (as it may, once payments have been out of equilibrium for some time) requires painful adjustments. This is where the symbol of fixity and the support of the international club of central bankers became crucial. The club made the commitment to exchange rate fixity credible both by raising the political cost of reneging on it and by reassuring the public that the means of achieving payments equilibrium at a bearable economic cost were available, in the form of bridge financing.

There are a number of reasons, however, why central bank cooperation was only partially successful in reaching even the limited goal of avoiding parity changes and could not succeed in solving the larger, systemic problems of the Bretton Woods system in the 1960s. In the first place, there was increasing pressure on central banks to pursue several goals with their one instrument, monetary policy. As long as the world rate of inflation was low, pursuing a fixed exchange rate served to achieve relative price stability. The central banker who was fortunate enough to have accumulated a comfortable stock of international reserves and a reputation for exchange rate stability could even occasionally use monetary policy countercyclically for internal purposes, provided that, on average, his policy was consistent with payments equilibrium at the existing parity. When, however, a rate of inflation abroad diverged widely (in either direction) from the domestic target rate of inflation, the tensions between internal and external balance were bound to result in parity changes. If a marked difference existed between the desired domestic rate of inflation and the actual rate of inflation abroad, even the assignment of monetary policy to overall payments balance and of fiscal policy to internal balance, as prescribed by Robert Mundell, would work only for the shortest of time spans. To this one should add that for many countries the problem was compounded by the unavailability of fiscal policy as a macroeconomic tool, leaving the central bank schizophrenic and leading in some countries (notably the United Kingdom but also the United States) to the adoption of a variety of controls on trade and capital flows.

Cooperation among central banks in the 1960s was by nature unable to deal with one crucial problem for the Bretton Woods system: insuring stable growth of international reserves at an internationally agreeable rate. Such stable reserve and monetary growth would in turn have led in the medium run to an internationally acceptable (presumably low) rate of inflation and hence would have made maintenance of fixed parities relatively easy. Because of the way the IMF system operated, it was almost impossible to solve the problem through central bank cooperation that accepted the system's rules. As long as foreign monetary authorities accumulated or gave up dollar reserves when there was a surplus or a deficit, it was U.S. monetary policy that determined the course of monetary expansion in both the United States and the rest of the industrialized world; monetary policy in the rest of the world essentially determined how much of non-U.S. monetary growth was backed by the accumulation of dollar assets, how much by the accumulation of domestic-currency assets. Within this framework, there was essentially only one form of central bank cooperation that could have solved the problem while recognizing the increased economic weight of the world outside the United States: having foreign central banks represented on the Fed's open-market committee, as Charles Kindleberger (1967) once suggested in a most perceptive proposal that was far too casually dismissed at the time he made it. But this, as all other solutions to the problem of the growth and composition of world reserves, would have required political commitments and often constitutional changes that were beyond the power of central banks to deliver. Discussions of more fundamental reform took place within the IMF and led to the creation and first issue of Special Drawing Rights (SDRs) in 1969 but foundered in 1974.

In brief, international cooperation among central banks was quite close at a technical level (the deputies who enacted it enjoyed a remarkable amount of authority) but could not compensate for a shortage of instruments effective for targets at both national and international levels. The rules of behavior for individual countries were simple, even if occasionally breached. There were no such rules at an international level or, if you wish, for countries issuing reserve currency. As long as the leading country followed a monetary policy that generally corresponded to the interests of the other major industrialized countries, tensions were kept at a level that could be dealt with through ordinary central bank cooperation to ensure stability of exchange-rates; however, once monetary policy in the United States diverged sharply from that desired by its major partners, as it did in the late 1960s, the breakdown of Bretton Woods became inevitable.

Central bank cooperation under Bretton Woods focused on helping individual countries maintain their parities, on supplementing the resources of the Fund where these were judged inadequate, or on remedying some technical defect in the system. In other words, cooperation focused on maintaining fixity of exchange rates as an (almost) ultimate goal of economic policy and on managing the process of creating international liquidity. In contrast, recent proposals and examples of policy coordination have focused, as mentioned earlier, on a different set of goals: the stabilization of world potential output, the minimization of spillovers from national macroeconomic policies, and the achievement of a sustainable pattern of current account balances. Moreover, in several recently proposed schemes, the exchange rate is considered an instrument, or at most an intermediate rather than ultimate target, of policy.

The shift of emphasis, of course, reflects the switch-over to floating exchange rates in 1973. That change marked the abandonment of one set of rules without the adoption of another. That it also marked a low point in international macroeconomic cooperation is not surprising, since the adoption of exchange rate flexibility was in good part motivated by failure to agree on a new system of fixed rates; unwillingness to sacrifice domestic objectives to internationally agreed ones; and a belief that the new regime would restore (this was thought to be its main merit) the autonomy of national macroeconomic and, particularly, monetary policy. Cooperation among central banks did not abruptly stop, but the emphasis of that cooperation shifted from macroeconomic concerns and exchange rates stabilization to regulatory and supervisory matters.

One might state that since 1973 three main factors have singly or jointly motivated renewed central bank cooperation for macroeconomic stabilization: (1) a perception that in circumstances where expansion or contraction is desirable for a majority of countries, joint action is needed, since individual expansion (or contraction) would be wasted in currency depreciation (or appreciation); (2) a belief that policy coordination might help correct large current-account imbalances and mitigate the foreign repercussions of changes in large countries' policy mixes;

and (3) a perception that exchange rates can become misaligned, besides becoming too volatile, and that such misalignments should be prevented or cured.

The OECD locomotive and convoy approaches to policy coordination, as well as the undertakings of the 1978 Bonn summit, reflect the first of these perceptions. Surplus countries were urged to adopt expansionary macroeconomic policies and act as "locomotives"to pull the rest of the world economy into growth. Since this might lead to deterioration of terms of trade for the locomotive country, the proposal was refined to suggest that the other countries should move "in convoy" and also expand their economies to offset the adverse impact on the locomotive country. The arguments that underpinned these efforts are in part reminiscent of those that led to the Louvre Accord. To quote the Group of Thirty (1988, 13) account:

> In the US the Carter Administration had reacted to the demand deflationary impact of the oil price rises by cutting taxes. It was argued that this was entirely appropriate as inflation would be constrained by the existence of excess capacity and/or wage/price guidelines. While US growth was reasonably good there was concern over the deteriorating current account position and the declining dollar. This in turn led to criticism of what were regarded as unduly restrictive policies in surplus countries such as Germany and Japan. It was argued strongly that easier policies in these countries would raise growth world-wide by lifting balance of payment constraints. There was also a suspicion that the United States was talking the dollar down in order to encourage both monetary and fiscal relaxation elsewhere, particularly in Germany.

What was different from current arguments is, of course, the view of the appropriateness of stimulative fiscal policy in the United States. The Bonn summit did call for stimulative measures in Germany and, to a lesser extent, in Japan, with the United States agreeing to raise domestic oil prices as its part of the bargain. As it turned out, the package was too late; when it began to be implemented, inflation and budget deficits were both rising.

Note that monetary cooperation was absent from the package and came into play only as the dollar depreciated sharply in the summer of 1978, leading to massive, partly joint, intervention by a number of major industrialized countries. Partly because it was massive and largely unsterilized and partly because the United States joined in and moved its monetary policy toward increased tightness, the intervention succeeded in putting a floor under the dollar.

There was little explicit policy coordination after 1979. Monetary policies initially converged as the fight against inflation became the overwhelming objective of monetary policy, but the move toward fiscal expansion in the United States and fiscal tightening in major OECD surplus countries in the 1980s was entirely uncoordinated. The resulting current account imbalances as well as the extraordinary rise in the dollar between 1980 and 1985 (which are discussed in more detail in the next section of this chapter) set the stage, however, for a number of policy coordination efforts motivated by the desire, on one hand, to correct current account imbalances and mitigate international cyclical spillovers and, on the other hand, to correct exchange rate misalignments. The Plaza agreement and the Louvre Accord are the two outstanding examples of such efforts.

The Plaza agreement—although it reaffirmed that fiscal policy should relieve current account imbalances, cyclical spillovers, and exchange rate misalignments—contained no explicit policy commitments except to encourage a further decline in the dollar, if necessary by intervention in the exchange market. That is, in view of the existing fiscal deadlock all hope for reducing current-account imbalances was put on the depreciation of the dollar. The dollar declined but the U.S. current account worsened further.

The Louvre Accord was a more ambitious undertaking. It contained explicit policy pledges by the G7 countries (except Italy). These have moved in what I will argue is the right direction: toward fiscal expansion by countries with large current-account surpluses and toward reductions in countries with major current-account deficits. The monetary part of the agreement, however, was left much less explicit. A desire to halt the decline in the dollar was clearly stated (the participating countries were to "cooperate closely to foster stability of exchange rates around current levels"), but the means by which this would be achieved were not described. The agreement on exchange rate stabilization seemed reasonably precise; but tensions arose fairly rapidly in the markets, and apparently among policy makers, when it became increasingly clear that the presribed elements of fiscal policy were, to put it politely, being implemented only slowly, especially by the United States.

In short, there have been several attempts at coordination of macroeconomic policy in the post–Bretton Woods era, with not entirely satisfactory results. The role of monetary policy in the process has been a particularly uneasy one, as it already was in the pre–Bretton Woods era. Ironically, in both cases the reasons are similar: central bankers are attempting to (and more often than not are pressured to) pursue conflicting targets with one instrument of policy. Whereas in the earlier period they were being asked to fight inflation and unemployment as well as to fix the exchange rate, in the later period they are being asked to help redress current account imbalances as well as to pursue domestic policy goals.

To evaluate the role that central bank cooperation could or should play in the future, it is important to understand current international imbalances and their origins, the subject of the next section.

## Current Imbalances and Their Origins

Output has been expanding steadily in major industrial countries since the trough of the last recession in the fourth quarter of 1982. Yet there will be little joyous celebration of the eighth anniversary of the longest recovery since World War II. Several factors contribute to the prevailing feeling of unease about the stability of the world economy and the sustainability of the recovery. Among these factors one may mention the obdurate and apparently secular rise in unemployment in most European countries, low growth in heavily indebted developing countries, a deterioration in the quality of bank assets that is not confined to the banks' loans to less developed countries, high real interest rates, the stock market crash of 1987, and the recent rise in inflation rates. For those attempting to coordinate international macroeconomic policy, however, it is the United States' double deficit (of budget and current account) and the fate of the dollar that have been at the center of recent concerns.

If I concentrate on these last imbalances, it is not because I believe them to constitute the only threats to international economic stability but because they shape current central bank cooperation and because their correction is, I will argue, a prerequisite to more fundamental international monetary reform. The facts are well known and the briefest of reminders of the dimensions of the problem will suffice.

The evolution of the current accounts of the United States, Japan, and Germany is given in Table 6.1. The figures tell a familiar story reflected in the growing net international indebtedness of the United States (the current account deficits cumulate to more than $570 billion over the years 1982 to 1987). The fiscal story, also well known, is summarized in Table 6.2, which pays special attention to the situation in the United States.

The main point of both tables is, of course, the trend increase in the ratio of the deficit to GNP in the United States in the 1982–1987 period as compared with the 1975–1980 average, in spite of the recovery in the United States. This increase indicates a structural rise in the full-employment budget deficit in the United States. The result is a significant increase in the federal debt-to-GNP ratio in the United States from

| TABLE 6.1 | The Evolution of Current Accounts | | | | | |
|---|---|---|---|---|---|---|
| | United States | | Germany | | Japan | |
| | $ billions | % GDP | $ billions | % GDP | $ billions | % GDP |
| 1975–1980 (average) | –1.1 | –0.2 | 0.3 | 0.03 | 4.8 | 0.4 |
| 1987 | –154.0 | –3.5 | 45.0 | 4.10 | 87.0 | 5.9 |

SOURCE: OECD, *Main Economic Indicators.*

TABLE 6.2    Central Government Fiscal Balances

|  | United States |  | Germany | Japan |
|---|---|---|---|---|
|  | $ billions | % GNP | % GNP | % GNP |
| 1975–1980 (average) | –59 | –2.8 | –2.3 | — |
| 1982 | –126 | –4.1 | –2.4 | –5.9 |
| 1983 | –202 | –5.6 | –1.9 | –5.6 |
| 1984 | –178 | –5.1 | –1.6 | –4.7 |
| 1985 | –212 | –5.3 | –1.3 | –3.9 |
| 1986 | –213 | –4.8 | –1.2 | –3.6 |
| 1987 | –156 | –3.3 | –1.4 | –3.3 |

NOTE: Dash = not available.
SOURCES: *International Financial Statistics*; IMF, *World Economic Outlook*.

a trough of 24 percent in December 1974 and a value of 27 percent at the end of 1980, to 44 percent at the end of 1987. Fiscal policy in the two largest OECD surplus countries, Germany and Japan, moved in the opposite direction. As a result of this movement, the debt-GNP ratios in these two countries, which had also been rising since the mid-1970s, began to stabilize in the early to mid-1980s. Yet another indication of the contrasting trend in fiscal policies can be found in an OECD estimate of the cumulative fiscal impulse for the years 1982–1985, which amounted to 4 percent of GNP for the United States and to –2.5 percent and –3 percent of GNP for Japan and Germany, respectively.

As for swings in exchange rates, suffice it to say that the dollar appreciated in nominal effective terms (as measured by the IMF) by 60 percent between the end of 1980 and March 1985 and had fallen back to 5 percent below its 1980 level by December 1987. In real effective terms (corrected for relative CPI inflation) the dollar had appreciated by 50 percent between 1980 and March 1985 but depreciated back to its 1980 level in the following thirty-three months. This difference has suggested to many observers that there have been gross misalignments in exchange rates since 1980 and to some that such misalignments still exist, in view of the United States' persistent current account deficit.

Most observers agree that it is urgent to reduce the U.S. current account deficit, lest a brutal adjustment take place and raise the specter of an inflationary recession, an international financial crisis, and an eruption of protectionism. There is less agreement on how that goal is to be achieved, what role international coordination of policy could play, and what form that coordination should take. Suggested solutions have included unilaterally reducing the U.S. budget deficit; coupling such reductions with fiscal (or, alternatively, monetary) expansion abroad; bringing the dollar down by one means or another; setting target zones for currencies, at levels that would substantially reduce current account imbalances or eliminate them entirely; or using more comprehensive schemes, such as the "extended target zone" proposal of Edison, Miller, and Williamson (1987). Adopting the proposal for extended target zones would, under present conditions, lower U.S. real interest rates to depreciate the dollar in real terms and achieve current account equilibrium; it would increase money supplies collectively to lower world interest rates and thus raise world nominal output (or at least prevent a recession); and it would let countries adjust their individual fiscal policies to reach their own internal balance targets.

This variety of proposals, together with deep disagreements on what level of the dollar should be the aim of central bank cooperation bewilders policy makers and unsettles markets. Contradictory estimates of the proper yen-dollar or deutsche mark–dollar rates have been put forward by McKinnon; by Branson, Dornbusch, and Feldstein; by Williamson; and by the G5 central bankers. One reason for so much variety is that these proposals are often based on different models (usually models of partial equilibrium) and on different starting assumptions. Without a simple, common general-equilibrium analytical framework, it is difficult to evaluate these proposals individually, to understand the reasons for their different conclusions, and to compare them with each other.

The elements of a simple general-equilibrium macroeconomic framework, which my colleague Hans Genberg and I have developed more fully elsewhere (see Genberg and Swoboda 1987a, 1987b), are presented later in this chapter; but four features of our model and of the questions we ask of it are worth bringing out here. First, the current account, the real exchange rate, and the real interest rate are jointly determined, endogenous variables; questions such as "By how much must the dollar depreciate in real terms to equilibrate the current account?" are meaningless until and unless we are told what brings about the depreciation of the dollar—and the improvement of the current account. Second, it is important to specify clearly what the instruments of policy are and to make sure that they are indeed, at least potentially, under the control of the authorities. It will not do just to assume that real interest rates can be set at will by the authorities (presumably by means of monetary policy). Third, the Tinbergen-Meade principle that you need as many instruments of policy as you have targets, to reach all of them, must be respected (see Meade 1951; Tinbergen 1952). Central banks must not be asked to target both the price level and the exchange rate independently. Fourth, we want to ask whether it matters which instrument we aim at which target, on the realistic assumption that information is less than perfect, or if we wish to establish some rudimentary rules for coordinating international macroeconomic policy; that is, we should be interested in Robert Mundell's well-known "assignment problem." These points are relevant to various current proposals.

The proposed analytical framework should also be able to explain, at least broadly, the origins of contemporary imbalances in current accounts. In keeping with the first feature of the model, one must be able to explain the joint behavior of the current account, the real exchange rate, and the real interest rate. The loose fiscal–tight monetary policy mix in the United States (together with the opposite mix in other countries) provided a familiar Mundell-Fleming pattern of high real interest rates and a rising dollar together with a deteriorating U.S. trade account until 1985. The subsequent depreciation can be at least partly explained by debt dynamics: The rising stock of U.S. debt held by foreigners creates a risk premium on the dollar. At the same time, the trade account must begin to improve if the current account is not to explode; and that requires some real depreciation of the dollar (income and wealth effects also come into play). The dynamics are very complicated, but the general pattern is clear. An initial appreciation of the dollar in real terms is followed by depreciation to a level below the initial one, and some overshooting on the downside as well as on the upside is likely. In brief, this view puts primary emphasis on fiscal policy (and secondary stress on monetary policy) to explain the behavior of the U.S. current account and of the real value of the dollar since 1981.

### A Simple Analytical Framework

This discussion will not repeat in detail the analysis Genberg and I developed in our two IMF Working Papers. Instead, I will briefly describe the framework we use, state some of the model's main conclusions, and then suggest some implications for the role to be taken by coordination of monetary and fiscal policy under fixed or floating exchange rates. The concluding part of this section suggests how the analysis can be applied to the current economic situation.

**The framework.** A slightly more general two-country model than that used by Mundell is probably the minimal structure required to evaluate the short- and longer-term effects of monetary and fiscal policy on the current account under flexible exchange rates. The model Genberg and I used is one such model; it assumes, for simplicity and with some claim to realism, perfect capital mobility (although we also show how that assumption can be relaxed). The model incorporates elements of the trade balance approach, since net exports are a function of the real exchange rate; and it incorporates elements of the saving-investment approach, since the current account is equal to the difference between national (government plus private) saving and investment. Absorption by the private sector depends directly on disposable income and inversely on the real rate of interest; disposable income is equal to output less taxes plus interest income on net foreign assets. Money market equilibrium is conventionally defined, and the domestic and foreign rates of interest are linked by the standard interest-parity condition. The stock of foreign assets is fixed in the short run; it varies with current account disequilibria in the long run. A flexible-price–full-employment version as well as a rigid-price–unemployment version of the model is provided. Although much of the analysis is for conditions of fixed-asset stocks and static expectations, the roles of changing expectations, of price-level dynamics, and of changing positions in net foreign assets are briefly investigated.

The analysis yields a number of conclusions that are relevant here. First, expenditure-changing policies are generally more effective instruments for affecting the current account than expenditure-switching policies. This is particularly true in the full-employment–flexible-price case but carries over to the fixed-price case. Second, fiscal policy has a comparative advantage over monetary policy in dealing with the current account as compared with internal imbalances under floating exchange rates. This advantage is most obvious in the full-employment case (since, in that case, monetary policy has no effect on the current account) but carries over to the case of unemployment and fixed domestic-currency prices of national export goods. Third, in accordance with the comparative advantage just noted, directing fiscal policy to the current account and monetary policy to the internal balance is a stable policy assignment, whereas using the reverse assignment will lead to a cyclical approach to equilibrium and may prove ultimately destabilizing. Fourth, with internationally integrated asset markets, it turns out that the real rate of interest depends only on world aggregate output and expenditure and not on the distribution of output and expenditure among countries or goods. In contrast, the current account depends on differences in autonomous (including government) spending between countries; such differences are also one of the main determinants of the real exchange rate.[1]

**Implications for policy coordination.** The implications of the framework for policy coordination seem rather straightforward. From a single country's point of view, there is the problem of internal coordination between the monetary and the fiscal authorities. Imagine that the authorities wish to pursue a current account target as well as an internal one (an output, price level, or nominal income target, whatever the merits of these alternatives). Monetary policy will have little if any influence on the current account; and, from considerations pertaining to stability of assignments in the short run, it is clear that fiscal policy is the instrument of choice for targeting the current account, monetary policy for targeting internal balance.

The problem is more complex in a multicountry setting. For simplicity, take the two-country case and assume, without questioning the wisdom of such targeting, that current accounts are targets of policy.[2] Assume also that there is agreement among countries on what the value of the current account should be. Now, rather than ask by how much the real exchange rate will or should change to bring the current account back into equilibrium after some initial fiscal or other disturbance, ask what policies are best assigned to the trade or current account, what policies to other objectives. Again to keep things simple, take the medium-run case, where prices are flexible and output is given at full employment, and consider the case where we start with current account equilibrium and try to maintain it. This last assumption allows us to bypass the effects of accumulating net foreign assets.

Table 6.3 shows the instrument assignments that suggest themselves under fixed and flexible rates (the latter case is the one Genberg and I analyzed). In the table, four instruments of policy are considered: monetary and fiscal policy at home (unstarred) and abroad (starred). Four targets can be reached with these four instruments, but the targets differ under fixed and flexible exchange rates. A fixed exchange rate ties national price levels together and endogenizes the distribution of the world money stock between the two countries issuing the currencies exchanged (national monetary policy loses its autonomy and must be devoted to keeping the nominal exchange rate, $E$, fixed). The nominal targets under fixed rates are therefore the world price level and the nominal exchange rate, to which the sum of the national money stocks (the world money stock, $M_w$) and their difference (the distribution of $M_w$) must respectively be assigned. The real targets are the current account and the world rate of interest, to which the difference and the sum of government spending in the two countries must respectively be assigned.

The same assignment of instruments to real targets obtains under flexible exchange rates. Here, however, the nominal exchange rate is no longer a target of policy but an endogenous variable; national monetary policy regains its autonomy and should be assigned to the national price level (or rate of inflation). Note that under both exchange-rate regimes, the real exchange rate is an endogenous variable. The exchange-rate regime influences whether the real exchange rate adjusts through inflation differentials, through changes in the nominal exchange-rate, or both.

Three broad conclusions emerge from this simple long-run framework.[3] First, as far as policy toward the current account is concerned, the focus should be on fiscal policy— more specifically on the difference in fiscal stances—and the real exchange rate should be left free to adapt under both exchange-rate regimes. Because the world fiscal stance plays an important role in determining the world level of real interest rates, coordination of fiscal policies is also required if the real variables are

TABLE 6.3    Long-Run Assignments

|  | Instrument | |
| Target | Fixed $E$ | Floating $E$ |
| --- | --- | --- |
| $P$ |  | $M$ |
| $P^*$ |  | $M^*$ |
| $P_w$ | $M_w = M + M^*$ |  |
| $E$ | $M - M^*$ |  |
| $CA$ | $G - G^*$ | $G - G^*$ |
| $r_w$ | $G + G^*$ | $G + G^*$ |

NOTES:
Blank cell = no instrument directly assigned to the target.
Definition of variables: $G$ = government spending; $M$ = money stock; $P$ = price level; $E$ = nominal exchange rate; $CA$ = current account; $r_w$ = world interest rate.
An asterisk identifies foreign variables; the subscript $w$ identifies world variables. The real exchange rate, $e = EP^*/P$, is endogenous under both exchange-rate regimes.
SOURCE: Author.

targets of policy. Second, under fixed exchange rates, some agreement on the desirable evolution of the world money stock and some means for effecting that evolution is required to achieve the world price level that corresponds to the target rate of inflation.

Finally, under both exchange-rate regimes, the real exchange rate is an endogenous variable that presumably adjusts to changes in tastes, technology, endowments, and relative asset positions. This fact suggests that targeting the real exchange rate as in some so-called target zone proposals is likely to be destabilizing, for two main reasons: First, unless the target value of the real exchange rate happens to correspond to the value that would represent an equilibrium, given all policy and behavior parameters, disequilibrium will build up in other variables of the system. Second, target zone proposals typically provide that the target real exchange rate be reached by means of monetary policy. According to the rationale expressed in Table 6.3, the assignment of monetary policy to the current account, through that policy's effect on the real exchange rate, is clearly inappropriate.

**Dealing with current international imbalances.** The general principles derived from the analytical framework do have some implications for determining the proper policy packages to deal with current international imbalances. The design of such packages requires, first, that current imbalances be identified; second, that there be some agreement on the goals to be reached; and, third, that there be some agreement on the way the world economy functions, that is, agreement on a minimal model of the world economy.

I will illustrate with a very simple version of the model Genberg and I developed in 1987. This model of the world economy under floating exchange rates is pictured in Figure 6.1. In the figure, G stands for government expenditure in the United States or, if you prefer, the stance of U.S. fiscal policy. $G^*$ stands for fiscal policy in the rest of the world—Europe and Japan if you wish. The line $CA$ represents the combinations of fiscal policies in the two regions that, taking into account current values of all other exogenous and predetermined variables, would yield current account equilibrium (or an agreed target value of the current account). Similarly, the $r_{w0}$ line represents those combinations of the two fiscal policies that would yield an appropriate, or target, level of real interest rates in the world. With symmetry of behavior parameters and perfect capital mobility, the $r_w$ lines would be 45-degree lines; that is, the world rate of interest would depend on the sum of government spending in the two regions. It is assumed that there is general agreement that $r_{w0}$ and current account equilibrium are legitimate and desirable goals of policy in the long run.

The remaining questions are, Where are we today, and how do we get from wherever we are to the target real interest rate and to current account equilibrium? Answers to the first question differ. Nevertheless, there is probably fairly general agreement that the U.S. current account deficit is too large—that we are below and to the right of the $CA$ line—and that current levels of real interest rates are too high—that we are above and to the right of the $r_{w0}$ line. These levels, in turn, imply that U.S. government expenditure is too high; it is above $G_0$, say at $G_1$. There is less agreement on where European fiscal spending is on the line segment $DE$. Suppose, for simplicity, that it is $G_0^*$ so that we are currently at $B$ in Figure 6.1. The combinations of the two countries' government expenditures that would maintain real interest rates at their current (high) level is given by the dotted line labeled $r_{w1}$.

Suppose that there is no change in fiscal stances—that $G$ remains at $G_1$ and $G^*$ remains at $G_0^*$. What would happen? Presumably, current account equilibrium would eventually be reestablished by the debt-dynamics mechanism. Increasing indebtedness of the United States would lead to a risk premium on the dollar; then real interest rates would rise in the United States and fall in the rest of the world. Net private saving would rise in the United States and fall abroad, and the $CA$ curve would gradually shift to the right until it intersected the $r_{w1}$ curve (now to be interpreted as a line of constant *average* world real interest rates) at $B$. The dollar would probably, though not necessarily, depreciate in real terms in the process; but the original target real interest rate would not be reached.

Alternatively, fiscal policy could be used to speed convergence to policy targets. One suggestion, made notably by Branson, would

## FIGURE 6.1  Three Paths toward Current Account Equilibrium

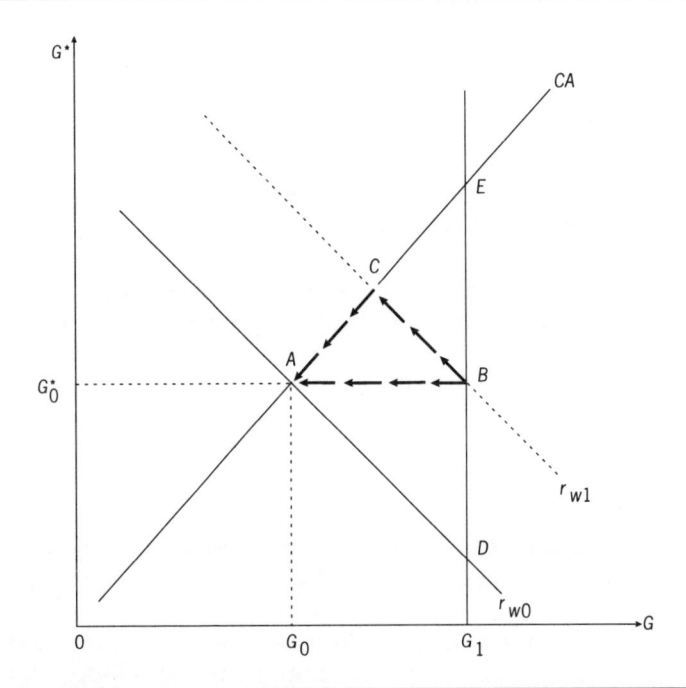

amount to moving directly from $B$ to $A$, leaving it to expansionary monetary policy in Germany and Japan to cushion the possible recessionary short-run impact of a reduction in U.S. government spending and to avoid too sharp a short-run nominal depreciation of the dollar. The Louvre Accord—with its emphasis on fiscal policy and its suggestion that exchange rates are about right, or what Branson has characterized as the G7 view—would seem to call for a movement from $B$ to $C$, where the decrease in U.S. government spending would be matched by an increase in government spending abroad, producing a return to current account equilibrium at the currently high level of world real interest rates. The increase in fiscal spending abroad that the latter strategy implies could again be justified by fear of the recessionary impact of the reduction in $G$ coupled with fear of the inflationary consequences of monetary expansion in the surplus countries. (To these fears could be added disbelief in the effectiveness of monetary expansion.) A third possibility would be to combine the U.S. budget cut with a temporary fiscal stimulus (if possible, of the supply-side variety) abroad; this would amount to moving from $B$ to $C$ and then to $A$ as the temporary stimulus is withdrawn.

Note that the basic element in all these policy packages is fiscal policy, particularly a reduction in the U.S. budget deficit. Little has been said about what would happen to the real exchange rate. Presumably the dollar would depreciate in real terms on impact, then appreciate in real terms, but this implies very little about what policy toward the nominal value of the dollar should be.

## What Role for Central Bank Cooperation?

The long-run considerations that have been discussed seem to leave little room for cooperation by central banks in solving current international imbalances. Instead, the accent is squarely on fiscal policy and the saving-investment balance. This does not mean that there is no case for cooperation by central banks or for coordination of monetary policy; rather, it means that the latter must be based either on short-run considerations or on traditional considerations involving reform of the international monetary system and must be independent of current account targeting. It is in failing to meet these criteria that several recent proposals for policy coordination or for targeting exchange rates seem to me inappropriate.

A brief illustration of why the proposals seem inappropriate is, for example, that parts of the assignment implicit in the Edison, Miller, Williamson (1987) extended target zone proposal run afoul of the assignments suggested in Table 6.3. More specifically, it is unlikely that using monetary policy to bring down real interest rates in the United States, to depreciate the dollar in real terms and thus to improve the current account, would succeed without creating an inflationary recession that fiscal policy, which is to be aimed at internal balance, would be hard put to prevent. Or take the suggestion so popular in Cambridge, Mass., that the dollar must depreciate by an extra 10 or 15 percent in real terms to correct the U.S. current account deficit. If this is a forecast, so be it; it may or may not be correct, depending on what will happen to various policies and on what part of the adjustment to the U.S. fiscal deficit has already occurred. If it is a policy prescription, we need to be told by what mechanism the dollar is to be brought down. Moreover, as a policy prescription, it has the double disadvantage of distracting attention from the crucial problem, fiscal policy and private saving, and of possibly fueling protectionist sentiment should it fail. Since we have tried everything (except the unmentioned proper fiscal policy), perhaps the only instrument left is protectionism—or so the argument might unfortunately be perverted.

What, then, is the role of monetary policy cooperation? I would argue that in the short run, as long as we have basically flexible exchange rates, it is fairly limited. After all, one role of that exchange-rate regime is to reconcile diverging monetary policies or to free monetary policy for use in achieving internal balance. There must, however, be some defenses against the competitive use of exchange rate depreciation for employment purposes, and some minimum of stability in national monetary policy is required for the world system to be stable. This does not imply tight coordination of policies, but it is true that some broad agreement on which countries should engage in expansionary or contractionary monetary policies might help to sustain a package of the *B*-to-*A* type illustrated in Figure 6.1.

I have argued so far that one thing that monetary cooperation should not want to do is to set *real* exchange rates. Stabilization of nominal exchange rates may, however, be pursued for reasons other than current account targeting. Ideally, a decision on stabilizing exchange rates could, in the long-run perspective of Table 6.3, take place whether or not there is coordination of fiscal policy. In reality and in the short run, the separation is not possible. In particular, a government probably should not try to fix the nominal exchange rate when wide fluctuations in real exchange rates are expected, lest such wide swings then require large allocations of domestic resources and cause high employment costs. The problem today is that uncertainty, in particular about fiscal policy, is so high that nobody knows with any precision where real exchange rates will have to go in the near future and by how much they might have to change. Lack of fiscal discipline is thus a major obstacle to stabilizing exchange rates.

These considerations suggest the following steps in coordinating international policy and in monetary cooperation. First, address fiscal imbalances. Second, while progress is being made on the fiscal front, confine exchange rate stabilization and monetary cooperation to smoothing operations and to massive interventions to establish a floor or a ceiling when utterly convinced of a gross misalignment. Third, once fiscal imbalances have been substantially redressed, start implementing exchange rate reform. If these steps are taken, progress can be made toward fixed exchange rates. The precise shape that the fixed exchange-rate system of the future will or should have is a topic for another discussion, but I am convinced that there will indeed be such a system.

WOLFGANG RIEKE　　　　　　　　　　　　CHAPTER 7

# Economic Policy and Exchange Rates: Experience and Prospects

The Bretton Woods system emphasized the need for cooperation but relied primarily on a set of clearly defined rules and U.S. monetary hegemony for its proper functioning. Its breakdown after a quarter century left major currencies floating against each other and presented multilateral cooperation with new challenges, especially the severe oil price shocks of the 1970s. In Europe, a regional system of exchange rate stabilization was put in place based on the deutsche mark (the "snake" system), later to be transformed into the more comprehensive EMS, aimed at creating a zone of monetary stability. This system sought to combine quasi-automatic adjustment and financing rules with cooperation procedures.

Responding to serious overshooting of dollar exchange rates, new global monetary cooperation efforts from the mid-1980s onward focused on stabilizing dollar exchange rates at realistic levels and fostering adjustment of large external imbalances in a noninflationary growth environment. Accompanying economic policy action in the various countries proved inadequate, however, to reduce external imbalances, and the focus on dollar exchange rate stabilization attracted increasing criticism. In Europe, the EMS showed that a rule-based system is workable between partners sharing common stability objectives. The role of the deutsche mark and of German monetary policy as a stable anchor was vital to the functioning of the EMS, but it also gave rise to criticism because intervention and adjustment burdens were felt to be asymmetric.

The experience with the EMS offers useful insights into the relative roles played by individual partners' self-discipline, by the good example of a key currency country, by agreed rules of the game, and by cooperation based on mutual respect. The absence of one or more of these elements may well explain the problems confronting global stabilization efforts. Cooperation between sovereign countries cannot be expected to compensate for lack of sound national policies, commonly agreed rules, and a key currency anchor. The economic policies of the United States and a stable dollar are likely to remain essential to the restoration of a more stable global monetary system.

## Global and Regional Cooperation: IMF and EMS

The IMF's Articles of Agreement prescribe that "each member undertakes to collaborate with the Fund and other members to assure orderly exchange arrangements and to promote a stable system of exchange rates" (Article IV, Section 1). For over twenty-five years, under the original Bretton Woods regime of fixed rates, member countries relied on intervention and monetary policy as prime instruments to comply with the statutory obligation to hold market exchange rates for their currency within a narrow margin around an agreed parity. The dollar served as major intervention currency and central anchor of the parity system, and the United States stood ready to convert officially held dollar balances into gold on demand (and to provide dollars in exchange for gold). Parity changes were subject to the Fund's approval, to be given only if "the change is necessary to correct a fundamental disequilibrium"[1] (like the proverbial elephant, never clearly defined but expected to be easily recognized). Imperfect capital mobility helped to keep intervention costs within limits that could be handled by an asset settlement system based on limited reserve holdings and supplemented by drawings on the IMF's resources in case of need.

Although the collaboration required by the Fund's Articles covered a broad range of activities (including furnishing statistical and other information, regular consultations on exchange restrictions and their policy background, and participation in financial support operations), coordination of economic and monetary policy in the IMF context was essentially limited to situations requiring recourse to the Fund's resources or involving a change in parity (though parity changes were often member governments' purely unilateral decisions that had to be endorsed by the Fund).[2]

The IMF system, based on a single-variable rule[3] centered on fixed parities, limited the need for cooperation, as well as its potential for conflict and its inherent costs. Some consider the hegemonial role of the United States to have been critical to the functioning of the system and believe the demise of the system became inevitable as soon as the American hegemony was challenged by other major players. It is more likely that the system broke down when the United States proved unable (or unwilling) to fulfill its key currency responsibility for global monetary stability and thus failed to provide a stable Nth currency anchor for the system. The turn to floating was tantamount to a vote of no confidence in the policy choices of the key currency country.[4]

The breakdown of the original dollar-based system briefly injected new energy into cooperative multilateral efforts aimed at redesigning a system of fixed but adjustable exchange rates based on more symmetrical adjustment and settlement obligations than those of the previous system. These efforts were soon abandoned, however, as fixed rates became generally recognized as unrealistic in a situation of sharply rising oil prices (with their diverse and unknown consequences for the balance of payments in each country), rampant world inflation, and sharply rising potential for capital flows.

The traditional academic arguments, which had long been advanced in favor of flexible exchange rates, soon proved to be inadequate as dollar rates became increasingly more volatile and—more important—tended to overshoot reasonable medium-term equilibrium ranges. The Anglo-American conversion to monetarist theology, however, provided new intellectual support for floating rates, since target-based monetary policy was found to be conceptually incompatible with fixed (or targeted) exchange rates. Moreover, the renewed preference for markets as the quintessential clearing mechanism was readily extended to the exchange markets. For countries with low inflation, floating was a means to shield their economies against imported inflation.

Not surprisingly, the new environment proved singularly infertile to economic and monetary cooperation at all levels. The IMF needed time to adjust to the new, unfamiliar circumstances and was forced to concentrate on more immediate issues such as the financing of large payments imbalances induced by high oil prices. Routine participation in multilateral efforts for macroeconomic coordination—for example, in the context of the Organization for Economic Cooperation and Development (OECD)—by the major player, the United States, proved perfunctory and inconsequential. The new environment did, however, favor ad hoc cooperation between the major players whenever they felt a need for it. The efforts made in 1978–79 to end the decline of the U.S. dollar, involving the extension of swap credit lines and the issue of nondollar-denominated "Carter bonds," are a case in point. The economic summits of the G7 nations regularly recognized the need for countries to put their houses in order and pursue mutually consistent policies within a medium-term strategy. The only direct attempt at coordinated macroeconomic policy made at the mid-1978 economic summit in Bonn proved to be largely counterproductive, because its effects coincided with the 1979 oil shock and only added to the problems of imbalance that had to be dealt with by countries individually.

In Europe, the currency "snake" offered an early alternative to generalized floating for countries that were willing to tie their fiscal and monetary policies to those of the Federal Republic of Germany. This practice left out Germany's major European partners, reducing the arrangement to a small "deutsche mark bloc"; but it usefully illustrated that exchange rates could be held at desirable and realistic levels between countries that shared similar concepts and objectives in economic, fiscal, and monetary policy.

The European Monetary System (EMS) reintegrated other major European partners into a more comprehensive regional system of fixed but adjustable central rates built on the experience with the currency snake; but the EMS encompassed a number of novel features, not all of which have fulfilled their inventors' high expectations. In its initial stage the system was helped to function by the relative weakness of the deutsche mark (against a rising U.S. dollar); however, the prime explanation of why the system has been more successful than it was expected to be is that all participants either made disinflation their top priority or felt enough pressure to meet the lower inflation standard set by the Federal Republic of Germany.

Widespread use of the deutsche mark for so-called intramarginal intervention—aimed at stabilizing individual EMS currencies' deutsche mark rates within the fluctuation bands, with the Bundesbank's consent but without its active participation—projected the deutsche mark into the role of $N$th currency within the system. This eventually gave support to the notion of "asymmetry," however—since the burden of financing imbalances and correcting them was felt to be unevenly distributed among participating countries—and prompted demands for changes in the intervention and settlement rules. The dominant role of the deutsche mark–dollar rate as a proxy for EMS exchange rate relations with the rest of the world, negating all calls for a common exchange rate policy based on the European Currency Unit (ECU), added fuel to the debate over the functioning of the EMS rules.

As inflation subsided from 1983 onward to more tolerable levels, some of Germany's partners called more insistently for shared responsibility in intervention, settlement, and monetary policy within the EMS as well as for common decision making on inflation, growth, and unemployment objectives and policies. They argued that eventually a system of fixed exchange rates with unrestricted capital movement will severely constrain national autonomy in monetary policy, making common policy choices and implementation imperative, and that economic and monetary integration would lead to establishment of a European central bank.

At the global level, effective economic and monetary cooperation resurfaced in early 1985. As exchange rates for the dollar increasingly overshot reasonable equilibrium ranges, observers became concerned that if the markets were left to themselves, the necessary adjustment to more realistic exchange rates would be disorderly and full of risk. No doubt, the strong wave of protectionist demands in the United States was also a powerful inducement for cooperation. Once begun, the cooperative efforts have kept the G5-G7 policy makers constantly involved, not least for fear of uncontrolled market reaction to signs of failing cooperation. The IMF has been involved in the process, both at the preparatory technical level and through its global surveillance function.

**Global Cooperation Refound: The G5-G7 Effort**

In 1985, the replacement of Donald Regan by James Baker as Treasury secretary ended a long period in which a U.S. policy mix of massive tax cuts in conditions of monetary disinflation existed together with benign neglect of the consequences of such policies for the dollar and the balance of payments. The return of the United States to active cooperation in economic policy and to intervention in the exchange market was welcomed by many countries, not only by the major industrial partners of the United States in the G5-G7. Even though it did not promise a rapid and radical turnabout in U.S. economic policy, especially as it applied to reducing the federal budget deficit, action by the United States formed a part of the basis for renewed cooperation and closer policy coordination.

The main focus of cooperation was, of course, the dollar's exchange rate in relation to other major currencies. By early 1985, the dollar was judged—except by a few extreme adherents to the markets-know-best philosophy—to have seriously overshot reasonable (equilibrium) levels. Accordingly, the efforts set in train initially by the G5[5] at the Plaza Hotel meeting on September 22, 1985—five months after the dollar had passed its peak and was already down 17 percent against the deutsche mark and 8 percent against the yen—sought to bring about a controlled further depreciation of the dollar (or appreciation of other major currencies) and at the same time to contain the perceived risks of too rapid and potentially harmful correction. The G5 recognized that adjustment of the large external imbalances called for more realistic exchange rates but that appropriate parallel macroeconomic policy action was also desirable, and in fact necessary, to bring about this external adjustment in a climate of continuing noninflationary growth in the United States and in the world economy.

Those responsible for the new U.S. cooperative strategy no doubt saw considerable merit in an increasing contribution to economic growth from net exports at a time when domestic impulses might be seen to weaken as the cyclical upswing aged. The rising protectionist pressures in the United States had added a new, worrying dimension to the deliberations of the G5 representatives and had called into question a policy that readily accepted the consequences of a rising dollar on U.S. trade. (The growth-oriented global adjustment strategy adopted by the G5 at the Plaza meeting on September 22, 1985, was followed only a few days later by the Baker Plan, which was announced in Seoul at the annual meetings of the IMF and the World Bank and which called for growth-oriented structural adjustment in highly indebted developing countries, supported by adequate new financing, as the only realistic way out of the international debt problem.)

As dollar rates moved down farther, the emphasis of cooperation efforts shifted to stabilization of exchange rates. The Louvre Accord of February 22, 1987, concluded by the G7 finance ministers and central bank governors[6] sought "to foster stability of exchange rates around current levels," leaving the markets guessing about ranges and trigger points for intervention or about action envisaged to give support to the stated intention. Specific policy undertakings of individual participants underlined the need for differential demand and supply-side reorientation favoring external adjustment without recession. Pursuing the multiple objectives of exchange rate stabilization, progressive adjustment of payments imbalances, and noninflationary growth was recognized as extraordinarily ambitious. The political obstacles were self-evident: In the United States policy makers lacked the political will to face up to the domestic causes of large external imbalances and their longer-term implications. In Germany, the government was unwilling to add to fiscal deficits that were already seen to be increasing sharply, because of tax cuts soon to go into effect and because of the built-in stabilizer effects of weaker-than-expected economic growth. Japan was committed to a comprehensive economic program to stimulate domestic demand.

There were other problems, some understandably never spelled out in clear terms by those involved in the political bargaining process. The

Louvre Accord incorporated the recognition that external adjustment could proceed within a reasonable time frame and without renewed pressure on exchange rates only if the changes in relative prices and profit incentives for foreign trade produced by exchange rate changes were accompanied by appropriate shifts in differential growth rates of domestic demand and output. The language of the accord, with its emphasis on "exchange rate stability around current levels," suggested that exchange rate modifications already achieved, together with the policies established or proposed by the various participants, were adequate to produce the desired results. This view was challenged by opponents of the coordination efforts, who were more prepared to allow exchange rates to move freely so as to bring about external adjustment and force countries into policy stances consistent with such adjustment. It was also criticized by those who supported coordination efforts but whose analysis led them to identify exchange rate levels other than the current ones as those at which stabilization promised to be successful and to be consistent with acceptable economic policy commitments.[7]

The debate on how to achieve external adjustment touches critically on the important issue of whether the exchange rate is to be an objective or an instrument, and on its linkages with other objectives, especially price stability. Developments associated with the earlier upward movement as well as with the more recent downward movement of the dollar rate testify to the complexity of the issue. It offers ample sustenance for disagreement, which can make coordination efforts involving exchange rate management difficult and controversial. Not only have such disagreements been aired from time to time between the Louvre participants, but they have also been part of the domestic debate in individual countries.

The German case may be particularly instructive, for a number of reasons:

- Because of its openness and its export orientation, the German economy is sensitive to exchange rate movements, including changes in the deutsche mark–dollar rate, even though dollar-related trade accounts for only about one-tenth of total foreign trade.

- Germany participates in the EMS, and the deutsche mark occupies the role of key currency in the operation of the system itself and in links with the dollar and third currencies.

- German economic policy is firmly committed to price stability. The Bundesbank acts as firm guardian of monetary stability and is endowed with full autonomy in monetary policy and with prime responsibility for exchange market policy.

German concern for the potentially disruptive effects of exchange rate movements on the economy and on the functioning of the EMS clearly favors efforts aimed at stabilizing exchange rates. At the same time, the desire for price stability and for effective control over monetary conditions tends to dampen enthusiasm for such efforts. At times, appreciation of the deutsche mark was accepted with equanimity because it benefited price stability, and any concerns raised by overshooting the monetary target and by other manifestations of imperfect control over monetary policy were set aside.

Experience with an earlier period of protracted deutsche mark appreciation in 1978 and 1979 had led the Bundesbank to tolerate overshooting its money supply target, but this was later recognized as rather problematic. The price stability imported through a rising deutsche mark rate proved elusive in the post-Bonn summit environment,[8] as the sharply rising oil price and the strong demand growth caused inflation to accelerate.

The more recent experience of, first, a strengthening of the deutsche mark from early 1985 to the end of 1987, followed by a weak spell lasting until mid-1989, was bound to reanimate these concerns. The rise of the deutsche mark was again accompanied by rapid growth of the monetary aggregates, exceeding the target growth foreseen by the central bank, but without adverse effects on price stability. Still, efforts to bring excessive monetary expansion under better control and, if at all possible, end the overshooting of the domestic monetary target were intensified for fear that inflationary pressures would emerge sooner or later. These efforts were further strengthened when, from the end of 1987 onward, the deutsche mark weakened once again against the dollar as the economy approached full capacity utilization. Insofar as this action succeeded in forestalling a further decline of the deutsche mark, it was also expected to support the role of the exchange rate as an instrument of external adjustment.

From the perspective of the United States, the concerns about possible implications of a weakened dollar also relate critically to the risks of accelerating inflation. This could affect monetary and financial market conditions in ways that could threaten continuing economic growth. More forceful fiscal action as the rise of the dollar was corrected might have eased the burden on monetary policy, perhaps even allowing interest rates to back off somewhat, while raising confidence abroad in the longer-term prospects for external adjustment. Since preelection circumstances were not favorable for such action, however, a holding operation involving other partners in efforts to keep the dollar stable or strengthen it somewhat, rather than let it decline, was clearly in the American interest.

The consequences of sharp dollar depreciation for domestic prices and costs were not entirely clear from past experience. After the 1985 turnabout of the dollar foreign suppliers showed considerable readiness to adjust profit margins; reduce production cost; and, partly in direct response to protectionist tendencies, shift production to the United States. In the absence of stronger wage pressures in the United States, the impulses from import prices did not translate into a sharply accelerating cost-price spiral, though they may have made it somewhat more difficult to bring inflation down farther. U.S. inflation remains essentially homemade, as are inflationary expectations, with their main focus on indicators of monetary conditions and prices of commodities, including oil; but in a climate of generally stronger world economic activity, further rapid depreciation of the dollar could well have a more forceful impact on inflation in the United States.

At the same time, it has been recognized that a marked strengthening of the dollar, against the existing inflation differential between the United States and other major countries, also entails certain risks, with effects on the financial markets that are difficult to foresee. Events surrounding the crash of 1987 are, of course, ever present in the minds of those responsible for monetary policy. Indeed, the reaction of dollar rates to temporarily less favorable trade figures can be taken as a warning signal. Concerted efforts among the G7 to influence market sentiment may be reasonably successful so long as external adjustment is seen to be well under way but may prove to be less effective when monthly or quarterly trade figures point to adjustment problems. These efforts may be especially unsuccessful if macroeconomic policy stances in major countries suggest that imbalances are likely to continue. The U.S. fiscal position is, of course, critically important here.

The situation in late 1988 was complicated by two uncertainties. One relates to the determination of the new U.S. administration under President Bush to deal with the savings-investment imbalance underlying the growth of the current account deficit and of external indebtedness. The other arises from the nature of the current investment-led strengthening of economic growth in the industrial countries. Stronger investment activity is to be welcomed on several grounds. It will help correct the adverse effects on the capital stock in various countries of past inflation followed by disinflation, misalignment of exchange rates, profit compression, and other conditions that did not favor an earlier recovery of investment activity.

In deficit countries like the United States higher investment will strengthen the basis for larger net exports in the future, whereas in the surplus countries it will assist the tendency toward greater domestic absorption in response to the appropriate price and profit signals, including those coming from exchange rate movements that occurred previously. In both groups of countries greater investment activity is also motivated by the desire to defend a competitive edge in world markets. Attempts to use forced adjustment of exchange rates to counteract the effects of stronger investment demand on the trade and current account balances of various countries might well be regarded as counterproductive, if the investment itself can be expected, in time, to help correct existing imbalances. Financing current deficits in the interim through adequate capital flows may be preferred. After all, economic development has historically relied on capital flows that were a natural component of overall equilibrium of payments.

In Europe, the role of capital flows was underlined in 1988 by the French finance minister, M. Pierre Bérégevoy, when he called for "effective recycling" of the large German current account surpluses as a contribution toward solving a dilemma confronting France and other European countries. To some observers the growing German surplus (and its counterpart deficits) has suggested the need for another realignment of EMS central rates to restore the competitive position of Germany's partners. Against that view it has been argued that in deficit countries price and cost indicators do not reveal a clear need for exchange rate adjustment and that trade and current account trends are affected by other factors, such as the decline of energy prices and the relative strength of domestic demand (including investment activity). Moreover, agreement to realign exchange rates could be interpreted by the public as willingness to resort again to an easy way out of a payments problem, and could call into question the seriousness of efforts designed to eradicate past attitudes to inflation, currency debasement, and monetary laxity.

It is assumed here that an unfailing commitment to monetary stability by its European partners is in Germany's interest as well as their own. In any case that commitment is basic to the longer-term functioning of the EMS. It reduces, and may eventually eliminate, the need for exchange rate adjustment as a means of establishing an *aussenwirtschaftliche Absicherung* (external safety shield) for surplus countries against the importing of inflationary impulses. Forgoing exchange rate adjustment in a situation of manifest external imbalance, however, carries obvious risks, especially in an environment of less restricted capital movements. The situation that existed before the last EMS currency realignment of January 1987 brought these issues into full focus and led to the Basel-Nyborg Accord of September 1987. This agreement between the EMS participants (see Frenkel, Goldstein, and Masson 1988, 1) stressed the need for ever more convergent economic policies and performance within a system of fixed but adjustable exchange rates and free capital movements, lest monetary policies in the EMS member countries face increasing difficulties. The accord also called on central banks to allow exchange rates to react more flexibly within the band and urged the banks to adjust short-term interest rates promptly in response to speculative pressures. It was also confirmed that realignments, if needed at all, should be as small and infrequent as possible.

**Economic Policy Coordination: The Merits and Limitations**

Coordination of economic policy may be viewed as an advanced stage of international cooperation, reaching beyond the level at which there is regular exchange of information and discussion of current policy issues without agreement on concrete policy action. Coordination constitutes, in the words of Henry C. Wallich (1984, 85), "a significant modification of national policies in recognition of international economic interdependence." Recognition of growing economic interdependence should indeed produce strong incentives for cooperation and policy coordination. It should be feasible to avoid mutually harmful and potentially escalating action even in the absence of active cooperation; but experience shows that incentives to act reasonably can be weak and that pretexts for acting unreasonably are ever present and need to be held in check, if only to preclude the need for even greater corrective action later. Even in the absence of harmful action there are undesirable spillover effects of individual countries' policies that cooperation can help to avoid or hold within manageable limits.

The case against policy coordination rests on a variety of concerns, with unwillingness significantly to modify national policy as the bottom line. Disagreement on matters such as the objectives to be pursued, the nature of the policy problem, the likely effects of particular policies, the instruments to be used, and the appropriate timing of specific measures figure prominently in any discussion of the limitations of coordination efforts. Opponents of coordination refer to real or purported obstacles arising from institutional, political, or other factors and claim, moreover, "that an emphasis on international coordination can distract attention from the necessary changes in domestic policy," and that

> the attempt to pursue coordination in a wide range of macroeconomic policies is likely to result in disagreements and disappointments that reduce the prospect for cooperation in those more limited areas of trade, defense and foreign assistance where international cooperation is actually necessary (Feldstein 1988, 3–4).

The case against coordination is weakened by the experience of the EMS. Its history offers insights into the contribution policy coordination can make to stabilizing exchange rates at reasonable levels. The success of the EMS in stabilizing rates between participating currencies has been greater than initially expected and is due to a combination of factors, which have been referred to earlier in this chapter. The commitment to fixed but adjustable central rates constitutes the necessary framework that encourages the EMS partners to pursue a variety of disciplined policies, individually and in concert.

It can be argued that, unlike the Bretton Woods system of fixed parities, the EMS discipline is not automatically enforced. That the EMS commitment to fixed rates has never been as strong as that of Bretton Woods is seen in Great Britain's absence from the exchange rate mechanism; in Italy's long-lasting insistence on a wider band (ended only in January 1990); in the heated pre-1983 debate in France about the merits of continuing adherence to the system; and in the serious risks of breakdown when the EMS was faced with the need for repeated realignments in its early phase. Once in the EMS, however, the participating countries accepted the exchange rate discipline as an important factor in the design of their economic policy. In this they had only limited success initially. The average rate of consumer price inflation in EMS countries declined from a peak of 11.6 percent in 1980 to 8.1 percent in 1983, but the dispersion remained substantial if measured against the lowest inflation rate (5.8 percent in 1980 and 5.3 percent in 1981).

Realignments were relatively frequent in the EMS until 1983. After 1983, the French government's insistence that inflation mentality, fiscal intemperance, and monetary laxity should not be allowed to revive was a key factor in lowering inflation rates in that country. Other EMS partners also tightened their policies around the same time. This change in attitude was tacit recognition that countries tolerating inflation had experienced no faster growth or higher employment than partner countries pursuing price stability as a matter of high priority. High-inflation countries had frequently adopted stop-and-go policies, which did not favor growth and high employment. Inflation proved to be a cause of social instability, rather than a pain reliever and a conciliator of excessive claims on available resources from the various sectors of the economy. The French government's decision to end heavy reliance on external borrowing, even though the country was far from seeing its credit standing impaired, can be interpreted as a clear manifestation of this change in attitude.

Regular consultation and cooperation at various levels, involving national governments and central banks, as well as the European Commission, is an important aspect of the EMS's functioning. Day-to-day operation of the EMS relies on central bank contacts in matters pertaining to intervention and its financing. The central banks also consult on interest rate policy when this is deemed desirable by one or more of them. As a matter of principle the purchase or sale of partner currencies requires the consent of the partner's central bank, except for obligatory intervention. The same requirements regulate the placement of intervention balances, normally in market instruments.

Coordinated intervention, as well as coordinated action on interest rates, has from time to time taken place within the EMS and, since 1985, occasionally in the wider context of the G7. Apart from day-to-day action in the exchange markets, exchange rate developments within and outside the EMS are regularly discussed by the European Economic Community (EEC) Committee of Governors, which gives special attention to intervention volumes and techniques and to the interaction of these with monetary policy and conditions, especially interest rates. The 1987 Basel-Nyborg Accord gave a new impetus to central bank cooperation within the EMS. Consultation and cooperation on a permanent basis also takes place in other bodies, including the Monetary Committee, and at the ministerial level.

It may be questioned whether all these EMS operations add up to effective coordination of economic policy and whether they produce corrective action based on mutually binding agreements that will significantly modify national policies. Policy formation within the EMS is often said to depend on the key role of the deutsche mark and on the dominance of the Bundesbank's monetary policy, which other partners feel constrained to accept as an "anchor" or standard for their own policy. The reality of EMS policy formation seems to involve several elements:

- *self-discipline* based on ever more widely shared objectives and concerns

- *good example* set by the key currency's country and accepted as a standard by its partners

- *rules* observed by participants in the exchange rate mechanism to assure its technical functioning

- *cooperation* sustained in a spirit of mutual respect and understanding, regardless of differences in economic power

An appropriate combination of these elements, rather than insistence on one or the other separately, appears to explain the relative success of the EMS; and the absence of one or more of these elements may well explain the problems confronting global stabilization efforts.

**Sound Economic Policies: The Role of National Self-Discipline**

Emphasis on self-discipline in policy formation suggests a variant of the well-known house-in-order philosophy adopted by the proponents of flexible exchange rates and monetarist orthodoxy. This philosophy was reflected in the Second Amendment of the IMF's Articles of Agreement, where the ability of countries to promote orderly underlying economic and financial conditions is set forth as a prerequisite for exchange rate stability.

It has long been recognized that stable underlying conditions are necessary for exchange rate stability, though they are not likely to be sufficient. Even with the best efforts there will be room for national objectives and outcomes incompatible with exchange rate stability, and these will give rise to additional variability as financial markets seek to exploit them. These imperfect conditions create the need for cooperative behavior, a stable anchor for exchange rates, and a set of rules to satisfy certain technical requirements of a functioning system.

The emphasis on self-discipline is based on the presumption that the major partners will only abide by rules that are self-imposed or market-imposed. At the global level, this presumption especially applies to the United States. Its economic weight, the lesser openness of its economy, and the international role of the dollar give the United States a special key currency status that has been only gradually reduced by the trend toward a multicurrency system. Experience demonstrates that exposure to market discipline cannot be relied on to force the United States to make prompt policy changes to correct conditions leading to serious external imbalances. On the contrary, from the end of 1980 onward the rising dollar helped to ease constraints on U.S. economic policy and was widely accepted as a vote of market confidence in the Reagan administration's policies. This is unlikely to have happened under a regime of fixed exchange rates; on the contrary, rising deficits in the trade and current accounts would have led rapidly to reserve losses and a loss of confidence.

The importance of self-discipline is duly recognized by eminent U.S. observers.[9] Indeed, sound national economic policy cannot forgo self-discipline that is based on simple truisms, including these:

- *Money* must be scarce. A policy that tolerates inflation will prove counterproductive over time.

- *Public debt* should be strictly limited. A rising share of public revenue and expenditure in total income will prove increasingly burdensome.

- *Current account deficits* and reliance on foreign borrowing to finance them need to be held in check, since they demonstrate a country's willingness to live beyond its means.

- *Market mechanisms* ought to have precedence over state regulation, and protectionism should be avoided.[10]

That it is inherently difficult to observe these principles explains the existence of certain institutional safeguards, for example, a legal commitment of the central bank to monetary stability, political autonomy of the central bank, a constitutional limitation on public sector borrowing, and anticartel legislation. Similar strictures are likely to be needed for the European Economic and Monetary Union to succeed, if it is set up within the next few years as intended by the heads of state and government of the European Community. At the global level, they would hardly be realistic in today's world; and they are also far from necessary, since global stabilization of exchange rates, and the closer economic policy coordination it involves, is not intended to end in full monetary integration. Voluntary adherence to such principles by the major countries, however, with the United States taking the lead, would serve three purposes:

- It would reduce the burden on official mechanisms of cooperation and economic policy coordination, avoiding strains with political overtones.

- It would allow the world economy to return to a system firmly anchored to the stability of a key currency.

- It would give the system a measure of symmetry, with major partners committed to self-discipline and smaller partners abiding by rules designed to assure consistency of policies and performance.

The breakdown of the Bretton Woods system and the success of the EMS both testify to the crucial role of a stable Nth currency anchor. In the gradually emerging multicurrency global system the responsibility for providing such an anchor would not fall so heavily on the United States as it did under the old Bretton Woods rules. A global system would presumably be affected by currency competition, involving the yen, deutsche mark (or ECU), and the U.S. dollar; but it could not rely wholly on currency competition to enforce the disciplines required for a stable system.

Cooperation and policy coordination can be helpful in dealing with the consequences of incompatibilities that are still likely to arise at the margin even though individual countries abide by the strictures of self-discipline. When coordination efforts are undertaken, they should support, not undermine, individual countries' commitment to sound policies. It would indeed seem contradictory to expect to use policy coordination to smooth out major incompatibilities or deal with their consequences if these conditions have been caused by the insistence of major countries on objectives and policies that are clearly incompatible with those of other countries and by the major economies' greater ability to resist market disciplines.

Self-discipline, currency competition, and coordination of economic policy will provide only the basic conditions for a viable system of stable exchange rates. This voluntary basis will have to be supplemented by certain rules of the kind agreed to by central banks in the EMS, to assure the proper functioning of the system. Only the combination of such basic conditions for stability of exchange rates, together with specific rules that will assure consistency of short- and medium-term action by policy makers in the participating countries, will produce a system that is more than a way station to stability.

The EMS experience suggests that expectations in the exchange market will be influenced favorably, and can in fact be tied down to a firm anchor even in the face of increasingly more integrated financial markets and unrestricted capital movements, if countries can establish the basic conditions and adopt the rules that have been discussed. Exchange restrictions, apart from their negative effects on confidence, are not likely to be too effective over time. Unrestricted capital movements may, in fact, add an additional dimension to discipline and will be seen as disciplinary by market participants. Willingness to act quickly to counteract a speculative attack, by changing short-term interest rates without fear of adverse effects the change may have on economic activity, will bring markets to accept the authorities' determination to defend exchange rate stability along with domestic monetary stability.

After a long period of floating rates and currency misalignment, market expectations cannot be expected to stabilize overnight. It took the EMS considerable time to move to a situation where markets can no longer be certain of measurable profits from speculating against individual currencies, if only because realignments are likely to be small and to leave market rates virtually unaffected.

The coexistence of major international currencies—such as the dollar, the yen, and the deutsche mark—adds to the difficulty of reining in global market expectations. For this reason, early attempts to restore a worldwide system based on fixed though adjustable exchange rates seem hazardous. The existence of large payments imbalances is also an obstacle to stabilizing global expectations; but these imbalances will not easily be corrected unless the major deficit country, the United States, practices self-discipline, especially in its fiscal policy.[11] Without U.S. restraint, forceful action by other major partners would not yield the desired results but could instead produce highly undesirable consequences in terms of inflation that they are unwilling to accept. Inaction by the United States, however, will gradually raise the cost of servicing the growing foreign indebtedness; and at some point market discipline will assert itself, forcing the United States to act. The country's first inclination will then be to minimize the cost to itself, with ever more serious consequences for other countries and for the world economy as a whole.

It may be argued that self-interest of just this kind led the United States to resume closer cooperation and policy coordination with the G5 in 1985 and the G7 in 1987. A more optimistic interpretation would be that the U.S. authorities saw the need for self-discipline but were politically able to bring it to bear only in a context of mutually agreed concessions. If this is the correct interpretation, there should be ample room for progress toward reducing existing imbalances and establishing favorable conditions for a more stable and lasting global exchange rate system.

PIERRE JACQUET
THIERRY DE MONTBRIAL                    CHAPTER 8

# Central Banks and International Cooperation

International monetary cooperation is a fashionable topic nowadays. Financial markets are eager to absorb any declaration by a finance minister or a central bank official and draw from it some inferences about the solidity and quality of the coordination process. This interest has brought into the limelight the main actors of monetary policy, notably the central banks of the United States and Germany and to a lesser extent those in other industrial countries. In this chapter we take a critical look at the role of the central banks in the process of international economic cooperation. Ours is not a central banker's point of view, but part of the central banks' influence on financial markets stems precisely from outsiders' assessment of their role and policies. The decision process within central banks will not be examined. The traditional secrecy that still pervades most central banks' inner politics makes it necessary to leave discussion of this subject to those who have directly experienced it. It may be as simplistic to call a central bank monolithic as it is for any institution. Nevertheless, this chapter will concentrate on the institution as a whole and will address the question of the central banks' place in the apparatus of international economic cooperation.

The discussion begins with description and analysis of the increasing importance of central banks and monetary policy in major industrial countries. In the second section, we turn to a brief conceptual survey of international economic cooperation. We then selectively and critically review some examples of international economic cooperation—in the interwar period, during and after the Bretton Woods era, within the European Monetary System, and through the Plaza-Louvre strategy. A final section draws some tentative conclusions.

### The Heyday of Central Banking

In times of financial and monetary strain, central banking generally acquires enhanced visibility and function. This happened during the interwar period, when cooperation among central banks began to be thought of in a systematic way. Cooperation in this period was shaped by the numerous financial rescues that had to be implemented, as well as by concern over the restoration and proper functioning of the gold standard. Central banks were prominent again in the 1960s, when monetary hurdles and speculation mounted and defense of the Bretton Woods parities became a concern. Of course from 1971 to 1973, the collapse of the convertibility of the U.S. dollar and of the system of fixed exchange rates brought central banking again into sharp focus. Floating, however dirty it was, and indeed in some sense because it was dirty, restored a significant margin of maneuver for central banks; increased the scope of their actions; politicized their role; and helped the development of a specific, discretionary, independent (even if not institutionally autonomous) central bank posture to fill the vacuum left when exchange rate rules disappeared. Central banks of major countries gradually emerged as vocal and powerful participants in international economic management.

Visibility of central banking appeared as a major phenomenon of the 1980s, on a scale notably different from earlier periods. Central banks in the G7 countries—but especially in the United States and West Germany, where their degree of institutional independence is much higher—acquired remarkable respect and an almost mythological status. This new charisma has many interrelated explanations, resting on contingent, structural, and theoretical analyses.

**Financial and monetary strains in the 1980s.** The polity of central banking in the 1980s was strongly influenced by two underlying forces: on the one hand, reaction to a decade of economic and monetary shocks as well as loose economic management in the 1970s and, on the other hand, liberalization and globalization of financial markets. Both of these forces played significant roles in boosting the status of central banking in the 1980s.

The need to correct a decade of loose economic management and inflation received generalized political support in the 1980s in industrialized countries and put a large part of the corrective responsibility on central banks. This responsibility increased their relative power within the national bureaucracies, to the extent that the ranking of economic objectives came to favor the one that defines their raison d'être, namely, price stability.

Progress in financial innovations and in worldwide liberalization brought with it five challenges: (1) It required complete deregulation and reregulation of financial markets, to cope with the need of these markets to grow and compete and with the new nature and distribution of risks that developed. (2) It blurred the measurement of appropriate monetary aggregates and fostered instability in money demand, presenting new challenges in monetary policy making, both to choose the right instruments and to understand their effects. (3) It made it more difficult to understand the linkages among national economic policies and among different spheres of economic policy. (4) It increasingly challenged traditional views about the determination of exchange rates. (5) It gave the financial decisions of private investors greater influence on policy making and on the development and effectiveness of economic and monetary policies. This influence increasingly required subtle market diplomacy by the monetary authorities in major countries. Central banks stood in the front lines to meet each of these challenges.

In the 1970s the world economy experienced many financial and monetary strains (possibly related to the mounting disorders of the decade and the policy reactions to them) that required contingent intervention by central banks. The first of these strains was the increased short term volatility of exchange rates and the emergence of significant, lasting misalignments in the first half of the 1980s. These developments revived the concept of managing exchange rates and called for central bank involvement and (forced) cooperation. Central banks were led to recognize that, although fluctuating rates indeed restored some autonomy in domestic monetary policy making, the persistence of misalignments could at some point challenge domestic objectives, notably price stability. Moreover, the overvaluation of the U.S. dollar raised fears of a hard landing, which were shared by many central banks. The coordination of economic policies since the Plaza agreement of September 1985, on which many (excessive) hopes have been placed, seems to rest essentially, if not exclusively, on central bank cooperation. In effect, the lack of adjustment in fiscal policies leaves to central banks the task of achieving the common objective of stabilizing exchange rates. We shall come back later to the nature and object of that coordination process.

The second strain on the world economy was the debt crisis that erupted with Mexico's default in August 1982. The crisis at once required central bank involvement. On the one hand, threats to the domestic banking systems in creditor countries called for specific lender-of-last-resort attention. On the other hand, central banks' policies also had to be directed toward developing countries. The Federal Reserve Board in the United States abruptly reversed its tight monetary management to ease domestic liquidity and the interest rates on which much of the Third World floating-rate debt was indexed. The Bank for International Settlements in 1983 organized the cooperation of central banks to alleviate temporary financial difficulties of central banks in indebted countries: Hungary, Mexico, Brazil, Argentina, and Yugoslavia received financial assistance.

The third strain was the stock market crash of October 1987. The crash, reviving the old ghosts of the 1929 crisis and the Great Depression, led central banks to feed the markets with adequate liquidity and to state firmly that they were cooperatively committed to that end. Here again, the financial stability of industrialized countries seemed to hinge upon central banks' behavior and was adequately supplied by easier liquidity.[1]

Finally, in the United States, the large increase in bank failures, attributable to domestic causes more than to the international debt crisis, called for active management under the jurisdiction of the Federal Reserve.

**Monetary policy and economic stabilization.** Besides the financial and monetary problems of the 1980s, theoretical fads and the practical division of labor between fiscal and monetary policies have certainly contributed to the prestige of central banking. Stagflation in the 1970s, and some unfortunate experiments to stimulate domestic demand, led to an increasing disgrace of fiscal policies as stabilization tools and an outright rejection of Keynesian prescriptions. The relative rigidity of fiscal policies, as well as a widespread conservative ideology, has fostered these reactions.

The conspicuous lack of flexibility in fiscal policy making increasingly transferred to central banks the task of macroeconomic stabilization. A case in point is the United States, where failure to take appropriate measures to reduce the budget deficit leaves the Federal Reserve with the tasks of controlling nascent inflationary pressures, preserving growth, avoiding a free fall in the dollar, sending appropriate signals to weary financial markets and protection-prone Congress, and occasionally redeeming the Treasury secretary's brinkmanship. Much of the current problem of imbalances in the world can be traced back to the 1981 U.S. policy mix, namely, an expansionary—and ironically for the Reagan administration, Keynesian—fiscal policy and, in the early period, a restrictive monetary policy. Whereas other industrial countries (including France from 1983 on) were concerned about the state of their public finances and adopted contractionary fiscal policies, the United States failed to take this aspect into account. U.S. politics and ideology still encourage fiscal inaction, and expectations for an early move by the Bush administration have not materialized at the time of writing. In Europe as well, fiscal inaction, in the face of repeated calls for joint reflation in the mid-1980s, was due to ideology and to a consequent lack of cooperation, since fiscal expansion could have been justified and effective only on a collective basis.

The lack of flexibility of fiscal policy does not derive from policy failure alone; inflexibility of the instrument is also grounded in the length of time it takes for fiscal policy measures to make their way into the economy (especially how long it takes for policy to influence interest rates, which have become ever more important variables following the liberalization of capital flows) and in the number of incompressible outlays of public spending that notably result from mature and sometimes overburdened social security systems. Moreover, imperfect theoretical knowledge still obfuscates the transmission mechanisms and predicted outcomes of specific fiscal measures and, together with political and ideological debates, prevents agreement on desirable policy actions.

Because of the shortcomings that have just been described, fiscal policy is generally recognized as not being suited for short-term stabilization in the face of financial and monetary disturbances, even if it does play a significant role in managing exchange rates. There is one qualification: the signals potentially sent to private agents through fiscal policy measures may easily translate into expectations that will significantly affect the economy in the short term. Short-term gearing of the economy, however, has become a task of monetary policy. Since short-term monetary and financial instability has increasingly required policy action, the role of monetary policy has been correspondingly enhanced, rightly or wrongly. Ideology has deepened the disgrace of fiscal policies. Stabilization of the internal value of money has been erected as a sine qua non of sound economic growth, sometimes irrespectively of timing or of any definition of the desired level of inflation or prices. Internal monetary stabilization has in some countries become an autonomous and predominant objective of economic policies and is related to the debate over independence of central banks, discussed in the next section.

In the current context of massive disequilibria in budgets and international payments, too much is expected of central bank policies. Part of the mythology of central banking is that international coordination will provide the anchor that gold was once supposed to represent. Whereas a gold anchor was thought to be automatic, central bank coordination, as the myth goes, promises to provide the anchor of collective reason in the face of disorderly economic policies. Ironically, the heyday of central banking comes at a time when there is, on the one hand, clear success in disinflation policies and, on the other hand, some conceptual disarray in monetary policy making and in the theoretical understanding of how instruments effectively work toward price stability. A strange situation obtains when monetary policy is supposed to solve the problem of macroeconomic stabilization (through price stabilization), but conventional monetary rules fail to explain the success in disinflation.[2] From first depending on a simple rule, monetary policy has now moved to a more pragmatic, muddling-through approach.

There is no paradox here: if a simple rule had been working, central banks would not be able to act in a discretionary way and would therefore remain rather low-key performers. In the same way that breaking the exchange rate rules in the early 1970s restored some room to maneuver, the failure of simple monetary rules in the early 1980s required more active, visible, and politically sensitive management. Discretion and short-term influence give central banks their relative power. Those central banks which enjoy that power could not be expected to support wholeheartedly institutional and formal—rather than episodic—coordination of monetary policies, nor any kind of binding exchange rate rule, for that matter.[3] Discussion of achievements of the so-called coordination process of the Plaza and Louvre agreements, and after, should not overlook these facts.

**Central bank independence and policy wisdom.** The considerable independence of central banks from government in the United States and in West Germany, together with the need for policy actions in these troubled economic times, has no doubt enhanced the visibility and respectability of central banking not only in these countries but internationally as well. The prominence of these central banks also stems from the influence of American economic policies on the world economy and from the expectations put on the Bundesbank once it became clear that the U.S. engine of growth could stall and needed to be rejuvenated through expansion in other industrialized countries. Moreover, such central bank governors as Paul Volcker and Karl Otto Poehl themselves acquired some of the mythological prestige conferred on their institutions. Although monetary policy has taken an increasing share of the burden in other countries as well, the relative dependence of central banks in these countries on their respective governments has prevented the emergence of a strong central bank power capable of defying the Finance Ministry or the office of the prime minister.

There are many dogmatic views about the independence of central banking, but institutional independence certainly does not mean full autonomy, even if it allows discretion. Many aspects of domestic economic policy making interact with monetary policy and cannot be ignored. Obviously, the nature of fiscal policies constrains the margin of maneuver available to makers of monetary policy. Moreover, even totally independent central bankers could not be entirely insensitive to domestic political pressures. Central banking is not immune to the narrow national perspective. Indeed, monetary policy, today as in the 1920s, is predominantly directed toward domestic goals.[4] This orientation makes any thought of an international directorate of central bankers premature, since the political commitment to subordinate some national objectives to the international common good is absent.

Some amount of independence is needed to promote the medium-term objective of price stability, to protect it from uncontrolled political pressures, and to establish it in the economic polity. At the same time, excessive independence can distract from the sensible view that price stability should be thought of not as an end in itself but as one essential ingredient to the achievement of stable growth and full employment. Excessive independence can create the illusion that fiscal and monetary policies must be decoupled. At a time when much emphasis is put on international coordination of economic policies, it should be recognized that a prominent concern should also be the *domestic* coordination of policies. In modern nation states, tax raising and public spending are prerogatives of the government. Unlike the international arena, where there is no world government to promote international public goods, a nation has a decision center that can make coordination attempts more realistic, if not easier to achieve.

Whether one likes it or not, neither policies nor markets are perfect; and that requires constant short-term compromising among objectives. Independence must therefore be constrained, to foster the emergence of a socially desirable compromise. One can argue that such a compromise, in democracies, is ultimately judged by voters, rather than delivered by the autonomous interplay of independent, separated powers. This argument, however, ignores the everlasting debate between different conceptions of modern democracies in the United States and some European countries, including the question of the separation of powers. In any case, full institutional independence of central banking is neither a prerequisite nor a sure recipe for policy wisdom. Moreover, it should be recognized that international economic cooperation is foremost political rather than technical. Independent central banks are not in a position to deliver the necessary commitment on a continuous basis and can even cause stalemates.

## A Typology of International Economic Cooperation

It is convenient to make a distinction between international cooperation under emergency conditions and cooperation under normal conditions.

The first is crisis management (provided one understands "crisis" as a condition of hardship requiring emergency measures), whereas the second basically aims at preventing undue fluctuations in economic variables such as exchange rates, interest rates, prices, growth, and balances of payments on current accounts.[5] One obvious lesson of history is that it is easier to obtain cooperation for crisis management than to secure continuous cooperation under normal conditions, for the simple reason that shared hardship at some point is likely to produce joint endeavors. The distinction between the two kinds of cooperation is not always clear-cut, however.

Emergency cooperation itself can be of two kinds: *ex ante* cooperation, designed to promote early recognition of an emergency situation and to prevent it from worsening, and *ex post* cooperation, undertaken once the crisis has occurred and the costs of noncooperative behavior have become blatantly obvious. There are several examples of *ex post* emergency cooperation in twentieth-century economic history. The most conspicuous are the limited cooperation that took place in the mid-1930s after the Great Depression and the post-World-War-II reconstruction. Somewhat lesser examples are the cooperation that took place after the collapse of the Bretton Woods agreement on exchange rates in the early 1970s, the management of the debt crisis from August 1982 on, and the monetary cooperation that took place after the October 1987 stock market crash. Of course, each of these successes has as its counterpart a failure of the corresponding *ex ante* cooperation.

*Ex ante* emergency cooperation is more difficult to find. Attempts to restore the gold standard in the 1920s may fit under this heading. A recent, conspicuous example is the G7 coordination process, which originated with the G5 meeting at the Plaza Hotel in New York in September 1985. The mounting risks that called for cooperation were several: risk of protectionism in the United States and in the world, of a hard landing of the U.S. dollar, of a collapse of the European monetary system, of generalized inflation, of recession in the United States, of a worsening of the debt crisis, and of a generalized financial crisis. One clear critical remark about that kind of joint initiative is that one would have liked it to happen much earlier.

An interesting question is whether appropriate and successful emergency coordination of the *ex ante* type is a process through which continuous cooperation in normal times can develop. Insofar as the current so-called Plaza-Louvre process is concerned,[6] strong doubts must be expressed. First, as Kindleberger (1986) recalls, "the attributes needed in crisis tend to atrophy in quiet times." Indeed, if coordination of policies is successful alleviating an emergency situation, the motivation to proceed tends to disappear with the emergency situation itself. Second, there is an ever-present temptation to overestimate the significance of contingent, dramatic events. It is still too early to interpret the 1985 U.S. reversal of posture with respect to the dollar as a lasting disappearance of benign neglect. A similar misinterpretation had already been made in the late 1970s, after the November 1, 1978, announcement by President Carter of the package painfully designed to halt the depreciation of the dollar.

Normal-times cooperation can itself be analyzed in three ways: through examination of the technical details of cooperation, by looking at the newly advocated coordination approach, and by viewing the process as part of an underlying system. Successful central bank cooperation abounds in the technical area and under the framework of the Bank for International Settlements. The BIS has developed a practice of regular monthly meetings of central bank governors. It has also developed many other formal and informal contacts among central bank officials. Consultation among central banks has therefore become quasi-permanent and successfully institutionalized. Although the BIS is traditionally centered on European cooperation, the Japanese and U.S. central banks take part in the network and attend the BIS monthly meetings. Besides running its operational division, the BIS produces studies on subjects related to monetary and economic policy making and issues occasional joint reports.[7] Technical cooperation among central banks has developed in many fields: In the face of financial innovation and deregulation, creating new challenges for international banking, technical cooperation has focused on prudential matters, establishing minimal harmonized measures for prudent operation, notably those concerning the level of capital requirements for banking institutions. Technical cooperation also provides a forum for communication on the evolution of media and systems of payments in the Group of Ten countries; on the question of risk in interbank relations; and on the related problems of security, compatibility, and maintenance of the banking system. Cooperation of this kind takes place through the establishment of a communication network among the central banks of the Group of Ten, which provides joint surveillance of international banking and financial markets. Finally, technical cooperation has led to the development of a strong statistical capability. The BIS provides the Group of Ten and Working Party 3 (WP3) of the Organization for Economic Cooperation and Development (OECD)[8] with data on international payments imbalances and has also developed an international financial and monetary data bank.

The coordination approach is directed toward positive exploitation of international interdependence for maximization of joint welfare and focuses on the strategic interaction of national policies, each of which has an impact on the welfare of other countries. Game-theory economists have recently developed a considerable coordination literature, with questionable relevance for policy making. The idea of Pareto-improving coordination would fit a politically centralized world, but it hardly fits a world of independent nation states that focus on domestic more than international concerns.[9] Moreover, the notion of welfare itself is highly subjective and therefore not directly measurable or comparable; and the aggregate welfare of a group of people is a political notion dependent on the organization of particular interests in the group. Reducing the government's objectives or the national well-being to a weighted average of inflation and unemployment, as in most models, does not look very promising. Hence, the coordination approach appears more appropriate as a part of emergency cooperation rather than as an effective and operational way of managing international economic relations.

Rather than focusing on the strategic interaction between economies, another school of thought, although it recognizes that regulation of the world economy is an international public good, stresses structural interdependence as a constraint on policy makers in independently framing their policies. In this systemic view, the world operates in an overall noncooperative way (in the "coordination approach" sense), the outcome of which depends on the framework in which the operation takes place. Cooperation is necessary in order to devise, maintain, and adapt the framework; therefore, one may speak of systemic cooperation.[10] The framework, or system, comprises a set of institutions, rules, and practices. This approach is congenial with the views, based on the thought of Knut Wicksell, expressed by James Buchanan:

> The *constitution* of policy rather than policy itself becomes the relevant object for reform. A simple game analogy illustrates the difference here. The Wicksellian approach concentrates on reform in the rules, which may be in the potential interest of *all* players, as opposed to improvements in strategies of play for particular players within defined or existing rules (Buchanan 1987).

A further argument is that the choice of strategies, and therefore the implementation of strategic coordination is not likely to be stable through the electoral cycle. Strategic coordination requires advanced understanding of international economic interactions and a desire to cooperate, which may have been learned through experiencing the costs of noncooperative behaviors and which may not necessarily be transmitted as such to the policy makers who come next.

The question addressed by systemic cooperation is in fact how to provide international public goods, as opposed to welfare maximization. The list of international public goods in the politico-strategic area includes peace through national defense and political cooperation. In the field of international economic relations, a liberal trade environment and international economic cooperation certainly qualify as international public goods. It is increasingly recognized that stable exchange rates are also an international public good. Orderly management of the exchange rate system is necessary to avoid the costs of competitive appreciation or depreciation. Recent experience of large and lasting misalignments also illustrate the potentially disruptive effect of floating rates on international trade relations. The question of whether a system of stable exchange rates is likely or not to induce sound and consistent domestic policies is more debatable. It is hard to think of any kind of exchange rate system that would have kept the Reagan administration from putting in place the economic policies it chose in 1981. Here is one clear limitation to the perfectibility of international economic cooperation, one that belongs to the larger set of issues raised by economic interdependence among politically independent nation states.

## Cooperation Experience

It is sobering to review the historical experience of and debate over central bank cooperation. Central bank cooperation has developed markedly in the twentieth century and now takes many forms. On some occasions and in some areas it has met significant success. From a global point of view, however, some achievements are debatable; and much of the current debate has been going on for a long time. In the current period, frustration comes from the fact that observers expect too much—indeed much more than it could ever deliver—from central bank cooperation.

**Central bank cooperation in the interwar period.** It is fair to assert that international economic cooperation started with central bank cooperation. Piecemeal financial cooperation among central banks occurred well before the twentieth century; but the notion of systemic international economic cooperation gradually, and in a still embryonic way, emerged in the interwar period. Paradoxically, cooperation started with the failure of the Genoa conference in 1922 to produce any kind of multilateral framework. Despite that failure, the conference was significant in that it took stock of the "economic costs of noncooperative behaviour" (Eichengreen 1985).

During the 1920s, central bank cooperation mainly focused on the exchange rate structure. International trade and payments in Europe were considerably strained by the consequences of wartime devastation, as well as by the economic and political problems linked with the question of war debts and reparations. European currencies frequently came under speculative attack. The fate of the German mark was linked to the large reparations required of Germany, and economic and financial prospects in France were conditioned on reparations payments and war-debt arrangements. British supremacy had ended, and the position of the United States was strengthened by its status as war creditor. Political tensions stemmed from the question of German reparations, but they were also caused by the war debts the Allies owed to the United States. A third cause of political tensions was the controversy between France and Britain over the question of security against Germany (Clarke 1967). There was a shared objective, however, in the gold stabilization of currencies, which was supposed to provide automatic regulation of the world economy. This objective implied successful prevention of a scramble for gold by central banks, as well as tighter business relations among them. In the 1920s the major countries sought to restore the gold standard at prewar parities for the pound sterling. Britain saw this objective as a major prerequisite to the restoration of its position as the major financial center. Other countries, especially the United States, preoccupied by international financial stability, thought it desirable to preserve the strength of London.

Cooperation among central banks slowly and episodically developed through the practice of stabilization credits to other central banks in difficulty, starting with the support loan granted by the Bank of England to the Austrian National Bank. Failure of the Genoa conference had left central banks with the task of cooperating, under the leadership of Benjamin Strong of the Federal Reserve, to try to stabilize currencies on a case-by-case basis (see Clarke 1967; Kindleberger 1984). Pressure mounted during the first half of the 1920s for Britain to restore the prewar gold parity of sterling, which was finally done (over Keynes's opposition) through the Gold Standard Act of April 1925.

It is now well known and documented that the gold standard did not exhibit the nice properties of smooth, automatic adjustment that the theory predicts. Central banks were predominantly concerned with their domestic economic objectives and although they paid lip service to the rules of the game, did not feel constrained to follow them. This disregard of the rules was particularly conspicuous at times when international aims conflicted with domestic objectives. In 1928–1929 for example, when the U.S. economy was booming and sterling came under severe pressure, the Federal Reserve chose not to lower interest rates. When, conversely, the Federal Reserve had lowered interest rates in 1927 to help counter speculation against sterling, this move also happened to fit a domestic context then characterized by recession, although some controversy arose as to whether the Federal Reserve had exposed the U.S. economy to undue inflationary risks or had helped nurture the rise of the stock market indices that would culminate and so dramatically reverse in 1929.

If central bank cooperation in the interwar period thus managed the reestablishment of the gold standard, it did not address the fundamental question of managing the system. That, according to the naive, theoretical, but unanimously held view, required subordination of domestic objectives to the maintenance of exchange rate stability. This subordination, it was assumed, would both constrain cooperation and make any further cooperation superfluous. This assumption was the basis of the feeling reportedly shared by Strong and Norman (Clarke 1967) that their task ended with the return of sterling to parity.

From mid-1928 on, strains in domestic economies accumulated, checked neither by international cooperation nor by successful domestic economic management. The return of sterling to an overvalued parity in the context of the 1920s and the stabilization of the French franc at an undervalued parity seriously contributed to those strains. The Bank for International Settlements was created in 1930 to promote the cooperation among central banks and to provide additional facilities for international financial operations, but this may be an illustration of defensive rather than active cooperation.[11] The role of the BIS remained subdued during the 1930s. After the international gold standard collapsed in the early 1930s, the June 1933 World Monetary and Economic Conference ended in outright failure to secure an agreement to stabilize exchange rates; however, the conference flatly recommended close and continuous cooperation between central banks, as well as an increasing role of the BIS to that end. The next major step in international cooperation occurred with the 1936 Tripartite Agreement,[12] inspired by a desire to check competitive devaluation of currencies. Although they were limited, the Tripartite declarations greatly emphasized consultation among Treasuries and central banks and therefore could be seen as a precursor of the current attempts at coordination. In both cases, concrete, specific mechanisms for the coordination of economic policies are conspicuously absent. The Tripartite declarations were directed toward currency markets, sending clear signals that day-to-day management of the exchange rates would maintain them within the agreed bands and that the days of beggar-thy-neighbor policies were gone.

There are a few lessons of current relevance to be drawn from the limited experience of central bank cooperation in the interwar period. First, it is important to stress the role of individuals, both in explaining how cooperation among central banks developed and also in understanding its limits. The Federal Reserve governor, Benjamin Strong, and the governor of the Bank of England, Montagu Norman, had developed a close friendship. Norman also had some affinities with the Reichsbank's Hjalmar Schacht, which could not have reduced his preexisting dislike for the French (see Clarke 1967; Kindleberger 1984). His relations with the Bank of France's Moreau were for this reason conflictive at best.

Second, exchange rate stability, even when based on a rigid rule such as the gold standard, is not sufficient in itself to deliver either sound domestic economic policies or appropriate coordination of these policies. The level at which stabilization takes place matters considerably; or, rather, it has clear implications for domestic policies that have to support the agreed rates. Moreover, statements of principle amount neither to proper understanding of the rules nor to a commitment to abide by those rules. Central banks' lip service to the gold standard rules of the game were clearly at odds with the practice they developed. Third, the outcome of central bank cooperation in the 1920s is debatable. Given the stated objective of reestablishing the gold standard with the prewar parity for sterling, one can consider it a clear success. One can, however, question the validity of such an objective in view of the political and economic circumstances prevailing in and among major industrialized countries, notably Britain and France. In any case, central banks were not able to manage the system successfully; and it collapsed in the most severe economic crisis of modern times. Fourth, political obstacles did clearly play a destabilizing role in international economic relations and acted as a strong impediment to the establishment of successful cooperation.

**Systemic cooperation under Bretton Woods.** Under the Bretton Woods system of fixed parities, central bank cooperation was again undertaken on a significant scale in the mid-1960s, against a background of accumulating monetary crises and mounting problems in the U.S. balance of payments. In the 1960s, the exchange rate was hardly thought of as a policy instrument that could be used to correct imbalances in international payments (see Solomon 1982). Defense of parities in the face of these imbalances and speculative capital movements required large-scale intervention. On the initiative of the U.S. Treasury in 1961 and under subsequent management by the Federal Reserve Bank of New York in 1962, a network of swap arrangements was established. These reciprocal credit facilities protected non-U.S. central banks against the risk of dollar depreciation, to the extent of the swap drawings by the United States.[13] In a further step to consolidate the system, the United States and seven other countries established a gold pool to try to stabilize the free-market price of gold in London. That gold pool collapsed in the aftermath of the sterling crisis of 1967 and the establishment in 1968 of the two-tier system.

There were many ways in which the making of international economic policy under Bretton Woods was different from that in the interwar period. One of these differences was that, as a reaction to the Great Depression, governments in the postwar period had a much more active role in the conception and implementation of domestic economic policies. They had become responsible for economic growth, full employment, and the welfare of their citizenry. Another difference was that the practice of international consultation had significantly developed through the multilateral bodies established under the Bretton Woods system. At OECD, consultation actively took place in the Economic Policy Committee and in Working Party 3 (WP3). The IMF statutes clearly specified the goal of promoting international monetary cooperation through its consultation machinery.

The process of consultation instilled in the minds of policy makers and of the public the reality of international interdependence, but it did not prevent frictions from developing. The major source of friction came to be the perceived passivity of the United States in the face of its balance of payments deficit. Moreover, the structure of that deficit—a strong surplus in the current account more than compensated for by capital outflows—contributed to the reluctance of other countries to engineer an appreciation of their currencies. The adjustment problem was again a major source of tensions.

Within the IMF, regular consultations have been fostered by the Group of Ten, which has gradually assumed an autonomous and vocal role in international economic matters. Closely related to WP3 by membership (the same countries make up both), the Group of Ten came to life during negotiations of the General Agreement to Borrow in October 1962. It was agreed that ten countries[14] would stand ready to lend to the Fund up to U.S. $6 billion, should the IMF and these countries consider supplementary resources necessary to support the international monetary system. The reason for these arrangements is to be found in the desire of the United States to secure sufficient financing for its balance of payments in the face of inadequate resources available from the IMF. The Group of Ten met both at the level of finance ministers and central bank governors, where initiatives could be taken, and at the deputy level, where substantive discussion and studies took place. The composition of the Group of Ten illustrates the politicization of international economic cooperation and the preeminence of finance ministers over the whole process, even if their countries have independent central banks. In effect, finance ministers kept the responsibility for adjustment of exchange rates. As long as a change in central parities was ruled out, central banks, willingly or unwillingly, had to bear the brunt of crisis management.[15]

The Group of Ten was instrumental in orchestrating emergency cooperation after President Nixon's decision on August 15, 1971, to terminate the convertibility of the dollar. This cooperation led to the Smithsonian agreement of December 1971.[16] The agreement was short lived, however, and could not restore proper functioning of the fixed exchange-rate system.

After the collapse of the Smithsonian agreement, discussions on the reform of the international monetary system took place within the Committee of Twenty, created for that purpose[17] and consisting of officials from the ministries of finance and central banks of each of the twenty IMF constituencies. That committee eventually (in 1974) produced an Outline of Reform, notably advocating an effective and symmetrical adjustment process, a regime of stable but adjustable exchange rates, recognition of floating as a useful technique in some circumstances, and the development of the Special Drawing Right as the principal reserve asset. This group was succeeded by the Interim Committee, similar in form, which was responsible for the implementation of reform. The committee's work, finalized in the 1976 Jamaica agreement and the adoption of the revised Article IV of the IMF Articles of Agreement, explicitly sanctioned floating as a legitimate option and advanced the view that exchange rate stability is not an end in itself but must be the result of orderly underlying economic and financial conditions. The pendulum had made a full swing, from the view that stability of exchange rates is required to foster orderly domestic policies to the reverse view that orderly domestic policies[18] are a prerequisite to exchange rate stability.

In the 1970s, a new forum for consultations at the highest political level was provided by yearly meetings of the heads of state and government of the seven most industrialized countries. Summitry alone has not produced any dramatic collective decision at the international level; however, it plays a helpful role in fostering political consultation, requires staff preparation, and may promote knowledge and use of the work done by multilateral institutions such as the OECD.[19]

One can draw a few lessons from the Bretton Woods experiment and from the 1971–1973 collapse of the system of fixed exchange rates. The first lesson, which became clear in the 1960s, is that large-scale intervention designed to avoid realignments undermines domestic monetary policies. Germany experienced this effect repeatedly, in 1961, 1968–1969, and again in 1971 (Solomon 1982). Since institutional independence fosters the drive for freedom of action, it is to be expected that independent central banks in the 1980s might not wholeheartedly support the formal reestablishment of a system of rigid rates.

Another lesson is that a crucial requirement for a stable exchange-rate system is the ability to change the official parities smoothly. The need to deter speculation around realignments is a delicate aspect of changing parities and requires that changes take place almost routinely. The reason is not exclusively economic. It has to do with the friction created by heightened international economic interaction in a world of jealously independent nation states. Without strong political cooperation, a system of fixed exchange rates will not be stable. Since the prospects for close and lasting political cooperation between the United States, Europe, and Japan are mixed at best, the structure of exchange rates has to be kept flexible enough.

A third lesson of Bretton Woods history and the collapse of fixed currency rates is that the exchange rate system has to accommodate changes in the underlying structure of relative economic power. The Bretton Woods system rested on both the ability and the willingness of the United States to exert hegemonic leadership, but this ability and willingness declined as European and Japanese economic might developed. Near the end of the century, it seems obvious that further meaningful changes are going to take place in the distribution of economic power in the world, notably with the emergence of Asian newly industrialized countries (NICs) as key players. Nascent changes should not be overlooked in the design of any new monetary arrangement.

A fourth lesson is that even though the pattern of hegemonic leadership no longer exists, adjustment obligations have to be symmetrical for deficit and surplus countries, lest the political stability of the system be seriously undermined. Ensuring this symmetry is a very difficult task indeed. It requires, on the one hand, sharing the costs of others' mistakes and, on the other, finding a way to make building external assets as costly as accumulating external debt.

**Some lessons of European monetary cooperation.** There is widespread agreement that the European Monetary System has been a successful cooperation attempt. The purpose of this section is to bring some qualifications to that judgment and to put the discussion in the broader context of European integration.[20] Since the European Monetary System is a good example of systemic cooperation and represents an attempt, absent in the Bretton Woods era, to develop and adapt to evolving conditions, it is useful for our purpose to discuss some of its features. The discussion will bring us back to the idea that systemic cooperation may induce more automatic coordination.

*Political, economic, and monetary integration.* Implicit in the 1957 Treaty of Rome, which established the European Economic Community, is the underlying resolve of the founders to work toward European political and economic integration. Marjolin (1986) argues that European initiatives in the 1960s were directed toward that goal and that after the failure of the Common European Defense initiative, further hope of political integration became subordinated to the possibility of economic integration through monetary cooperation. This argument provides a political interpretation of the European Monetary Union initiative of the late 1960s, which culminated in the Werner Report.[21]

Debate at that time focused on the different routes toward economic integration and opposed two main streams of analysis. The "monetarists" argued that monetary cooperation would be instrumental in progress toward economic integration. Conversely, the "economists" replied that without a prior convergence of economic policies, attempts at monetary integration would be short lived and even counterproductive.[22] Analyzed according to this division, the EMS looks like a move along the "monetarist" route. One cannot know what would have happened in the absence of the EMS; but it is clear that, within the system, substantial convergence of economic policies (toward disinflation) has successfully taken place. A conspicuous example of the EMS tendency toward convergence is the reversal of French economic policy in 1983. In that case however, there was widespread agreement on the need to disinflate. Both the proponents of staying within the system and those who advocated leaving the EMS shared this view. Opinion therefore hinged less on the relative priority to give to the different economic objectives than on the political symbolism of the system and the perception that Germany was not sharing enough of the burden.

The extent to which the EMS has contributed to installing so-called natural (as opposed to strategic) cooperative behavior is certainly debatable. The clear priority given to the fight against inflation may be seen as the major factor behind a closer convergence of monetary policies.[23] Padoa Schioppa (1985) argues that the EMS has helped to change the way policy decisions are made and objectives are ranked in member countries. One can argue that it is the commitment to the system, rather than the system itself, that may have fostered such an evolution. Believing that technical solutions may bring forth political change is largely an illusion.[24]

The current situation, however, highlights the limits of the "monetarist" approach. It is clear that further monetary cooperation requires political cooperation and integration and will entail further loss of autonomy in monetary policy. That is, closer central bank cooperation will have to be decided at the highest political level and certainly will not be left to central banks alone. These conditions apply to the creation of a European central bank as well.[25]

The need for political cooperation is one reason why the European Commission has proposed changing the route toward integration. The proposal to create a single market and remove remaining trade barriers in the EC by the end of 1992 can be seen as an attempt, through market and economic integration, to constrain further monetary cooperation.[26] The clear ranking of objectives that is implicit in the 1992 plan, namely free capital movements and stable exchange rates, requires some loss of national autonomy in the making of monetary and economic policy.

*EMS shortcomings.* The experience of the EMS highlights two main areas where progress is still needed if the exchange rate mechanism is to function smoothly. The first area is the practice of realignments; the second is the question of asymmetry.

It is true that, not only have realignments been possible, but they have been generally implemented through collective decision and in the absence of major speculation; however, negotiation of realignments has usually been tense, political, and geared toward domestic political benefits. Any change in official parities creates domestic problems. In devaluating countries, the costs are damaged credibility of economic policy making and weakened confidence in the currency. In appreciating countries, there is opposition from the sector of export-oriented industries. These problems again illustrate the difficulty of managing smooth realignments in a system of adjustable rates.

The experience of the EMS suggests that asymmetry is not only a technical question. The EMS is essentially symmetric in design, with the obligation to defend parities equally distributed between deficit and surplus countries. EMS practice, however, has restored asymmetry, notably through intramarginal interventions. The central banks of surplus countries, especially Germany, refrained from intramarginal defense of the exchange rates because they feared loosing control over the domestic money supply. Conversely, the central banks of deficit countries intervened to make the weakness of the currency less obvious to the markets.[27] In the end, the burden of intervention, and of adjustment, still falls primarily on countries that have deficits or weak currencies.

The question of asymmetry is complex. One cannot logically argue that one of the successes of the EMS has been the convergence of economic policies toward disinflation and, at the same time, that asymmetry is a major failure of the system. In effect, asymmetry, together with the commitment to make the system work, required member countries to align their economic policies on Germany's and hasten the disinflation process. Of course, when the problem of inflation seems to abate, and when there seems to be a major difference between the preferred rates of inflation among member countries, asymmetry is seen as a major political problem.

From these shortcomings of the EMS one may conclude that the system as it works was adapted to the circumstances of the late 1970s and to those of the first half of the 1980s but that it is not, in its current state, adequate for the 1990s. It must now evolve, lest it collapse.

**The Plaza and Louvre coordination experiments.** The looming crises of the 1980s again drew attention to the need to cooperate. The process put in place through the Plaza-Louvre strategy, described in detail by Funabashi in *Managing the Dollar*, aims at institutionalizing the policy coordination that began as an experiment in ad hoc, emergency cooperation. There are many flaws in that process: lack of clarity, unclear commitment, contradictory signals from participants since the original Plaza Accord, and outright failure of monetary cooperation in some instances (notably in the summer of 1987). Most of all, the objective of stabilizing the value of the dollar needs some further thought and qualification.

Although stability of exchange rates is desirable, that does not mean it must be secured as soon as an acute awareness of the costs of earlier instability stimulates enough political will to rally around that objective. To put it differently, stabilizing the exchange rates at their current level requires appropriate domestic economic policies to sustain those rates. The major failure of the Plaza-Louvre process is that it has largely neglected, despite declarations to the contrary, to back up the accords on exchange rates with a binding commitment to domestic adjustment. This failure is an outright consequence of the predominance of domestic political concerns in the United States. Overnight, the overvalued dollar, together with the policies followed in other countries, became in 1985 the United States' scapegoat for its balance of payments problem.

When sudden enthusiasm for cooperation appeared in the fall of 1985, it was, although welcomed, highly contingent and political.[28] In the United States, it had become (politically) clear that an overvalued dollar was doing some harm to farmers and exporters and that it could endanger the traditional free-trade orientation of American economic policies. Protectionist tendencies in the U.S. Congress threatened to grow out of control. In West Germany, the Bundesbank and the Finance Ministry were concerned about the potential inflationary effects of a weak deutschemark, as well as about the risk of a hard landing for the U.S. dollar and the potential disruptive effect of that development on the European Monetary System.[29] In Japan, much of the politics of international economic relations became dominated by the bilateral trade conflict with the United States and eventually favored alleviating the strains of that conflict through a gradual and controlled appreciation of the yen. In France, stability of exchange rates had been a long-advocated objective; but the whole coordination exercise initiated at the Plaza also appeared as a way to exert pressure on West Germany to reflate. Although it is desirable that cooperation benefit every participant, the Plaza Accord apparently stemmed from narrow national interests more than from a proper assessment of the need for collective management of the world economy for the common good.

A cynical view of the G7 is that they have been prisoners of their own failing strategy—that once the whole process started, it became necessary to let the markets believe that economic coordination was working satisfactorily, lest the markets cause a free fall of the dollar. From the beginning, G7 cooperation was not allowed to fail. G7 history reveals an amazing mixture of official declarations of success (understandably directed to market stabilization) together with little evidence that anything at all is taking place in terms of domestic adjustment. The evolution of international and domestic imbalances was surprisingly satisfactory at the end of the 1980s, but this was not the result of policy change. Believing that future evolution will validate and strengthen this trend places an undue faith in Providence. One can understand why the so-called secret accord on exchange rates was kept so vague: imprecision diminishes the risk of aggressive testing by the markets. They cannot really be convinced that no significant coordinated move will happen as long as the G7 still meet.

If this interpretation of events is true, G7 coordination strategy is phony. That view may be excessively negative, and one lesson of history is that the worst outcome is never certain, anyway. Optimists will say that nothing better could be devised in the current situation and that there is ample ground for satisfaction. Moreover, Funabashi's account confirms that coordination, not only of intervention policies but of policies on interest rates, has actually taken place occasionally between central banks. It is hard, however, to find any clear evidence that such coordination, when it occurred, was motivated by international rather than selfish domestic concerns.

Alone among the G7, Japan fulfilled some of the promised agenda, through a clear fiscal expansion in 1987. As Funabashi explains, external pressures have traditionally played a significant (but not exclusive) role in the Japanese decision-making process. Clearly, however, domestic political pressures, especially from constituencies hurt by *endaka* (high yen), were instrumental in the expansion. Moreover, although the G5-G7 apparatus may have relayed some external pressures, the pressures which really matter from the Japanese point of view, almost exclusively, are those from the United States. For these reasons, it is farfetched to interpret the Japanese fiscal expansion as a success of the G7 coordination strategy.

Another coordination issue is stabilization of the U.S. dollar. Stabilization has rested entirely on monetary policies; coordination of market diplomacy (through appropriate statements by central bank officials and ministers of finance); and the use of published U.S. statistics to judge the evolution of the current account, the fiscal deficit, and inflation. Coordination of central banks has played a major role in attempts to stabilize the dollar, but central banks have from the outset been skeptical about the role of monetary coordination taken in isolation. Officials of central banks have emphasized the need for adjustment of fiscal policy, especially in the United States. During the whole process, finance ministers have constrained central banks to act despite their reluctance to do so. Failure of the U.S. administration to get appropriate deficit reduction measures through Congress has put an additional burden on central banks.[30]

A further criticism of the G7 process is that, even in its "hard" components, such as the agreement on the set of statistics on which to base discussion and coordination and the choice of a number of indicators to serve as guides for adjustment requirements, one does not quite see what it adds to the work of the existing WP3 and Group of Ten.[31] One answer could be that the identical composition with that of the annual summits of industrialized countries is likely to have the G7 activities endorsed at the highest political level. Actually, however, nothing could prevent the summit participants' endorsing the work of the Group of Ten as well. Moreover, WP3 and the Group of Ten do work on a set of international statistics, most of them coming from the BIS. One rather gets the impression that supporting the G5 and then the G7 has been an ad hoc choice designed to suit the self-interest of U.S. international economic diplomacy. Besides, the United States used G2, G3, and G5 structures as well with the purpose of advancing its national interest.[32]

It is true that the practice of consultation has greatly developed under the auspices of the G7 and that it represents a success in international cooperation. The benefits of consultation are not unambiguous, however. As it has developed, consultation has become more commonplace; therefore, it attracts less attention among participants.[33] This acceptance may indeed show that the world is going international; but, since nation states stick to their national prerogatives, it also poses the risk of installing a routine, in which everybody knows what the others think, knows that pressure put on the others is motivated by domestic political concerns, and expects nothing significant from the process. International consultation is a public good, but it also has its own limits.

Finally, the current problems in the international economy seem to be problems not so much of current exchange rates as of inadequate domestic economic policies. This statement brings us back to the everlasting debate between internationalists and those we may call domesticists.[34] The latter contenders highlight the need for every one to put his house in order (ironically, this was part of the first Reagan administration's message to the world); the former focus on the requirements for collective management. This is a yet-unresolved dilemma. Effective constraint on governments may be instrumental in facilitating reasonable domestic economic policies, but governments generally will accept only those constraints that they feel are in their national interest.

**Concluding Comments**

There is no perfect, even optimal, solution to the international economic problem of reconciling interdependence with the existence of independent nation states. We must face the sad but inescapable fact that we live in a world of second bests, in which any international arrangement will be incomplete and will be more political than technical.

The signals sent by markets, as well as the expressed preferences of policy makers, suggest that the international economy needs some kind of anchor. Recent plans for coordination of economic policies attempt to respond to that need. In examining the process itself, however, one discovers that policy makers, and central banks for that matter, clearly lean toward discretion, or ad-hoc solutions, rather than toward systematic cooperation or, even less, systemic rules. At the same time, statements are issued to try to convince markets and outside observers that the lack of clear, specific, and public commitment is a deliberate strategic choice and that, indeed, the process is moving gradually toward implementing a systemic approach. The whole strategy for reconciling interdependence with national autonomy, therefore, rests on an illusion. The myth of all-powerful central bank cooperation is part of that illusion, sustained by the lack of any commitment to fiscal policy adjustment. It is a useful myth: without it, exchange rates would be much less stable than they are. The risk of a hard landing for the dollar has not disappeared, however; and if markets discover they have been guided by a myth, more instability will come.

The problem of the international anchor remains unsolved. Such an anchor has to be provided through collective management; and, for stable, regime-preserving cooperation in collective management, some clear rules are needed. The reason is not the debatable assertion that rules induce discipline; it is, rather, that they make the anchor visible and real. Departure from the rules is always possible, but it is conspicuous and therefore requires justification. Rules on exchange rates are probably the most palatable. A system of stable but adjustable rates might contribute to anchoring the international economic system; but, as we have argued several times in this discussion, the system itself has to be both stable and flexible. The conditions needed to make the G7 body an appropriate framework for running such a system are very stringent indeed. What is required beyond the current practice is (1) a commitment to specified, public targets; (2) a commitment to fiscal as well as monetary cooperation to establish credibility of the previous commitment; (3) a process for adjusting the targets. Only the last requirement may, or even must, remain vague, to keep speculation at a distance.

The contention that true international economic cooperation may come through gradualism is hardly convincing. It requires instead a major departure from, rather than an improvement of, the current practice. It requires political will and commitment and is, unfortunately, not to be expected for some time to come.

JACOB A. FRENKEL
MORRIS GOLDSTEIN
PAUL R. MASSON                                              CHAPTER 9

# International Coordination of Economic Policies: Issues and Answers

> Coordination of macroeconomic policies is certainly not easy; maybe it is impossible. But in its absence, I suspect nationalistic solutions will be sought—trade barriers, capital controls, and dual exchange-rate systems. War among nations with these weapons is likely to be mutually destructive. Eventually, they, too, would evoke agitation for international coordination.
>
> —James Tobin (1987)

> I believe that many of the claimed advantages of cooperation and coordination are wrong, that there are substantial risks and disadvantages to the types of coordination that are envisioned, and that an emphasis on international coordination can distract attention from the necessary changes in domestic policy.
>
> —Martin Feldstein (1988)

This chapter discusses the scope, methods, and effects of international coordination of economic policies. Coordination is defined here, following Wallich (1984, 85), as "a significant modification of national policies in recognition of international economic interdependence." The existence of a number of comprehensive surveys of the literature on coordination makes the task easier.[1] This discussion can, therefore, be selective and focus on a number of key issues that impinge on the advisability and practicality of strengthening policy coordination among the larger industrial countries. The purpose is to identify and evaluate factors that merit attention in any serious examination of the subject.

The first three sections of the chapter cover economic policy coordination in the widest sense and analyze the scope for and of coordination. Dimensions of coordination covered include benefits of coordination, the applicability of the "invisible hand" paradigm to decentralized economic policy decisions, barriers to coordination, the range and specificity of policies to be coordinated, the frequency of coordination, and the number of participants to be included in the coordination exercise. The second section of the chapter narrows the discussion to monetary and fiscal policies and turns to the methods of coordination. The evaluation of these methods emphasizes the broad issues of rules versus discretion, single-indicator versus multiple-indicator approaches, and hegemonic versus more symmetric systems. The last section is still more specific. It addresses the issue of gains from coordination and confronts the problem of how to infer the effects of policy coordination, in a world where there is uncertainty about the links between policies and target variables.

**Benefits of Coordination**

The most logical starting point is to ask why international policy coordination would be beneficial in the first place. After all, if, in the domestic economy, the working of the invisible hand under pure competition translates independent decentralized decisions into a social optimum, why should not the same principle apply to policy decisions by countries in the world economy?

The answer is that economic policy actions, particularly those of larger countries, create quantitatively significant spillover effects—or externalities—for other countries and that a global optimum requires that such externalities be taken into account in the decision-making calculus.[2] Coordination is then best seen as a facilitating mechanism for internalizing these externalities. This conclusion can perhaps be better appreciated by emphasizing the departures from the competitive model in today's global economy. Cooper (1987) has identified several such departures, and his analysis merits some extension here.

Unlike the atomistic economic agents of the competitive model, who base their consumption and production decisions on prices that are beyond their control, larger countries exercise a certain degree of influence over prices, including the real exchange rate. The existence of this influence of course raises the specter that they will manipulate such prices to their own advantage and at the expense of others. Two examples are frequently cited—one dealing with inflation and the other with real output and employment. Under floating rates, a Mundellian (1971) mix of tight monetary policy and loose fiscal policy allows an appreciated currency to enhance a country's disinflationary policy strategy—but at the cost of making it harder for trading partners to realize their own disinflation targets. Similarly, under conditions of high capital mobility and sticky nominal wages, a monetary expansion under floating rates leads to a real depreciation and to an expansion of output and employment at home. The other side of the coin, however, is that output and employment contract abroad.[3] Seen in this light, the role of coordination is to prevent—or to minimize—such intentional as well as unintentional beggar-thy-neighbor practices. Most international monetary constitutions have injunctions against "manipulating" exchange rates or international reserves.

The existence of public goods—and their role in the resolution of inconsistencies among policy targets—constitutes a second important point of departure from the competitive model. When there are $N$ currencies, there can be no more than $N - 1$ independent exchange rate targets. Similarly, not all countries can achieve independently set targets for current account surpluses.

Adherents of decentralized policymaking—sometimes rather inappropriately labeled the German school—argue that such inconsistencies provide no justification for intervention.[4] Much as in the competitive model, the economic system will generate signals—in the form of changes in exchange rates, interest rates, prices, and incomes—that will lead to an adjustment of targets such that they eventually become consistent. If, however, the path to consistency involves large swings in real exchange rates or, even more problematically, the imposition of restrictions on trade and capital flows, then reliance on decentralized policy making may not be globally optimal. Implicit in this conclusion is the notion that a certain degree of stability in real exchange rates and an open international trading and financial system are valued in and of themselves, that is, they are public goods. (In contrast, the market signals that resolve supply and demand inconsistencies in the competitive model are not regarded as public goods.) If that concept of public goods is accepted, there is a positive role for coordination, both to identify target inconsistencies at an early stage and to resolve them in ways that do not produce too little of the public good(s).[5] It is possible for groups of countries who value the public good highly to attempt to obtain more of it by setting up regional zones of exchange rate stability or of free trade, and some have done exactly that (these attempts include the establishment of the European Monetary System [EMS]);[6] but the essence of a public good is that it will tend to be undersupplied as long as some large suppliers or users act in a decentralized fashion.

Once the realm of atomistic competitors is left and that of nontrivial spillovers of policies is entered—be it through goods, asset, or labor markets—the possibility arises that choices made independently by national governments would not be as effective in achieving their objectives as policies that are coordinated with other governments.[7] A popular example suffices to illustrate the point. Whereas any single country acting alone may be reluctant, for fear of unduly worsening its external balance, to follow expansionary policies designed to counter a global deflationary shock, coordinated expansion by many countries will loosen the external constraint and permit each country to move closer to internal balance.

The existence of spillover effects and public goods establishes a presumption that there can be valid reasons for deviating from the tradition of decentralized decision making when it comes to economic policy, that is, that there is scope for coordination. This presumption is reinforced by two empirical observations. The first is that the world economy of 1990 is considerably more open and integrated than that of 1950, or 1960, or even 1970. Not only have simple ratios of imports or exports to GNP increased but also—and probably more fundamentally—global capital markets are more integrated.[8] With larger spillovers, there is more at stake in how one manages interdependence. Second, there is by now widespread recognition that the insulating properties of floating exchange rates are more modest than was suspected before their introduction in 1973.[9]

**Barriers to Coordination**

A presumption that cooperation could be beneficial is not the same as a guarantee, however; nor does it preclude the existence of sometimes formidable obstacles to implementation.

Suppose national policy makers have a predilection for inflationary policies but are restrained from implementing them by the concern that relatively expansionary monetary policy will bring on a devaluation (or depreciation). Yet, as outlined by Rogoff (1985), if all countries pursue such inflationary policies simultaneously, none has to worry about the threat of devaluation. Here, coordination may actually weaken discipline by easing the balance of payments constraint. In a similar vein, as noted by Feldstein (1988), there is the potential risk that a coordinated attempt to stabilize a pattern of nominal or real exchange rates could take place at an inappropriately high aggregate rate of inflation. The proposals put forward by U.S. Treasury secretary Baker and U.K. chancellor Lawson, at the 1987 annual meetings of the Fund and the World Bank, for a commodity-price-basket indicator as a potential early-warning signal of emerging aggregate price developments address just such a concern.[10] Equally troublesome would be a coordination of fiscal policies that caused the larger countries to have an aggregate fiscal deficit that put undue upward pressure on world interest rates. The basic point is straightforward: there is nothing in the coordination process in and of itself that reduces the importance of sound macroeconomic policies.[11] There can be coordination around good policies and coordination around bad ones—just as with the exchange-rate regime, where there are good fixes and bad fixes, good floats and bad floats.[12] Welfare improvements are not automatic.

It is only realistic, too, to acknowledge that there are barriers to the exercise of coordination. Four of the more prominent barriers are worth mentioning.[13] First, international policy bargains that involve shared objectives can be frustrated if some policy instruments are treated as objectives in themselves. Schultze (1988), for example, offers the view that it would have been difficult to reach a bargain on target zones for exchange rates in the early 1980s, given President Reagan's twin commitments to increased defense spending and reduced taxes. In some other countries, the constraints on policy instruments may lie in different areas, including structural policies; but the implications are the same.

Second, there can at times be sharp disagreements among countries about the effects that policy changes have on policy targets. In some cases, these differences may extend beyond the size to even the sign of various policy-impact multipliers.[14] The harder it is to agree on how the world works, the harder it is to reach agreement on a jointly designed set of policies.

Third, although most countries have experienced a marked increase in openness over the past few decades, there remain huge cross-country differences in the degree of interdependence. Large countries—the United States is the classic case in point—are generally less affected by other countries' policies than are small ones. Coordination, as Bryant (1987) recently emphasized, is not a matter of altruism. It is rather the manifestation of mutual self-interest. To the extent that large countries are less beset by spillovers and feedbacks than small ones, the formers' incentive to coordinate on a continuous basis may be lower.[15] In this regard, the high degree of trade interdependence shared by members of the European Monetary System can be seen as a positive factor in reinforcing that group's incentives to coordinate.

Finally, as Polak (1981) has reminded us, as a national priority, international bargaining typically ranks below domestic bargaining. More specifically, the compromise of growth and inflation objectives at the national level may leave little room for further compromise on demand measures at the international level.

These barriers to coordination should not be overestimated: one of the clearest examples of true coordination—the Bonn economic summit of 1978—occurred just when domestic bargaining over the same issues was most intense;[16] the growing integration of capital markets—of which the global stock market crash of October 1987 was but one reminder—has brought the implications of interdependence home to even large countries; and continued empirical work on multicountry models should be able progressively to whittle down the margin of disagreement on the effects of policies. Still, as readers of Sherlock Holmes stories will be aware, sometimes the most telling clue is that the hounds *didn't* bark. If the scope for coordination is to expand beyond the efforts of the past, these obstacles will need to be overcome.

**The Scope of Coordination**

When the scope of coordination is explored, a key issue concerns the appropriate range and depth of policies to be coordinated.

The case for supporting a wide-ranging, multi-issue approach to coordination is that such an approach increases the probability of concluding some policy bargains that benefit all parties,[17] that favorable spillover effects are generated across negotiating issues, and that improved economic performance today depends as much on trade and structural policies as on exchange rate and demand policies. Exhibit A is the Bonn economic summit of 1978, where commitments by Japan and the Federal Republic of Germany to accelerate growth were exchanged for a commitment by the United States to come to grips with its inflation and oil problems. The agreement on macroeconomic and energy policies reached at this summit has been credited with reinforcing progress on the Tokyo Round of multilateral trade negotiations (Putnam and Henning 1986).

The defense of a narrower approach to coordination rests on the arguments that negotiation costs rise rapidly with the spread of issues under consideration (Artis and Ostry 1986); that prospects for implementation of agreements dim as the number of jurisdictional spheres expands (that is, finance ministers can negotiate agreements; but fiscal policy is typically the responsibility of legislatures, and monetary policy is the province of independent central banks); and that heated disputes on some issues (such as the stance of monetary and fiscal policies) can frustrate the chance for agreements in other areas (like defense and foreign assistance) where coordination might be more fruitful (Feldstein 1988). In addition, a case could be made that coordination is likely only in areas where there is a consensus about the effects of common policies (Cooper 1988).

In view of these conflicting considerations, it is hard to fault present institutional practices on the range of coordination. Those practices entail high-frequency coordination on narrow issues in a multitude of forums (such as the International Monetary Fund, the Organization for Economic Cooperation and Development, the Bank for International Settlements, and the General Agreement on Tariffs and Trade;[18] less frequent (say, biannual) and wider coordination at a higher level in more limited forums (such as the IMF's Interim Committee or the Group of Seven major industrial countries); and even less frequent (annual), still wider coordination at the highest level (heads of state and of government at the economic summits). Thus, there are occasional opportunities for multiissue bargaining, but without the exponential increase in negotiation costs that might ensue if such bargaining were the order of the day. All in all, this is probably not a bad compromise.

The depth of coordination is the degree of specificity and disaggregation within a given policy area. Here, two issues arise—one dealing with fiscal policy and the other with structural policies. A strong implication of recent research is that an aggregate measure, such as the central or general government fiscal deficit, is not likely to be a good guide to the effects of fiscal policies on macroeconomic variables such as the current account, the exchange rate, and the rate of interest.[19] The reason is that such effects depend on *how* the deficit is altered—that is, whether the means chosen are taxes or expenditures, expenditures on tradables or those on nontradables, taxes on investment or taxes on saving; whether fiscal action is taken by a country with a current account surplus or by one with a deficit; and whether the policies are anticipated or unanticipated. These differences suggest that more specificity in coordination—quite apart from its positive effect on the ability to monitor the implementation of agreed-on policies—would be desirable. It is notable that the Louvre Accord of February 1987 among the Group of Seven specified not only quantitative targets for budget deficits but also some quantitative guidelines for how these overall fiscal targets were to be achieved.[20]

In the area of structural policies, a good case can also be made for specificity—but on somewhat different grounds. Here, coordination may often best be interpreted, not as the simultaneous application of the same policy instruments in different doses or directions across countries, but rather as the simultaneous application of different policy instruments[21]—with each country adopting the policy best tailored to its particular structural weakness.[22] In some cases, this may imply reducing impediments to labor mobility or to market-determined wages; in others, it may mean increasing incentives for private investment relative to those for private saving; and, in still others, it may mean changes in the trade and distribution system. The simultaneous application of the policy measures across countries may be necessary to overcome the blocking tactics of domestic pressure groups and to enhance the credibility of the exercise. Again, the depth or specificity of coordination can be as relevant as the range.

Another salient issue concerns the question of *when* to coordinate. There has been, and continues to be, wide variation in the frequency of coordination across different forums—ranging from one-of-a-kind meetings like the 1971 Smithsonian conference on exchange rates to the nearly continuous discussion and decision making by the executive boards of the IMF and the World Bank.

One position is that, because of the constraints that exist, true coordination cannot be expected to be more than an episodic, regime-preserving effort. Dini (1988) has recently argued that international considerations still play only a small part in policy making and that only at times of crisis is a common interest in coordinated action clearly recognized.[23] Some might even go farther and argue that the reservoir of international compromise should be conserved for situations when there is a high probability of a policy deal and when failure to reach an agreement would carry a high cost.

Our view is that both the likelihood and effectiveness of coordination will be enhanced when it is a regular, ongoing process—for at least three reasons. First, the potential for multiperiod bargaining expands the opportunities for policy bargains (by facilitating, for example, phasing of policy measures). What should count in assessing the gains to coordination is the present discounted value of welfare-improving policy agreements over an extended period—not the welfare change in a single period. Second, as suggested in the game-theoretic literature, the existence of repeated bargaining strengthens the role of reputational considerations in coordination.[24] In contrast, when coordination is a once-and-for-all or episodic exercise, there is a higher risk that agreed policies will never be implemented. This risk exists because of the much-discussed problem of time inconsistency, that is, the temptation to renege on earlier policy commitments when it later becomes advantageous to do so.[25] To be effective, a coordination agreement needs to pass through the market filter of credibility, and credibility is more likely to be established if sticking to the agreement enhances reputation. A reputation for adherence in turn allows profitable bargains to be struck in the future. Third, once coordination is established as a routine, ongoing process, there is likely to be more freedom of policy maneuver for all participants than when negotiations are conducted in a crisis atmosphere and when disagreements—which are inevitable—may be inappropriately seen as signaling the collapse of coordination itself.[26]

As any good newspaper reporter knows, the three Ws of *why*, *what*, and *when* are not sufficient for writing a story. One also has to bring in the fourth W, namely *who* should coordinate. Again, existing practice does not provide a definitive answer. Among the industrial countries, we have the Group of Seven and the Group of Ten. For the developing countries, there are the Group of Twenty-four and the Group of Seventy-seven; and on the executive board of the Fund, where industrial and developing countries alike are represented, there are twenty-two representatives of various country groupings—a Group of Twenty-two.

Among the factors that should influence the size of the coordinating group, three seem to stand out. First, to the extent that the raison d'etre of coordination is the internalization of externalities, the group should include those countries whose policies generate the largest externalities. This principal argues for including the largest industrial countries. Second, there is the general proposition that the costs of negotiation, and conflicts that might endanger the continuity of the exercise, increase significantly with the number of players. This proposition argues for a relatively small group. The third factor, however, is that a small group runs the risk of concluding policy agreements which are beneficial to the direct participants—but which are not satisfactory to those countries absent from the coordination table.[27]

In light of these considerations, it is worth mentioning two features of recent coordination efforts by the Group of Seven. One of them, proposed at the Venice economic summit in 1987 and incorporated in subsequent coordination meetings, is the addition of aggregate indicators for the Group of Seven as a whole to the list of individual country indicators. Aggregate indicators for the group may include such variables as the growth rate of real GNP and of domestic demand, the interest rate, the current account position, and the real exchange rate. A strong motivation for such aggregate indicators is that they can be helpful in gauging the impact of G7 coordination agreements and actions on the rest of the world, with particular reference to the developing countries. For example, it has been estimated that each 1 percent change in real GNP in the industrial countries is associated, if all else remains the same, with approximately a 3 percent change (in the same direction) of export earnings in developing countries. Similarly, a 1 percent change in world interest rates implies roughly a $3 billion–$4 billion change in net interest payments by capital-importing developing countries. In short, aggregate indicators can be seen as an analytical instrument for helping to evaluate whether a given policy package for the larger countries is also in the interest of others.

A second notable feature is that the managing director of the Fund participates in these Group of Seven coordination meetings. Since the Fund's membership includes not only the larger industrial countries but also the smaller industrial countries, as well as most of the developing countries, one rationale for the managing director's participation is that it provides a systemic perspective on and evaluation of proposed policy agreements—while still keeping the meeting small enough for administrative efficiency.

## Methods of Coordination

In this section, the focus shifts from whether to coordinate to how to coordinate. More specifically, the advantages and disadvantages of alternative methods of coordination are discussed, with particular attention to the issues of rules versus discretion, single-indicator versus multiindicator approaches, and hegemonic versus symmetric systems.

**Rules or discretion.** It is not surprising that many of the issues that have emerged during the long and continuing debate on the relative merits of rules as compared with discretion in domestic economic policy should have resurfaced in the dialogue on international coordination of economic policy. After all, the present system of managed floating, even as it has evolved since the Plaza agreement of September 1985, is much closer to a pure discretion model than to a pure rules model. In this regard, the gold standard with its automatic mechanism of specie flow, the adjustable peg system with its clear implications for the subordination of domestic monetary policy to the exchange rate (except during fundamental disequilibria), the EMS with its parity grid and divergence indicator, target zone proposals with their trigger for coordination discussions whenever the actual exchange rate threatens to breach the zone, and pure floating with its complete prohibition on all official intervention in the exchange market—all can be considered less discretionary than the present exchange rate system. The debate is thus not about what is but rather about what should be.

Those who support a more rules-based approach to international economic policy rest their case on essentially four arguments. First, the most promising route to eliminating any excess demand for coordination in the world economy is not by increasing the supply but rather by decreasing the demand (or the need) for coordination.[28] That decrease in demand, in turn, can best be brought about by the application of simple policy rules, such as the maintenance of a fixed exchange rate. In the process, one would eliminate—so the argument goes—most of the negotiation costs and burden-sharing conflicts that are intrinsic to more discretionary systems. Second, rules are regarded as the only viable mechanism for imposing discipline on economic policy makers who might otherwise manipulate the instruments of policy for their own objectives.[29] Third, rules are regarded as enhancing the predictability of policy actions and thereby improving the private sector's ability to make informed decisions about resource allocation.[30] Fourth, by preempting destabilizing fine tuning, rules are championed as providing protection against the lack of knowledge about how the economy operates.

The main counterarguments in favor of a discretionary approach are the following: First, rule-based adjustment systems often turn out to be less automatic in practice than in theory. For example, the automaticity of the specie-flow mechanism under the historical gold standard was often undermined by the proclivity of authorities to offset or sterilize the effect of gold flows.[31]

Second, rules will impart discipline to the conduct of macroeconomic policy only to the extent that the penalties for breaking the rules are significant enough to ensure that the rules are followed. The Bretton Woods rule that countries should consult with the Fund when there was a cumulative parity change of 10 percent or more, although complied with in a technical sense, fell short in a substantive way of its original purpose. The discussion surrounding the revision of the original Gramm-Rudman deficit-reduction targets in the United States is a more recent case in point. History could in fact be considered just as kind to the proposition that the policy regime adjusts to the amount of discipline that countries want to have as to the reverse proposition (Goldstein 1980, 1984; Frenkel 1982; Frenkel and Goldstein 1986). Also, care needs to be taken to separate the effects of policy rules from other influences on economic outcomes. In this connection, the oft-made argument that the EMS was a major determinant of the 1979–1985 disinflation in Europe would seem to stand on shaky ground.[32]

Third, it is by no means clear that rules are necessary to obtain the benefits of greater predictability of policy. For example, the practice of preannouncing money supply targets—sometimes accompanied by announcements of public sector borrowing requirements—provides the markets with information on the authorities' policy intentions but stops well short of a rigid rule.

Finally, although rules diminish the risk emanating from fine tuning, they increase the risk stemming from lack of adaptability to changes in the operating environment.[33] The idea of a crawling peg rule based on inflation differentials drew quite a few supporters in the 1960s as the right antidote for sticky nominal exchange rates. Yet its neglect of the need for *real* exchange rate changes now seems more serious in light of the real economic disturbances of the early 1970s.[34] More recently, the crumbling of the link between narrow monetary aggregates and the ultimate targets of monetary policy in the face of large-scale financial innovation and institutional change has reminded us anew of the limitations of policy rules.

In light of these considerations, there may not be any attractive alternative to conducting economic policy coordination in a judgmental way.

**Single or multiple indicators.** Even after the choice is made between rules or discretion, there remains the decision of whether to coordinate around a single indicator or around a set of indicators. A regime of fixed exchange rates or target zones is an example of the former approach, whereas the ongoing Group of Seven coordination exercise is an example of the latter.

There are two main considerations that are typically advanced to support the single-indicator approach. One is that it avoids over-coordination of policies by preserving for each country freedom of action over those policies not used to reach the single target variable. Thus, for example, if the exchange rate is the focus of coordination, monetary policy will be constrained, but other policies will be less affected. Implicit in this line of argument is the view that attempts to place many policies under international coordination will ultimately prove self-defeating and may even induce national authorities to compensate by exercising greater independence in uncoordinated policy instruments, such as trade policy.[35]

The second, and probably more important, defense of a single-indicator approach is that it sends a clear signal to markets about the course of future policy. If, for example, the monetary authorities commit themselves to maintain a fixed exchange rate within a given band, then movements of the exchange rate provide an unambiguous guide for monetary policy. A similar message would derive from setting a nominal income target for monetary or fiscal policy and leaving the exchange rate to be determined by the market. In contrast, a multiindicator approach increases the authorities' scope for discretion, since they can appeal to the conflicting messages coming from different indicators. In cases where the authorities' past record of policy performance has been weak and where a single objective of policy (such as disinflation) is predominant, a single-indicator framework for coordination can carry significant advantages in the battle to restore credibility to policy.

Relying on a single policy indicator can also carry substantial risks. Perhaps the most serious one is that the single indicator can send weak—or even false—signals about the need for changes in other policies that are not being coordinated. This is perhaps best illustrated by considering the problem of errant fiscal policy under a regime of fixed exchange rates or of target zones.

First, consider fixed rates. With high capital mobility, a fiscal expansion will yield an incipient positive interest-rate differential, a capital inflow, and an overall balance of payments surplus, not a deficit. Here, exchange rate fixity helps to finance—and by no means disciplines—irresponsible fiscal policy (Frenkel and Goldstein 1988). Only if and when the markets expect fiscal deficits to be monetized will they force the authorities to choose between fiscal policy adjustments and devaluation.[36] The better the reputation of the authorities, the longer in coming will be the discipline of markets, that is, the exchange rate will provide only a weak and late signal for policy adjustment. In this connection, it is worth observing that, whereas the EMS has produced a notable convergence of monetary policy, convergence of fiscal policy has not taken place (Tanzi 1988; Holtham, Keating, and Spencer 1987).

Next, consider the same fiscal expansion under a target zone regime, where the zones are to be defended by monetary policy. In such a scenario, the appreciation of the currency induced by the fiscal action will prompt a loosening of monetary policy to keep the rate from breaching the zone. Here, coordination around a single indicator, namely, the exchange rate, will have exacerbated—not corrected—the basic cause of the problems.[37] The single indicator would have sent the wrong signal for policy adjustment.

In contrast, a multiindicator approach to coordination—assuming that the list of indicators included monetary and fiscal policy variables—would not be susceptible to this weak- or false-signal problem.[38] This is because such an approach goes directly to the basic stance of fiscal and monetary policies, rather than passing through the medium of the exchange rate. If, for example, the impetus for coordination were a misalignment of exchange rates, and if the root cause of the misalignment were an inappropriate stance or mix of monetary and fiscal policies, the multiindicator approach would be appealing.

A multiindicator approach is not all a bed of roses, either. All effective approaches to coordination require a consistency of policy instruments and targets within and among countries, but this requirement of consistency or compatibility can take an added prominence when authorities make public a set of targets and intended courses for policy instruments.[39]

Two aspects merit explicit mention. One is that exchange rate targets—or even concerted views on the existing pattern of exchange rates—must be consistent with the announced course of monetary and fiscal policies. Without that consistency, attempts to provide the market with an anchor for medium-term exchange rate expectations are likely to prove fruitless.

The second point is that the credibility of multiple policy targets also hinges on the constraints on policy instruments. Two such constraints are the striking inflexibility of fiscal policy in almost all industrial countries, and the limited ability of sterilized exchange-market intervention to affect the level of the exchange rate over the medium term (unless, of course, it provides a signal about the future course of policies).[40] A relevant concern is that limitations on other policy instruments may cause monetary policy to be left with too heavy a burden—it may wind up with primary responsibility for maintaining internal and external balance. In such a case, any contribution that a multiindicator approach to coordination could make to enhancing the predictability of policies would also be diminished. This is so because a shock to the system—such as the October 1987 global stock market crash—might lead market participants to wonder whether monetary policy would serve its internal or its external master.

**Hegemony or symmetry.** Yet another key methodological issue associated with coordination—particularly when it involves joint decision making—is whether one country should, by common consent, have a predominant voice in the course of policies or, alternatively, whether that influence should be shared more evenly. In this respect, the historical gold standard, the Bretton Woods system, and the EMS are all often regarded as hegemonic systems, whereas the ongoing Group of Seven coordination process would qualify as a more symmetric exercise.[41]

Hegemonic exchange rate systems have typically operated under what might be called an implicit contract between the leader and the satellite countries.[42] Under Bretton Woods, the leader (that is, the United States) carried the obligation to conduct prudent macroeconomic policies, perhaps best summarized as resulting in a steady, low rate of inflation. This obligation was reinforced by the leader's commitment to peg some nominal price—in that case, the price of gold. Since there can be no more than $N - 1$ exchange rates among $N$ countries, the leader was passive about its exchange rate. The satellite countries committed to peg their exchange rates within agreed margins to the leader. As a reaction to the competitive depreciation of the 1930s, cumulative exchange rate adjustments greater than 10 percent were to be placed under international supervision and were to be taken only under conditions of "fundamental disequilibrium." By virtue of their exchange rate obligations, the satellites sacrificed independence in their monetary policies but expected to import stability from the leader.

With the benefit of hindsight, it is not surprising that this implicit contract came under strain from two main directions (in addition to Triffin's [1960] well-known "confidence problem.") One strain was the breakdown (after the mid-1960s) of discipline by the leader. The satellites then came to see it as exporting inflation rather than stability. The response was for the satellites to sever their formal links with the leader (in the early 1970s) and thereafter to seek stability through other mechanisms, including national money supply targeting and regional exchange rate arrangements. The second strain was an excessive rigidity of nominal exchange rates in the face of fundamental disequilibrium that produced a misalignment of the leader's real exchange rate in the late 1960s. The leader then abandoned the commitment to be passive about its exchange rate.

The implicit contract in the EMS is similar in many ways to that under Bretton Woods. Although there is no formal leader, most observers regard the Federal Republic of Germany (and its Bundesbank) as the de facto leader.[43] Germany follows macroeconomic policies that export price stability and antiinflationary credibility to the others. It is noteworthy that although there have to date been eleven realignments in the EMS, none of them has resulted in a revaluation relative to the deutsche mark, thus leaving Germany's reputation as an exporter of stability intact. Other participants in the exchange rate mechanism of the EMS can be characterized as tying their hands on domestic monetary policy so as to make credible both their exchange rate obligations and their inflation objectives.[44] Exchange rate adjustments are placed under common supervision. When realignments do take place, they do not always provide full compensation for past inflation differentials. In this way, the resulting real appreciation for high-inflation countries can act as a disincentive to inflation (by penalizing exports, output, and employment), while the leader receives a gain in competitiveness that provides some compensation for its export of antiinflationary credibility.[45] Monetary policy in Germany is typically regarded as the anchor and is considered disciplined enough to do away with the need to peg to some outside nominal price.

Although there have clearly been periods when large countries have exerted a stabilizing influence on the system, it is hard to accept that hegemony is a necessary characteristic of a well-functioning system of international coordination. There are several reasons. First, careful study of alleged hegemonic systems, including the gold standard, reveals that the amount of cooperation needed for smooth functioning was substantial (Eichengreen 1987). The coordinated actions of September 1987 on interest rates in the EMS, when Germany and the Netherlands lowered their rates and France raised its rate, are an example of such cooperation. Second, much of what passes for the stabilizing influence of hegemony can also reflect common objectives. Again, the EMS serves as a useful laboratory. In the early 1980s, disinflation was the top priority in virtually all EMS countries. Since Germany had the best reputation for price stability, there was a commonality of interests in trying to converge to the German inflation rate. Now, however, some observers argue that both because of the progress already made with inflation and because of the high unemployment rates that prevail in some EMS (and potential EMS) countries, it is time to give greater weight to objectives other than controlling inflation. If such a decision were made, it would probably result in a more symmetric EMS, quite apart from shifts among members in relative economic size or reputation.[46] Third, attempts to reinstate a hegemonic approach to coordination when economic realities no longer support it could be counterproductive. In the present context, there appears to be no obvious candidate that combines an unblemished record for economic stability, a dominant position in international trade and finance (relative to other members of the coordination group), and a willingness to accept the requisite responsibilities.

### Coordination When Effects Are Uncertain

An important aspect of the policy coordination process is the lack of knowledge about the effects of policies and hence about whether a particular policy choice is likely to have beneficial or harmful effects.[47] For instance, Feldstein has argued that "uncertainties about the actual state of the international economy and uncertainties about the effects of one country's policies on the economies of other countries make it impossible to be confident that coordinated policy shifts would actually be beneficial" (Feldstein 1988, 10). Evidence of this lack of knowledge can be gleaned from a comparison of existing multicountry models that was made at the Brookings Institution.[48] The second-year multiplier effects on GDP of a standardized increase in government expenditure in the United States ranged from 0.4 to 2.1, whereas the transmission effects on GDP in the rest of the OECD area ranged from slightly negative to 0.7. Moreover, estimates of single parameters—for instance, the interest elasticity of investment or the direct substitution effect of government spending on private consumption—often have very large standard errors relative to estimated coefficients.

Lack of knowledge about the functioning of the world economy—which we will term model uncertainty—should be distinguished from disagreement about the correct view of the world, which may or may not involve recognition by policy makers that their view of the world may be incorrect.[49] In an extreme case, each policy maker may be convinced that he has the truth but that others do not. Then, each may think that he can fool the others into reaching agreements that they mistakenly believe are in their best interest. Disagreement among policy makers will be discussed in this chapter, but first we will consider the question of model uncertainty.

**Model uncertainty.** A natural way to treat model uncertainty is to formulate a general model that includes the various possible models (assuming that they constitute a relatively small set) as special cases with different parameter values—that is, treat model uncertainty as parameter uncertainty. If we can formulate the problem as finding the optimal policies (either coordinated or uncoordinated) in the presence of ranges of possible parameter values, then Brainard's (1967) analysis applies. Brainard shows that in general there is a trade-off between close attainment of targets and increases in the variance of the target variable. For instance, suppose that, starting from a situation where policy is set to hit a target exactly, an oil price shock threatens to produce a suboptimal outcome; should an attempt be made to use the policy instrument to counteract fully the effect of the shock? Since the effect of the policy instrument is uncertain, attempting to counteract the shock fully may in fact more than offset its effect. The main lesson from Brainard is that policy should be less activist in the presence of model uncertainty and should not attempt to respond fully to shocks.[50] That is, policy makers in general should not engage in fine tuning of policy instruments.

What is the lesson about gains that may result from international coordination of policies? On the surface, policy coordination may seem to be more activist than independent pursuit of policy goals by the countries concerned; but that presumption is not correct. On the contrary, policy coordination may rule out certain types of activist policies, such as the use of the exchange rate in a beggar-thy-neighbor fashion (as when competitive depreciation is used to generate employment or appreciation to achieve quick disinflation). The question is whether the existence of uncertainty increases the gap between coordinated policies—which, by definition, are fully optimal if problems of time inconsistency are ruled out—and uncoordinated policies.

It turns out that there is a useful distinction between uncertainty about the effects of policies in the country taking the action (which we will call domestic multiplier uncertainty) and uncertainty about the effects on the home country of policy moves taken abroad (which we will call transmission multiplier uncertainty). For domestic multiplier uncertainty, there are no general results to show whether an increase in uncertainty will increase or decrease gains from policy coordination. In the case of the latter uncertainty (which is larger, the greater is the variance of transmission multipliers), there is an unambiguous increase in the gap between coordinated and uncoordinated policies and hence an increase in the gains from policy coordination (Ghosh and Ghosh 1986; Ghosh and Masson 1988a). The appendix to this chapter demonstrates these findings in a simple algebraic model. Uncoordinated policies, because they do not correctly capture the endogenous nature of foreign policy making (that is, the reaction of policy abroad to moves made at home), do not properly take into account this element of uncertainty. Policy coordination, in contrast, internalizes uncertainty about the effects of policy moves made abroad. Thus, the gains to be expected from policy coordination may be larger than is suggested by the simulation of deterministic models that use point estimates of parameter values and ignore uncertainty.

This conclusion emerges from the model simulations performed by Ghosh and Masson (1988a). In their paper, a two-country global model of the United States versus the rest of the world was used to quantify gains from policy coordination. Ranges for parameters were established from a survey of empirical work, and three possible models were considered: a midpoint estimate and the high and low extremes of the range. Policy makers (and private agents) were all assumed to assign the same probabilities to these possible models and to set optimal policy on the basis of expected utility maximization. It was shown that uncertainty in most parameters increased the gain from coordinated policy choices relative to independent maximization of utility—that is, uncertainty increased expected gains from policy coordination.

A recent instance—the stock market crash of October 1987—may help to make concrete the argument and illustrate its real-world relevance. It could be argued that the shock to stock prices also produced greater uncertainty about underlying transmission mechanisms. There was concern in central banks at the time of the crash that liquidity should be increased, to avoid possible bankruptcies among investment houses and a crisis of confidence in the real economy. A central bank acting alone, however, would run the risk that by increasing the money supply and lowering interest rates it might provoke a run against the currency, exacerbating financial collapse. In such circumstances, the absence of cooperation among monetary authorities might lead them to increase liquidity by less than the optimal amount; therefore, the uncertainty concerning effects on exchange markets should be an incentive for enhanced coordination. Of course, the need for coordination would depend on the nature of the shocks and the perceived risks. Paradoxically, the fact that the shift out of equities into other assets was generalized across major countries may have minimized the need for coordination in October 1987.

**Disagreement about models.** Uncertainty may or may not be associated with disagreement among policy makers about the correct representation of reality. If policy makers disagree (one or each is therefore necessarily wrong), then, as Frenkel and Rockett (1988) point out, coordination agreements may lead in the end to losses rather than gains, relative to uncoordinated policymaking. Frankel and Rockett calculate that coordination between the United States and the rest of the OECD is about equally likely to worsen welfare as to improve it, when models are chosen from those represented in the Brookings model-comparison conference cited earlier and when coordination involves setting policies to maximize joint utility (assumed to depend on both regions' output and inflation performance).

The significance of this result has been questioned on two grounds. First, it has been argued that coordination is unlikely if one of the partners to an agreement believes that the other is using the wrong model and believes that the agreed policies will be demonstrably worse for that country than the alternative, uncoordinated policy (Holtham and

Hughes Hallett 1987). In this case, there is the danger that the agreement might be abandoned by one of the parties. In addition, the perception that one of them had taken advantage of the other might preclude later beneficial cooperation. If some of the cases considered by Frankel and Rockett (1988) are ruled out, the conclusion that coordination has a good chance of being harmful is considerably weakened.

The second qualification is to suggest that the models probably do not adequately represent the nature of disagreements among the policy makers. Ghosh and Masson (1988b) start from alternative estimated variants of a standard two-country open-economy model (Oudiz and Sachs 1984), which contains about the same degree of reduced-form multiplier uncertainty as the models considered by Frankel and Rockett. They show that if policy makers learn from observations on endogenous variables about the probabilities to be assigned to each of the models, using Bayesian learning,[51] they converge rather quickly to the assumed, "true" model. This suggests that the experiment performed by Frankel and Rockett is rather artificial. It may be that the range of disagreement among the models compared in the Brookings conference is in fact larger than that between policy makers; some of the models can clearly be ruled out of court. Alternatively, policy makers' views of reality are much more subtle than those represented by the models—they are models after all—and policy setting cannot be represented by such simple optimization exercises.

Furthermore, attempts to date to evaluate the effects of policy coordination using models—which conclude that gains for the major industrial countries are likely to be small[52]—may not give an adequate assessment for at least four additional reasons. First, from a comparison of optimal uncoordinated with optimal coordinated policies, it may not be possible to generalize to the relevant comparison of suboptimal policies. In particular, the link between pressures for protectionism, on the one hand, and recession and exchange rates, on the other, could result in quite a different "counterfactual" (that is, what would happen in the absence of coordination) than that assumed in these studies.[53] Second, some of the gains (but also no doubt some of the losses) from coordination may be unobservable (unwritten pledges to alter policies in the future) or may be difficult to separate from less ambitious forms of cooperation (exchange of information across countries) or may extend beyond the realm of macroeconomic policy (joint measures to combat terrorism or to harmonize international fare schedules for air travel, for example). Third, a judgment that gains from coordination are small presupposes some standard of comparison and does not imply that they are not worth obtaining. For instance, are the gains from international coordination small relative to the gains from coordination of policies across different economic agencies within a national government, or are they small relative to the costs of coordination? Fourth, and related to the first point, empirical estimates of gains from coordination have typically compared policies that do not exploit the incentive governments have to adhere to agreements in order to enhance either their reputations for consistency or their credibility with the private sector. Currie, Levine, and Vidalis (1987) argue, in contrast, that comparison of "reputational" policies shows large gains.

We believe that international economic policy coordination is likely to lead to good domestic policies and for that reason is a valuable mechanism for promoting global welfare.

## Appendix

## The Effects of Model Uncertainty on Gains from Coordination

To illustrate the different effects of uncertainty concerning domestic multipliers and transmission multipliers, consider a simple two-country model in which the goal of monetary policy is price stability ( $p = 0$ ); the central bank's loss function is given by $V = E(p^2)$.[54] Inflation depends on domestic monetary policy ($M$) and foreign monetary policy ( $M^*$ ), as follows:

$$p = \theta_1 M + \theta_2 M^* + \varepsilon,$$

where $\theta_1$ and $\theta_2$ are stochastic parameters that capture domestic and transmission multipliers respectively (with $\theta_1 > 0$, $\theta_2 \gtrless 0$, but $\theta_1 + \theta_2 > 0$) and $\varepsilon$ is an inflation shock facing both countries (assumed to be positive), and observable by the two governments. Symmetric relationships are assumed to describe the foreign country (variables indicated by $^*$).

In the absence of uncertainty about multipliers, both independent policy making and coordination (i.e., maximization of a joint welfare function $W = 0.5 V + 0.5 V^*$) yield the same optimal policies, since there are as many targets as instruments; and so price stability can be achieved exactly in each case. Such is not the case when $\theta_1$ and $\theta_2$ are uncertain, however. If we suppose that they are stochastic (though identical in the two countries) and have means $\mu_1$, $\mu_2$ and variances $\sigma_1^2$, $\sigma_2^2$, respectively, then optimal policies will be the following. Under independent policymaking, each country's optimum policy will be

$$M = M^* = -\varepsilon/(\mu_1 + \mu_2 + \sigma_1^2/\mu_1), \tag{1}$$

whereas coordination will yield

$$M = M^* = -\varepsilon/[\mu_1 + \mu_2 + (\sigma_1^2 + \sigma_2^2)/(\mu_1 + \mu_2)]. \tag{2}$$

It is clear that, in general (1) and (2) will not be the same; there will be gains from policy coordination. (Since the countries are assumed to be identical and the shock to be symmetric, an increase in $W$ will yield an increase in both $V$ and $V^*$, increasing both countries' welfare). Moreover, it can be shown that the gains are an increasing function of transmission multiplier uncertainty ( $\sigma_2$ ), but increases in domestic multiplier uncertainty ( $\sigma_1$ ) have ambiguous effects. The reason for the ambiguity is that the values for optimal $M$ given by (1) can be either greater or less than those given by (2). Increases in $\sigma_1$ will tend to reduce $M$ in both cases (i.e., make monetary policy less activist)[55] but can increase or reduce the gap between them, depending on the relative values of means and variances of the parameters. Therefore, gains from coordinating policies can either increase or decrease as a result of an increase in domestic multiplier uncertainty.

NOTES AND REFERENCES

1  Rudiger Dornbusch and Steve Marcus, "Introduction"

*Note*

1. See Cooper (1989) and Federal Reserve Bank of Boston (1989) for extensive discussion of these issues.

*References*

Baxter, M., and A. Stockman. 1989. "Business Cycles and the Exchange Rate Regime: Some International Evidence." *Journal of Monetary Economics*, May.
Cline, W. 1989. *United States Adjustment and the World Economy*. Washington, D.C.: Institute for International Economics.
Cooper, R., et al. 1989. *Can Nations Agree?* Washington, D.C.: Brookings Institution.
Federal Reserve Bank of Boston. 1989. "To Coordinate or Not Coordinate: A Panel Discussion." In *International Payments Imbalances in the 1980s*.
Frankel, J. 1985. "Six Possible Meanings of Over-valuation: The 1981–85 Dollar." In *Essays in International Finance*. Princeton, N.J.: Princeton University Press.
Frankel, J., and Ken Froot. 1987. "Using Survey Data to Test Standard Propositions Regarding Exchange Rate Expectations." *American Economic Review*, March 1987.
Frankel, J., and Richard Meese. 1987. "Are Exchange Rates Excessively Variable?" In *NBER Macroeconomics Annual*. Cambridge, Mass.: MIT Press.

Frankel, J., and K. Rockett. 1989. "International Macroeconomic Policy Coordination When Policy Makers Do Not Agree on the True Model." *American Economic Review,* June.

Friedman, M. 1988. "Why the Twin Deficits are a Blessing." *The Wall Street Journal,* December 14.

Ito, T. 1988. "Foreign Exchange Rate Expectations: Micro Survey Data." NBER Working Paper no. 2679. National Bureau of Economic Research, Cambridge, Mass., August.

McKinnon, R. 1988. "Monetary and Exchange Rate Policies for International Financial Stability: A Proposal." *Journal of Economic Perspectives,* winter.

———. 1989. "Sound Dollar Tells Business: Think Long." *The Wall Street Journal,* June 15.

Mundell, R. A. 1968. *International Economics.* London: Macmillan.

———. 1971. *Monetary Theory.* Pacific Palisades, Calif.: Goodyear.

Mundell, R.A., and A. Swoboda, eds. 1968. *The International Monetary System.* Chicago: University of Chicago Press.

Shaffer, J. 1989. "What the U.S. Current Account Deficit Has Meant for Other OECD Countries." *OECD Studies,* spring 1988.

Swoboda, A. 1989. "Financial Integration and International Monetary Arrangements." Graduate Institute of International Economics, Geneva. Mimeo.

Williamson, J. 1989. "The Case for Roughly Stabilizing the Real Value of the Dollar." *American Economic Review,* May.

Williamson, J., and M. Miller. 1987. *Targets and Indicators: A Blueprint for the International Coordination of Economic Policy.* Washington, D.C.: Institute for International Economics.


## 2  Stanley Fischer, "Recent Debt Developments"

*Notes*

A radical change in debt strategy took place following Secretary Brady's speech in March 1989. This chapter is based on a paper, originally delivered at the annual meetings of the IMF and the World Bank in September 1989, that examines the debt situation as it appeared at that time. I am grateful to John Underwood of the Bank's Debt and International Finance Division for advice and assistance.

1. The three options are (1) one-third of debt service coming due during the rescheduling period (usually one year to eighteen months) forgiven, remainder rescheduled at regular (near-market) rates over fourteen years, including eight years of grace; (2) reschedule over twenty-five years, with fourteen years of grace, at market interest rates; (3) reschedule debt service coming due during the rescheduling period (the "consolidated" amounts) at reduced interest rates, at one-half of market rates, or three and a half percentage points below market rates, whichever is less, over fourteen years with eight years of grace.

2. Included in this group of countries are Bolivia, Cameroon, Congo, Costa Rica, Dominican Republic, Egypt, Honduras, Jamaica, Morocco, and Syria.

## 3  Anne O. Krueger, "Decision Making at the Outset of the Debt Crisis: Analytical and Conceptual Issues"

*Notes*

1. Capital flows can take a number of forms. Direct investment, purchase of equities, long-term lending by either private or public entities, and foreign aid (which is often lending by public entities at concessional rates of interest) are the main ones. In most situations, owners of capital in the exporting country and those importing capital in the receiving country will choose the techniques of financing most suited to the investment at hand. One would expect a combination of equity and debt financing from commercial markets in addition to concessional financing from governments.

In practice, except perhaps for sub-Saharan Africa, the composition of capital flows in the years prior to the debt crisis was a minor contributor to later difficulties. For purposes of this paper, the terms "borrowing" and "capital inflows," and "lending" and "capital outflows," will be used interchangeably. See Hope and McMurray (1984) for an early discussion of the inappropriate composition of African debt-servicing obligation. Hope was chief of the World Bank's Debt Division at that time.

2. Governments can encourage private firms to borrow from abroad by raising the domestic rate of interest above that prevailing abroad after allowance is made for exchange rate changes. In these circumstances, private savings can, in effect, finance public sector deficits while capital inflows finance private investment. It is also possible for private firms to invest in activities that are privately profitable but which do not exhibit social profitability. This is especially important in instances where governments have provided high levels of protection to domestic producers of import-competing goods.

3. These difficulties typically culminate in a balance of payments crisis. See the "Debt Crises of the 1970s" section of this chapter for a discussion.

4. See Krueger (1986) for a fuller analysis of the role of capital flows as it was then envisaged.

5. See World Bank, *World Development Report*, 1985, 17ff.

6. Ibid., 33.

7. See Krueger (1987, 276) for a calculation.

8. Data from *World Development Report*, 1987, 24.

9. See de Vries (1987) for a documentary history of Fund-supported programs.

10. See Diaz-Alejandro (1981, 124).

11. See *World Development Report* 1985, 27, for a fuller description of the Paris Club and its evolution. Box figure 2.4a lists the various reschedulings over the period after 1975 and indicates the parties involved in the rescheduling.

12. Data from *World Development Report*, 1985, 23.

13. For an account of the events leading up to the Mexican debt crisis and its initial resolution, see Kraft (1983).

14. In reality, there were two "debt crises": one was for sub-Saharan African countries, and the other was for middle-income countries that were heavily indebted to the commercial banks. The sub-Saharan African problems were even more severe and intractable than those of the middle-income countries: even during the 1970s, it was estimated that per capita incomes in sub-Saharan Africa had fallen. Sub-Saharan African debt was small contrasted with that of the heavily indebted middle-income countries, however; for that reason, world attention focused on the latter. For purposes of the present paper, focus will be on the middle-income countries. Although the origins of the problem for the African countries lie in much the same variables—highly inappropriate domestic economic policies, exacerbated by the worldwide recession—resolution of those problems will probably require a longer time horizon and considerable concessional finance once policy reforms are undertaken. They are thus more appropriately viewed as a problem of foreign aid and of starting growth than they are of restoring creditworthiness and resuming growth.

15. See Kraft (1984) and de Vries (1987) for discussion of the U.S. role. The secretary of the Treasury and the chairman of the Federal Reserve Board were active supporters of the Mexican program. The United States did extend bridging loans to Mexico but made clear that these were temporary until the IMF could act.

16. It was not until Secretary Baker addressed the annual meetings of the World Bank and the International Monetary Fund in Seoul in September 1985 that the United States—the largest shareholder in the World Bank—withdrew its opposition to any increase in World Bank nonproject lending of more than 10 percent of its total lending portfolio. One of the conceptual confusions surrounding the debt crisis was the perceived dichotomy between "balance of payments" lending and project lending. This issue is discussed further in the section of this chapter titled "The Policy Response in Hindsight."

17. A fourth component was essential globally: world economic growth had to be sufficiently rapid, and markets of the developed countries had to be sufficiently open, so that developing countries that did alter their policies could successfully change their current account balances.

18. The Fund had already been expanding its lending significantly and finally achieved agreement of the Interim Committee for a quota increase of SDR90 billion in February 1983. As is well known, the United States Congress finally passed the quota increase, but only after a hard-fought battle. For particulars of Fund resources and other issues, see de Vries (1987).

19. See Fischer (1987) for a survey of the proposals that have been made.

20. See, for example, *The Economist*, December 11, 1982, 11, 69.

21. See Cline (1983) for calculations which, at the time, appeared very reasonable. When the average annual real rate of growth of the middle-income countries had exceeded 5 percent in the 1970s, it was difficult to believe that interest obligations of 1–2 percent of GNP could constitute a severe bottleneck to

resumed growth. Even now, the macroeconomic orders of magnitude do not appear overwhelming. See Feldstein (1987).

22. See, for example, Krugman (1985).

23. I have elsewhere estimated that if the rate of growth of world trade had exceeded the interest rate by three percentage points in every year since 1982, oil-importing developing countries' 1986 exports would have stood at $521 billion, contrasted with an actual $371 billion. See Krueger (1989).

24. See *World Development Report*, 1983, chap. 3, for an analysis of this phenomenon.

25. This continues to be a major problem. In late 1988, it was reported that the United States was very unhappy with the International Monetary Fund because it had refused to lend to Argentina in circumstances in which Fund officials questioned the adequacy of the Argentine policy package. See *The Wall Street Journal*, September 26, 1988, 3. The American bridging loan to Mexico in October 1988 raises the same set of issues.

26. This appeal is in large part spurious. A country may have several projects it wishes to undertake: if a foreign creditor will fund any of these, it frees resources for additional projects of the country's choosing.

27. There are also important issues concerning the role of the World Bank and IMF in influencing developing countries' trade policies and the role of GATT, as the multilateral international trade organization. Those issues are well beyond the scope of this paper.

28. I ignore here the institutional rigidities that are thought by some to give rise to an imperfectly functioning secondary market in debt.

29. In some reschedulings, finance ministers had to sign as many as several thousand agreements individually. More costly, however, has been the urgent need for top economic officials to focus on the imminent debt rescheduling, rather than on longer-term economic programs.

30. Whereas World Bank project loans disburse at a rate consistent with the expenditures on an investment project, World Bank structural adjustment lending usually disburses over a period of less than two years. Once the loan is fully disbursed, there is no mechanism (except for the promise of yet another loan) by which adherence to the terms of the loan may be monitored nor incentive for their observance.

31. An urgent part of any reform program is a dismantling of protectionist barriers to imports and an increased incentive to produce exportables. This implies greater uniformity of incentives among economic activities. Exports must grow rapidly enough to permit the financing of growth of import demand, or the programs cannot succeed.

*References*

Cline, William R. 1983. *International Debt and the Stability of the World Economy.* Washington, D.C.: Institute for International Economics, September.

de Vries, Margaret. 1987. *Balance of Payments Adjustment, 1945 to 1986: The IMF Experience.* Washington, D.C.: International Monetary Fund.

Diaz-Alejandro, Carlos. 1981. "Southern Cone Stabilization Plans." In *Economic Stabilization in Developing Countries*, ed. R. Cline and Sidney Weintraub. Washington, D.C.: Brookings Institution.

Feldstein, Martin. 1987. "Muddling Through can be Just Fine." *The Economist*, June 27, 21–25.

Fischer, Stanley. 1987. *Resolving the International Debt Crisis*. National Bureau of Economic Research Working Paper no. 2373. Cambridge, Mass.

Hope, Nicholas, and David W. McMurray. 1984. "Loan Capital in Development Finance, the Role of Banks, and Some Implications for Managing Debt." In *Problems of International Finance: Papers of the Seventh Annual Conference of the International Economics Study Group*, ed. John Black and Graeme S. Dorrance. New York: St. Martin's Press.

Kraft, Joseph. 1984. *The Mexican Rescue*. New York: Group of Thirty.

Krueger, Anne O. 1986. "Aid in the Development Process." *World Bank Research Observer* 1, no. 1, 57–78.

———. 1987. "Aspects of Capital Flows between Developing and Developed Countries." In *Economic Policy in Theory and Practice*, ed. Assaf Razin and Efraim Sadka. New York: Macmillan.

———. 1989. "Resolving the Debt Crisis and Restoring Developing Countries' Creditworthiness." In *International Debt, Federal Reserve Operations, and Other Essays*. Carnegie-Rochester Conference Series on Public Policy, ed. Karl Brunner and Allan H. Meltzer, vol. 30. Amsterdam: North-Holland.

Krugman, Paul. 1985. "International Debt Strategies in an Uncertain World." In *International Debt and the Developing Countries*, ed. Gordon W. Smith and John T. Cuddington. Washington, D.C.: World Bank.

Kuczynski, Pedro-Pablo. 1988. *Latin American Debt*. New York: Twentieth Century Fund.

## 4    Jesús Silva-Herzog, "Problems of Policy Making at the Outset of the Debt Crisis"

*Notes*

1. Presidential elections set for July 4, 1982, were an additional complication. It was important to reach that date with as little economic and political unrest as possible.

2. The size of those deposits denominated in dollars—the so-called mex-dollars—amounted to around $11 billion. Foreign exchange resources to face a massive withdrawal—some signals were already appearing—simply did not exist. The exchange rate for the conversion into pesos was not considered, by the depositors, to be a favorable one.

3. This operation was without precedent. The BIS dealt only with its industrial member countries. The roles of the Federal Reserve, the Bank of England, and the president of the BIS were crucial. The bridge loan, to be repaid with the IMF

line of credit that we also began to negotiate, was finalized some days later. The especially supportive position of Spain in this operation has to be acknowledged.

4. In the recent past a number of other countries had, of course, suspended payments and restructured foreign debt; however, never before had a problem as large as ours erupted. On the other hand, a useful example was the then-recent restructuring of the Nicaragua debt, in which Mexico's authorities had played an active role.

5. The group was formed by Citibank, Bank of America, Chase Manhattan, Chemical Bank, Bankers Trust, Manufacturers Hanover, Bank of Montreal, Société Générale, Lloyds Bank, The Bank of Tokyo, Swiss Bank Corporation, Deutsche Bank, Morgan Guaranty Trust, and Banamex. The last named left the group after the nationalization of the Mexican private banking system, on September 1, 1982.

6. This is a good place to emphasize, however, that the debt crisis appeared as a surprise for the rest of the participants. Even though there were some voices of caution for the rapid process of external indebtedness of the developing countries, nobody was able to forecast the explosion of the crisis. It is helpful to remember this, to place in the proper perspective the forecasting ability of economists, academicians, and government experts.

7. A few days after the debt crisis began, the annual meeting of the governors of the IMF and the World Bank took place in Toronto. The meeting was heavily dominated by the Mexican debt crisis. In conversations with a number of finance ministers from Latin America, it was evident that they failed to recognize the impact of the Mexican crisis on their own economies, although in a matter of days we all were facing serious problems. This failure showed a clear lack of perception of today's interdependence.

## 5    Roberto Junguito, "The Colombian Debt Problem"

*Notes*

As minister of finance in the Betancur government, the author was a participant in the events described in this chapter.

1. Lora and Ocampo (1988) argue that in the nonorthodox phase the distortions began to be significantly corrected, a view disputed by Garay and Carrasquilla (1988), among others.

2. The need to adjust the economy and the characteristics of the new adjustment program were publicly announced by the president at the end of July.

3. See the IMF reports (1985a, 1985b, 1986). These reports give the Fund's views on the design and success of the Colombian adjustment program.

4. See Stallings (1988). The author of this excellent review of adjustment programs argues, however, on the basis of the memorandum, that the minister

of finance favored the standby and that his opinion was overridden by the president. This argument does not take due account of the fact that precisely what was being sought was support for the rapid execution of the adjustment program, since there existed the threat that the standby would be imposed if the program were not undertaken.

5. The program presented to the commercial banks in December 1984 was called Colombia's Economic Program and External Debt-Management Strategy. The results of the December 1984 meeting with the Banks as well as that held in February 1985 were detailed in another memorandum to the president, "Propuesta del Chairman del Comité de Bancos Internacionales," February 19, 1985 (see Junguito 1986).

6. The April 1985 internal and confidential report on Colombia was somehow taken off the IMF premises in Washington and published in the Colombian daily, *El Tiempo*. In fact, the economic team did not know about the report, except from some positive news expressed the previous day by Mr. de Larosière, managing director of the IMF.

7. Mr. Volcker's note, which in his own words outlined his understanding of Colombia's preferred approach, described a possible Colombia-IMF-IBRD scenario, in which actions and compromises were assigned to the actors, including the commercial banks.

8. The financial conditions for the jumbo loan approved and subscribed to by the commercial banks appeared in the section "Economic Information Memorandum" in a publication (República de Colombia 1985) sent to commercial banks by the government.

9. The actual Colombian proposal has been published (República de Colombia 1988).

*References*

Garay, L., and A. Carrasquilla. 1988. "Dinámica del Desajuste y Proceso de Saneamiento Económico en Colombia en la Década de los Ochentas." *Coyuntura Económica*, October.
IMF. 1985a. "Colombia: Recent Economic Developments," June.
———. 1985b. "Colombia: Staff Report for the 1985 Article IV Consultation." Executive Board Summary EBS/85/149.
———. 1986. "Colombia: Recent Economic Developments," November 13.
Junguito, Roberto. 1986. *Memoria del Ministro de Hacienda: Julio 1984–Septiembre 1985*. Bogotá: Banco de la República, Departamento Editorial.
———. 1988. "History's Debt Crisis Lessons." *The International Economy*, May–June.
Lora, E., and J. A. Ocampo. 1988. "Estructura Económica, Políticas de Ajuste y Distribucion del Ingreso: La Experiencia de los Ochentas." *Lecturas de Macroeconomía Colombiana*. Bogotá: Tercer Mundo Editores. An earlier version was published in 1986 by Wider Publications, Helsinki.

Ministerio de Hacienda y Crédito Público. 1984. "Memorando, Reuniones FMI–Banco Mundial," October 2. The memorandum was printed in the Colombian press. It was published later in Junguito (1986).
Presidencia de la República de Colombia. 1984. "Alocución del Presidente de la República de Colombia, Belisario Betancur." In *El Consenso de Cartagena.* Bogotá, June 27.
República de Colombia. 1983. *Cambio con Equidad: Plan Nacional de Desarrollo, 1983–86.* Departamento Nacional de Planeacion. Bogotá.
———. 1985. *The Republic of Colombia: Term Credit Facility.* Bogotá, June.
———. 1988. *External Financial Needs 1989–1990.* Bogotá, July.
Stallings, Barbara. 1988. "The Political Context of Economic Decision Making: Chile, Peru and Colombia in the 1980s." University of Wisconsin, Madison.

6     **Alexander K. Swoboda, "The Changing Role of Central Banks in International Policy Coordination"**

*Notes*

1. The intuition behind these results is that changes in aggregate demand relative to current output should affect the intertemporal terms of trade (the real interest rate) and not the commodity terms of trade (the real exchange rate), and that changes in the composition of spending will have the opposite effect. See Genberg and Swoboda, (1987a).

2. Why current accounts should or should not be targets of policy is discussed in Genberg and Swoboda, (1987b). The remainder of this section and the next section, "Dealing with Current International Imbalances," draw heavily on an unpublished paper I wrote in 1988 and from which the discussion is reproduced with some modifications.

3. For additional, especially short-run, implications under floating rates, see Genberg and Swoboda (1987b).

*References*

Branson, W. H. 1988. "International Adjustment and the Dollar: Policy Illusions and Economic Constraints." Paper presented at the IMF-HWWA Seminar, Hamburg, May.
Edison, Hali J., Marcus H. Miller, and John Williamson. 1987. "On Evaluating and Extending the Target Zone Proposal." *Journal of Policy Modelling* (New York), no. 1 (spring): 199–224.

Genberg, H., and A. K. Swoboda. 1987a. "Policy and Current Account Determination under Floating Exchange Rates." IMF Working Paper no. 69.
———. 1987b. "The Current Account and the Policy Mix under Flexible Exchange Rates." IMF Working Paper no. 70.
Group of Thirty. 1988. *International Macroeconomic Policy Coordination*. New York and London.
Kindleberger, Charles P. 1967. *The Politics of International Money and World Language*. Princeton Essays in International Finance, no. 61. Princeton, N.J.: Princeton University Press.
Swoboda, A. K. 1988. "International Adjustment and the Dollar: A Case of Misplaced Emphasis?" Comment on Branson (1988). Mimeo.
Meade, J.E. 1951. *Theory of International Economic Policy: The Balance of Payments*. Oxford: Oxford University Press.
Tinbergen, Jan. 1952. *On the Theory of Economic Policy*. Amsterdam: North-Holland.

## 7 Wolfgang Rieke, "Economic Policy and Exchange Rates: Experience and Prospects"

*Notes*

1. Article IV, Section 5 (J) of the original IMF Agreement.

2. A recent study makes the point that "the macroeconomic coordination which took place was largely the result of the automatic discipline imposed by the system, and when it failed it did so because the discipline was not automatic (for example in the case of the United States)" (Group of Ten 1988, 9).

3. Term used in an IMF paper (1988, 9) to distinguish from cooperation using a number of indicators as in G7 discussions (multiple-variable rule).

4. See the thorough discussion of the "redundancy problem" and its implications in Giavazzi and Giovannini (1988). The authors quote O. Emminger (1977, 53):

> A system of fixed rates can only function so long as the key-currency country, by its domestic stability—i.e. monetary stability and economic stability in general—enables the other member countries to maintain fixed exchange rates without imposing undue strains on their own domestic stability.

5. United States, Japan, Federal Republic of Germany, United Kingdom, France.

6. The G7 are the G5 plus Italy and Canada.

7. The work of C. Fred Bergsten may best represent this line of argument.

8. At the G7 summit held in Bonn in 1978, the German government agreed to a fiscal program designed to stimulate domestic demand with a view to reducing the large surplus in its trade and current accounts.

9. See, for example, Blumenthal (1988):

> Clearly as the United States is the world's largest economy, its $140 billion annual current account deficit . . . casts an unsettling shadow over all aspects of worldwide economic governance. . . . Management of this stark macroeconomic reality will require disciplined policies by the U.S. and the cooperation of its trading partners.

10. The list draws on Sievert (1988).

11. See Wolfensohn (1988):

> The fundamental problems can be overcome if the new president can convince the American people that it is now necessary to get back to a balanced position, that for the next two years we must work our way out of our debt problems and live within our means. The issue, of course, is not just one for the U.S.; it is of critical importance to the rest of the world.

*References*

Blumenthal, Michael W. 1988. "Managing the Macro-Economy." *World Link*, no. 8 (October).

Emminger, O. 1977. *The DMark in the Conflict between Internal and External Equilibrium, 1948–75*. Essays in International Finance, no. 122. Princeton, N.J.: International Finance Section, Princeton University. Quoted in Giavazzi and Giovannini (1989).

Feldstein, Martin S. 1988. "Distinguished Lecture on Economics in Government: Thinking about International Economic Coordination." *The Journal of Economic Perspectives* 2, no. 2 (spring).

Frenkel, Jacob A., Morris Goldstein, and Paul Masson. 1988. "International Coordination of Economic Policies: Scope, Methods, and Effects." In *Economic Policy Coordination*, ed. Wilfried Guth. Washington, D.C.: International Monetary Fund.

Giavazzi, F., and A. Giovannini. 1988. *Limiting Exchange Rate Flexibility: The European Monetary System*. Cambridge, Mass.: MIT Press.

Group of Ten. 1988. *International Macroeconomic Policy Coordination*. Group of Thirty Report. New York and London.

International Monetary Fund. 1988. "International Coordination of Economic Policies." Unpublished.

Sievert, Olaf. 1988. "Weise, Mahner, und Propheten." *Frankfurter Allgemeine Zeitung*, August 13.

Wallich, Henry C. 1984. "Institutional Cooperation in the World Economy." In *The World Economic System: Performance and Prospects*, ed. Jacob Frenkel and Michael Mussa. Dover, Mass.

Wolfensohn, James D. 1988. "We Need Partners, Not Consultants." *World Link*, no. 8 (October).

## 8 Pierre Jacquet and Thierry de Montbrial, "Central Banks and International Cooperation"

*Notes*

Helpful comments by our colleague Jacques Edin are gratefully acknowledged.

1. The restoration of confidence after the stock market crash, notably conspicuous in investment planning by companies, was instrumental in containing the crash's impact on economic activity. It is possible to argue, but not to prove, that central banks' policies fostered that restoration of confidence.

2. See Friedman (1988) for useful comments on the factual success of anti-inflationary policies associated with a failure of the conventional prescriptions of monetary policy to explain that success.

3. The Bundesbank, in particular, is understandably reported (Funabashi 1988) to be rather skeptical about both coordination of monetary policies and international exchange rate rules. Its commitment to the EMS is one exception, easily explained by the observation that within the EMS the Bundesbank has captured the remaining degree of freedom and so far provides the monetary anchor for the system. The EMS thus reinforces its relative power, in spite of the constraint that it also represents and the subordination that it implies to the exchange rate management decided by the Finance Ministry.

4. In the 1920s, Federal Reserve Governor Strong wrote to the Bank of England Governor Norman in response to the latter's "statements of principles for central bank cooperation" that "the domestic functions of the bank of issue are paramount to everything," and that no "surrender of sovereignty" should be attempted under the guise of cooperation (Clarke 1967).

5. These conditions were defined as early as 1935, in a report by the RIIA (1935).

6. David Mulford is a vocal advocate of this process. See Mulford (1988).

7. Such as *Recent Innovations in International Banking*, 1986.

8. WP3 consists of representatives from the finance ministries and central banks of the ten largest OECD countries and discusses international payments and monetary problems.

9. A Pareto improvement makes everyone at least as well off as he was before. This notion is to be distinguished from a change that makes some players better off at the expense of others' becoming worse off.

10. Kenen (1988) uses the concept of "regime preserving" cooperation. Regime "improving" may also be a legitimate concern.

11. Einzig (1932, 18) thus describes one of the raisons d'être of the BIS: "to devise arrangements whereby the countries wanting support could participate in the authority which determines the terms of support. To ask for and receive assistance would thereby appear less humiliating, and unpopular terms would become more palatable." The first years of the BIS saw conflicts, not the least of which was the reported attempt by the French to use the structure for advancing their own political interests, notably with respect to reparations.

12. Parties to the agreement were the United States, the United Kingdom, and France. See the analysis in Eichengreen (1985).

13. These arrangements initially involved nine foreign central banks and the Bank for International Settlements and amounted to U.S. $900 million. In 1981, they amounted to more than $30 billion. See Solomon (1982).

14. The G7 countries plus Sweden, Belgium, and the Netherlands. Switzerland, although not a member of the IMF, associated itself with the arrangement.

15. This is another illustration of how independent central banks can lose freedom of action in a tightly managed exchange rate system.

16. This agreement enforced a realignment of exchange rate parities with a devaluation of the U.S. dollar and increased margins of fluctuations.

17. The United States, and in particular its Treasury secretary, John Connally, wanted to circumvent the Group of Ten's widespread criticism of the United States (Solomon 1982).

18. One does not find a proper definition of such policies. Generally, it is easier to comment on *ex post* consequences of policies rather than to produce effective *ex ante* guidelines.

19. Nonetheless, Kindleberger (1986) eloquently voices his doubts about summitry: "The commitment to consultative macroeconomic policies in annual summit meetings of the seven heads of state has become a shadow play, a dog-and-pony show, a series of photo opportunities—whatever you choose to call them—with ceremony substituted for substance."

20. This section draws on Jacquet (1988).

21. The 1970 Werner report presented a plan for the attainment by stages of economic and monetary union.

22. The main proponents of the "monetarist" approach were France, Belgium, and Luxembourg; Germany, Italy, and the Netherlands represented the "economist" approach.

23. Convergence, moreover, needs to be distinguished from coordination. Neither actually implies the other.

24. The choice of any technical mechanism of cooperation in the field of international monetary relations is foremost political. It is nevertheless possible that focusing on the technical aspects can be instrumental in persuading the domestic constituencies to accept the loss of national autonomy implied by such cooperation.

25. In his analysis of the optimal currency area, Robert Mundell (1968) concludes that the optimal area is the region. Of course, the concept of region is predominantly political and cultural, not economic.

26. For discussion of the reasons behind the choice of the 1992 proposal as the major European initiative in the 1980s, see Delors (1986).

27. As in the case of the gold standard, one can argue that central banks under the EMS unsurprisingly interpreted the rules of the game with a view to the domestic interest. The small concessions made by the Bundesbank in the Basel-Nyborg agreement of the fall 1987 simply illustrate that the maintenance of the EMS and of German leadership within the system both have become part of the Bundesbank's perceived interests, which required some indications of goodwill.

28. Funabashi (1988) provides illuminating insight into the nature of this cooperation.

29. The commitment of the Bundesbank to the EMS is relatively recent and stems from its de facto leadership of monetary policy within the system. See note 3.

30. See Funabashi (1988). Some critics also note the failure of Germany to expand. This would certainly help reduce the huge German current account surplus, but the significance of a German fiscal expansion has been somewhat overplayed. It will not solve the U.S. external imbalance problem. On the other hand, it is the key to a successful growth strategy in Europe.

31. Save for the fact that it is a *new* structure and therefore acquires a new legitimacy and becomes a new symbol of the determination to cooperate.

32. The United States and Japan in their bilateral relationship seem to constitute their own G2. When Germany is included, they become the G3.

33. The public media still pay attention to consultation, but that might change as well.

34. See, for example, Nau (1984).

*References*

Buchanan, James M. 1987. "The Constitution of Economic Policy." *The American Economic Review*, June.

Clarke, Stephen V. O. 1967. *Central Bank Cooperation: 1924–1931*. New York: Federal Reserve Bank of New York.

Delors, Jacques. 1986. "Quels ressorts pour l'Europe." *Politique Etrangère*, no 4.

Eichengreen, Barry. 1985. "International Policy Coordination in Historical Perspective: A View from the Interwar Years." In *International Economic Policy Coordination*, ed. Willem H. Buiter and Richard C. Marston. Cambridge: Cambridge University Press.

Einzig, Paul. 1932. *The Bank for International Settlements*. 3d ed. London: Macmillan.

Friedman, Benjamin M. 1988. "Lessons on Monetary Policy from the 1980s." *Journal of Economic Perspectives* 2, no. 3, 51–72.

Funabashi, Yoichi. 1988. *Managing the Dollar: From the Plaza to the Louvre*. Washington, D.C.: Institute for International Economics.

Jacquet, Pierre. 1988. "The European Monetary System and European Monetary Integration." In *Tokyo Club Papers*, no. 2. Tokyo: Tokyo Club Foundation for Global Studies.

Kenen, Peter B. 1988. *Managing Exchange Rates.* Chatham House Papers, The Royal Institute for International Affairs. London: Routledge and Kegan Paul.
Kindleberger, Charles P. 1984. *A Financial History of Western Europe.* London: George Allen and Unwin.
———. 1986. "International Public Goods without International Government." *The American Economic Review* 76, no. 1 (March).
Marjolin, Robert. 1986. *Le travail d'une vie. Mémoires 1911–1986.* Paris: Editions Robert Laffont.
Mulford, David C. 1988. "Economic Policy Coordination and the Foreign Exchange Market." Remarks at the Association Cambiste Internationale, Honolulu, Hawaii, May 28. Washington, D.C.: Department of the Treasury.
Mundell, Robert A. 1968. "A Theory of Optimum Currency Areas." Chap. 12 in *International Economics.* New York: Macmillan.
Nau, Henry R. 1984. "La Reaganomie au service de l'économie mondiale." *Politique Etrangère,* no 4.
Padoa Schioppa, Tommaso. 1985. "Policy Cooperation and the EMS Experience." In *International Economic Policy Coordination,* ed. Willem H. Buiter and Richard C. Marston. Cambridge: Cambridge University Press.
Royal Institute for International Affairs. 1935. *The Future of Monetary Policy.* Report on International Monetary Problems by a Group of the Royal Institute of International Affairs. London: Oxford University Press.
Solomon, Robert. 1982. *The International Monetary System 1945–1981.* New York: Harper and Row.

## 9     Jacob A. Frenkel, Morris Goldstein, and Paul R. Masson, "International Coordination of Economic Policies: Issues and Answers"

*Notes*

This chapter is based in large part on a paper presented at a conference organized by the IMF and HWWA-Institut für Wirtschaftsforschung, National Economic Policies and Their Impact on the World Economy, held in Hamburg, May 5–7, 1988, and published under the title "International Coordination of Economic Policies: Scope, Methods, and Effects," in *Economic Policy Coordination,* ed. Wilfried Guth (Washington, D.C.: International Monetary Fund, 1988): 149–92. A new section on the uncertain effects of policy replaces a section that dealt with model simulations.

    We are indebted to colleagues in the IMF Research Department and to Hali Edison, Martin Feldstein, Atish Ghosh, Pieter Korteweg, and Jacques Melitz for helpful comments on an earlier draft.

1. See the surveys by Artis and Ostry (1986), Cooper (1985), Fischer (1987), Hamada (1979), Horne and Masson (1988), Kenen (1987), Polak (1981) and Wallich (1984).

2. Evidence on the size of spillover effects from policy actions by the major industrial countries is discussed in the latter part of this section.

3. The conclusion that a monetary expansion under floating rates affects real output in opposite directions at home and abroad is associated with the Mundell (1971)–Fleming (1962) model. For a recent evaluation of this model, see Frenkel and Razin (1987b); a broader survey of the international transmission mechanism can be found in Frenkel and Mussa (1985). Econometric models are more divided on whether a monetary expansion under floating rates has negative transmission effects on real output abroad; see Helliwell and Padmore (1985) and Bryant et al. (1988).

4. We regard the label as inappropriate both because the proponents of decentralized macroeconomic policy making—including Corden (1983, 1986), Feldstein (1988), Niehans (1988), Stein (1987), and Vaubel (1985)—are geographically quite diverse and because some prominent German economists, such as Poehl (1987), have stressed the importance of coordination.

5. Corden (1986) has recently argued that there may be a case for asking large countries to slow their speed of adjustment to desired policy targets so as to dampen movements in real exchange rates that could cause difficulties for others.

6. Another constraint on regional attempts to create more of the public good is that they may divert or discourage its production outside the region; the argument here is analogous to the concepts of "trade creation" and "trade diversion" in the customs union literature.

7. To reach this conclusion, it is necessary to assume no player has sufficient policy instruments to achieve all its policy targets simultaneously and that coordination alters the trade-offs among policy targets; see Gavin (1986). Without those assumptions, the motivation for coordination would disappear in the absence of uncertainty about the effects of policies (see "Coordination When Effects Are Uncertain," later in this chapter).

8. See Fischer (1987) and Frenkel (1983, 1986).

9. See Goldstein (1984). This is not to say that the insulating properties of floating rates are inferior to those of alternative regimes. Indeed, it is hard to see any other exchange rate regime surviving the shocks of the 1970s without widespread controls on trade and capital.

10. On the possible use of commodity price indicators in the conduct of monetary policy, see Heller (1987).

11. See Bocklemann (1988) for a similar conclusion.

12. See Frenkel (1985).

13. Another barrier is disagreement over forecasts for key economic variables over the medium term; on this point, see Tanzi (1988).

14. See Bryant et al. (1988) and Helliwell and Padmore (1985) for a comparison of open-economy multipliers from different global econometric models. Frankel and Rockett (1988) illustrate the sensitivity of welfare effects of coordination to the selection of the "right" versus the "wrong" economic model.

15. See Fischer (1987). Dini (1988) goes farther to argue that when the incentives to coordinate differ widely among group members, there may be a tendency for bilateral bargains to take place among those who have the most to trade.

16. See Putnam and Bayne (1984). At the same time, the Bonn summit is regarded in some quarters as illustrative of the pitfalls of coordinating macroeconomic policies when the economic outlook is changing rapidly.

17. See Putnam and Bayne (1984).

18. Another example of high-frequency coordination is that among central banks of the largest countries on exchange-market intervention tactics.

19. See Frenkel and Razin (1987a).

20. For example, the Louvre communiqué states that

> the United States Government will pursue policies with a view to reducing the fiscal 1988 deficit to 2.3 percent of GNP from its estimated level of 3.9 percent in fiscal 1987. For this purpose, the growth in government expenditures will be held to less than 1 percent in fiscal 1988 as part of the continuing program to reduce the share of government in GNP from its current level of 23 percent.

See International Monetary Fund (1987).

21. Because coordination of structural policies typically involves different policy instruments, individual countries' actions—unlike their actions under coordination of fiscal policies—cannot be evaluated with reference to an aggregate policy indicator that would be desirable from a global perspective.

22. This is not to deny the helpful role that harmonization of structural policies—ranging from adopting similar tax provisions to implementing common regulations concerning movements of goods, labor, and capital—could play in certain circumstances.

23. Those who hold the view that international factors have minimal influence on policy making sometimes also argue that countries' policy commitments in coordination agreements represent policies that would have occurred even in the absence of such agreements. According to this view, coordination affects only the timing of policy announcements: countries delay such announcements until coordination meetings so that they can present a dowry to the others.

24. See Buiter and Marston (1985).

25. The classic references to what is called the time inconsistency of policies are Kydland and Prescott (1977) and Calvo (1978).

26. As Poehl (1987, 19–20) notes:

> International cooperation does not necessarily imply that all parties must agree on all details at all times. It is important that we regard it as a process of maintaining stability in our increasingly interrelated world economy.... The process of international cooperation may be difficult and burdensome, even frustrating at times, but there is no alternative to it.

27. It is precisely because of the risk of collusion among the coordinating countries that Vaubel (1985) favors decentralized decision making.

28. See Polak (1981) and Kenen (1987).

29. It is in this context that the problems of time inconsistency and moral hazard often surface.

30. Advocates of rules also argue that, once the public knows better what the authorities will do, markets will demand less of a risk premium to hold the authorities' financial obligations.

31. See Cooper (1982) and U.S. Congress (1982).

32. Kenen (1987) cites a regression of the *change* in the inflation rate between 1979 and 1985 on both the *level* of the inflation rate in 1979 and a zero-one dummy variable denoting participation in the exchange rate mechanism of the EMS. The sample comprised twenty-two industrial countries. The EMS dummy variable was not statistically significant, whereas the level of the inflation rate in 1979 was. Note that this finding does not preclude a helpful role of the EMS in disinflation, since participation could still have reduced the output *cost* of disinflation (see, for example, Giavazzi and Giovannini [1988]); but this is a different story.

33. As developed in Polak (1988), the need for rules to guard against the dangers of fine tuning has receded, since economic policy in most industrial countries is now oriented much more toward the medium term. Fischer (1987) makes the complementary point that the state of our knowledge about the effects of monetary and fiscal policy is too rudimentary to justify policy rules. Niehans (1987) expresses doubts that rules could be relied upon to reduce international disturbances.

34. On the limitations of purchasing-power parity rules, see Frenkel (1981).

35. See Frenkel (1975).

36. The literature on "speculative attacks" deals with just this phenomenon; see, for example, Flood and Garber (1980).

37. See Frenkel and Goldstein (1986). This missing link between exchange rate movements and fiscal policy under target zones is being increasingly recognized. Whereas first-generation target zone proposals spoke only of monetary policy, second-generation proposals have added a policy rule or guideline for fiscal policy; contrast Williamson (1985) with Williamson and Miller (1987).

38. The list of indicators noted in the communiqué of the Tokyo economic summit included growth rates of gross national product, interest rates, inflation rates, unemployment rates, ratios of fiscal deficits to GNP, current account and trade balances, money growth rates, international reserve holdings, and exchange rates.

39. There is also the question of the proper *assignment* of policy instruments to policy targets.

40. On inflexibility of fiscal policy, see Tanzi (1988); on intervention, see Mussa (1981) and Jurgensen (1983).

41. This characterization is not universally shared. Williamson and Miller (1987), for example, regard the gold standard and Bretton Woods as more symmetric systems.

42. See Frenkel and Goldstein (1988).

43. See Giavazzi and Giovannini (1986).

44. In practice, high-inflation countries have sometimes resorted to capital controls during exchange rate crises to avoid the choice of having to give up either monetary independence or the exchange rate target.

45. To the extent that the EMS produces greater stability and predictability of exchange rates, all members also share any efficiency gains associated with moving closer to a single currency.

46. On a more symmetric EMS, see Holtham, Keating, and Spencer (1987). The proposals on the EMS put forward to the European Community Monetary Committee late in 1987 by Minister of Finance Balladur of France can be seen as prefacing such a symmetric development of the EMS.

47. This section draws on previous work by one of the authors, in particular, Ghosh and Masson (1988a, 1988b).

48. See Bryant et al. (1988).

49. It is true that a high degree of model uncertainty is likely to be associated with disagreement about the functioning of the world economy.

50. This conclusion may not apply to general models where there are many targets and instruments, however. We are indebted to David Kendrick for this point.

51. Based on the principles developed in the eighteenth century by Thomas Bayes and applied in this century to economic decision making.

52. See Oudiz and Sachs (1984), McKibbin and Sachs (1988), and Taylor (1985).

53. See Schultze (1987) and Bryant et al. (1988). As an example of the difficulties associated with identifying the "counterfactual," contrast Feldstein's (1988) appraisal of the likely evolution of exchange rates in the absence of the Plaza agreement with that of Lamfalussy (1987).

54. This appendix is based on Ghosh and Ghosh (1986) and section 1 of Ghosh and Masson (1988a).

55. This need not be true in general, however.

## References

Artis, Michael, and Sylvia Ostry. 1986. *International Economic Policy Coordination*. Chatham House Papers, no. 30. Royal Institute of International Affairs. London: Routledge and Kegan Paul.

Bockelmann, H. 1988. "The Need for Worldwide Coordination of Economic Policies." Paper presented at conference Financing the World Economy in the Nineties, School for Banking and Finance, Tilburg University. Tilburg, March 1988.

Brainard, William C. 1967. "Uncertainty and the Effectiveness of Policy." *American Economic Review* 57 (May): 411–25.

Bryant, Ralph. 1987. "Intergovernmental Coordination of Economic Policies." In Volcker et al. (1987), 4–15.

Bryant, Ralph, and Richard Portes, eds. 1987. *Global Macroeconomics: Policy Conflict and Cooperation*. London: Macmillan.

Bryant, Ralph, et al., eds. 1988. *Empirical Macroeconomics for Interdependent Economies*. Washington, D.C.: Brookings Institution.

Buiter, Willem H., and Richard C. Marston, eds. 1985. *International Economic Policy Coordination*. New York: Cambridge University Press.

Calvo, Guillermo A. 1978. "On the Time Consistency of Optimal Policy in a Monetary Economy." *Econometrica* (Evanston, Ill.), no. 46 (November): 1411–28.

Cooper, Richard N. 1982. "The Gold Standard: Historical Facts and Future Prospects." *Brookings Papers on Economic Activity* (Brookings Institution, Washington, D.C.) 1: 1–45.

———. 1985. "Economic Interdependence and Coordination of Economic Policies." Chap. 23 in vol. 2 of *Handbook of International Economics*, ed. Ronald Jones and Peter Kenen, 1194–1234. Amsterdam: North-Holland.

———. 1987. "International Economic Cooperation: Is It Desirable? Is It Likely?" Lecture presented at the International Monetary Fund, October.

———. 1988. "U.S. Macroeconomic Policy, 1986–88: Are the Models Useful?" In Bryant et al. (1988), 255–66.

Corden, W. Max. 1983 "The Logic of the International Monetary Non-System." In *Reflections on a Troubled World Economy: Essays in Honour of Herbert Giersch*, ed. Fritz Machlup et al., 59–74. London: Macmillan.

———. 1986. "Fiscal Policies, Current Accounts and Real Exchange Rates: In Search of a Logic of International Policy Coordination," *Weltwirtschaftliches Archiv* (Tubingen) 122, no. 3, 423–38.

Currie, David, Paul Levine, and Nicholas Vidalis. 1987. "Cooperative and Non-Cooperative Rules for Monetary and Fiscal Policy in an Empirical Two-Bloc Model." In Bryant and Portes (1987).

Dini, Laberto. 1988. "Cooperation and Conflict in Monetary and Trade Policies" International Management and Development Institute, U.S.–European Top Management Roundtable, Milan, February 19.

Eichengreen, Barry. 1987. "Hegemonic Stability Theories of the International Monetary System." Discussion Paper no. 193, Centre for Economic Policy Research, London, July.

Feldstein, Martin. 1988. "Distinguished Lecture on Economics in Government: Thinking about International Economic Coordination." *The Journal of Economic Perspectives* 2, no. 2 (spring).

Fischer, Stanley. 1987. "International Macroeconomic Policy Coordination." NBER Working Paper no. 2224. National Bureau of Economic Research, Cambridge, Mass., May.

Fleming, J. Marcus. 1962. "Domestic Financial Policies under Fixed and under Floating Exchange Rates." *Staff Papers* (International Monetary Fund, Washington, D.C.), 9 (November): 369–79.

Flood, Robert and Peter Garber. 1980. "Market Fundamentals versus Price Level Bubbles: The First Tests." *Journal of Political Economy* (Chicago) 88 (August): 745.

Frankel, Jeffrey, and Katharine Rockett. 1988. "International Macroeconomic Policy Coordination When Policy Makers Do Not Agree on the True Model." *American Economic Review* 78 (June): 318–40.

Frenkel, Jacob A. 1975. "Current Problems of the International Monetary System: Reflections on European Monetary Integration." *Weltwirtschaftliches Archiv* (Tubingen) 3, no. 2, 216–21.

———. 1981. "The Collapse of Purchasing Power Parities during the 1970's." *European Economic Review* (Amsterdam) 16 (May): 145–65.

———. 1982. "Turbulence in the Market for Foreign Exchange and Macroeconomic Policies." The Henry Thornton Lecture. London: City University Centre for Banking and International Finance.

———. 1983. "International Liquidity and Monetary Control." In *International Money and Credit: The Policy Roles*, ed. George M. von Furstenberg. Washington, D.C.: International Monetary Fund.

———. 1985. "A Note on 'the Good Fix' and 'the Bad Fix.'" *European Economic Review* (New York) 1–2 (June–July).

———. 1986. "International Interdependence and the Constraints on Macroeconomic Policies." *Weltwirtschaftliches Archiv* (Tubingen) 122, no. 4.

Frenkel, Jacob A., and Morris Goldstein. 1986. "A Guide to Target Zones." *Staff Papers* (International Monetary Fund, Washington, D.C.) 33 (December): 633–70.

———. 1988. "The International Monetary System: Developments and Prospects." Paper presented to Cato Institute Conference, February. (Also published in *Cato Journal* 8 [fall 1988].)

Frenkel, Jacob A., and Michael Mussa. 1985. "Asset Markets, Exchange Rates and the Balance of Payments." In *Handbook of International Economics*, ed. Ronald Jones and Peter Kenen, vol. 2. Amsterdam: North-Holland.

Frenkel, Jacob A., and Assaf Razin. 1987a. *Fiscal Policies and the World Economy*. Cambridge, Mass.: MIT Press.

———. 1987b. "The Mundell-Fleming Model: A Quarter Century Later." *Staff Papers* (International Monetary Fund, Washington, D.C.) 34 (December).

Gavin, Michael. 1986. "Macroeconomic Policy Coordination under Alternative Exchange Rate Regimes." Unpublished, Federal Reserve Board, September.

Genberg, Hans, and Alexander Swoboda. 1987. "The Current Account and the Policy Mix under Flexible Exchange Rates." International Monetary Fund Working Paper no. 70, October.

Ghosh, Atish, and Swati Ghosh. 1986. "International Policy Coordination When the Model Is Unknown." Geneva, December. Mimeo.

Ghosh, Atish, and Paul R. Masson. 1988a. "International Policy Coordination in a World with Model Uncertainty." *Staff Papers* (International Monetary Fund, Washington, D.C.) 35 (June): 230–58.

———. 1988b. "Model Uncertainty, Learning, and the Gains from Coordination." International Monetary Fund Working Paper no. 114, December.

Giavazzi, Francesco, and Alberto Giovannini. 1986. "The EMS and the Dollar." *Economic Policy Review*, April, 455–73.

———. 1988. "Interpreting the European Disinflation: The Role of the Exchange Rate Regime." *Información Comercial Espannola* (Madrid), May.

Goldstein, Morris. 1980. *Have Flexible Exchange Rates Handicapped Macroeconomic Policy?* Special Papers in International Economics, no. 14. Princeton, N.J.: Princeton University Press, June.

———. 1984. *The Exchange Rate System: Lessons of the Past and Options for the Future.* IMF Occasional Paper no. 30. Washington, D.C.: International Monetary Fund, July.

Gotur, Padma. 1985. "Effects of Exchange Rate Variability on Trade: Some Further Evidence." *Staff Papers* (International Monetary Fund, Washington, D.C.) 32 (September): 475–512.

Hamada, Koichi. 1979. "Macroeconomic Strategy and Coordination under Alternative Exchange Rates." In *International Economic Policy: Theory and Evidence*, ed. R. Dornbusch and J. Frenkel, 292–324. Baltimore: Johns Hopkins University Press.

Heller, H. Robert. 1987. Address before the International Economic Working Group in Washington, D.C., March 24.

Helliwell, John F., and Tim Padmore. 1985. "Empirical Studies of Macroeconomic Interdependence." Chap. 21 in vol. 2 of *Handbook of International Economics*, ed. Ronald Jones and Peter Kenen, 1107–51. Amsterdam: North-Holland.

Holtham, Gerald, and Andrew Hughes Hallett. 1987. "International Policy Coordination and Model Uncertainty." In Bryant and Portes (1987).

Holtham, Gerald, Giles Keating, and Peter Spencer. 1987. *EMS: Advance or Face Retreat.* London: Credit Suisse First Boston Ltd.

Horne, Jocelyn, and Paul R. Masson. 1988. "Scope and Limits of International Economic Cooperation and Policy Coordination." *Staff Papers* (International Monetary Fund, Washington, D.C.) 35 (June). (First published in *IMF Survey* March 9, 1987.)

International Monetary Fund. 1987. *IMF Survey,* March 9, 73.

Johnson, Manuel H. 1988. "Recent Economic Developments and Indicators of Monetary Policy." Address before the Money Marketeers of New York University, New York, March 15. Unpublished, Board of Governors of the Federal Reserve System, Washington, D.C.

Jurgensen, Philippe. 1983. *Report of the Working Group on Exchange Market Intervention.* Washington, D.C.: Department of the Treasury.

Kenen, Peter B. 1987. "Exchange Rates and Policy Coordination." Brookings Discussion Papers, no. 61, October. Brookings Institution, Washington, D.C.

Kydland, F., and E. Prescott. 1977. "Rules Rather than Discretion: The Inconsistency of Optimal Plans." *Journal of Political Economy* (Chicago) 85 (June): 473–91.

Lamfalussy, Alexandre. 1987. "Current Account Imbalances in the Industrial World: Why They Matter." In Volcker et al. (1987).

Lucas, Robert. 1976. "Econometric Policy Eveluation: A Critique." In *The Phillips Curve and Labor Markets,* 19–46. Carnegie-Rochester Conference Series on Public Policy, ed. Karl Brunner and Allan H. Meltzer, vol. 1. Amsterdam: North-Holland.

Masson, Paul R. 1988. Steven Symansky, Richard Haas, and Michael Dooley. 1988. "MULTIMOD: A Multi-Region Econometric Model." In *Staff Studies for the World Economic Outlook.* Washington, D.C.: International Monetary Fund.

McKibbin, Warwick J., and Jeffrey D. Sachs. 1988. "Coordination of Monetary and Fiscal Policies in the Industrial Countries." In *International Aspects of Fiscal Policy,* ed. Jacob A. Frenkel. Chicago: University of Chicago Press.

Mundell, Robert A. 1971. *The Dollar and the Policy Mix.* Essays in International Finance, no. 85. Princeton, N.J.: Princeton University Press, May.
Mussa, Michael. 1981. *The Role of Official Intervention.* Occasional Paper no. 6. New York: Group of Thirty.
Niehans, Jurg. 1987. "Generating International Disturbances." In *Toward a World of Economic Stability: Optimal Monetary Framework and Policy,* ed. Y. Suzuki and M. Okabe, 181–218. Tokyo: University of Tokyo Press.
Oudiz, Gilles, and Jeffrey D. Sachs. 1984. "Macroeconomic Policy Coordination among the Industrial Economies." *Brookings Papers on Economic Activity* (Brookings Institution, Washington, D.C.) 1: 1–75.
Poehl, Karl Otto. 1987. "Cooperation—A Keystone for the Stability of the International Monetary System." First Arthur Burns Memorial Lecture, at the American Council on Germany, New York, November 2.
Polak, Jacques J. 1981. *Coordination of National Economic Policies.* Occasional Paper no. 7. New York: Group of Thirty.
———. 1988. "Economic Policy Objectives in the Major Industrial Countries and Their Effects on Policymaking." In *Economic Policy Coordination.* Washington, D.C.: International Monetary Fund.
Putnam, Robert D., and Nicholas Bayne. 1984. *Hanging Together: The Seven-Power Summits.* Cambridge, Mass.: Harvard University Press.
Putnam, Robert D., and C. Randall Henning. 1986. "Bonn Summit of 1978: How Does International Economic Policy Coordination Actually Work?" Brookings Discussion Papers in International Economics, no. 53, Brookings Institution, Washington, D.C., October.
Rogoff, Kenneth. 1985. "Can International Monetary Policy Cooperation Be Counterproductive?" *Journal of International Economics* (Amsterdam) 18 (May): 199–217.
Schultze, Charles. 1988. "Prepared Remarks: Macroeconomic Policy." In *International Economic Cooperation,* ed. Martin Feldstein. Chicago: University of Chicago Press.
Stein, Herbert. 1987. "International Coordination of Economic Policy." *The AEI Economist* (American Enterprise Institute, Washington, D.C.), August.
Tanzi, Vito. 1988. "Fiscal Policy and International Coordination: Current and Future Issues." Paper presented at Conference on Fiscal Policy, Economic Adjustment, and Financial Markets, Bocconi University, January 27–30.
Taylor, John. 1986. "An Econometric Evaluation of International Monetary Policy Rules: Fixed versus Flexible Exchange Rates." Stanford University, October. Mimeo.
Tobin, James. 1987. "Agenda for International Coordination of Macroeconomic Policies." In Volcker et al. (1987), 61–69.
Triffin, Robert. 1960. *Gold and the Dollar Crisis: The Future of Convertibility.* New Haven, Conn.: Yale University Press.
U.S. Congress. 1982. *Report to the Congress of the Commission on the Role of Gold in the Domestic and International Monetary Systems.* Washington, D.C.: Government Printing Office, March.
Vaubel, Roland. 1985. "International Collusion or Competition for Macroeconomic Policy Coordination? A Restatement." *Recherches Economiques de Louvain* 51 (December): 223–40.

Volcker, Paul A., et al. 1987. *International Monetary Cooperation: Essays in Honor of Henry C. Wallich.* Essays in International Finance, no. 169. Princeton, N.J.: Princeton University Press, December.

Wallich, Henry C. 1984. "Institutional Cooperation in the World Economy." In *The World Economic System: Performance and Prospects,* ed. Jacob Frenkel and Michael Mussa, 85–99. Dover, Mass.: Auburn House.

Williamson, John. 1985. *The Exchange Rate System.* Policy Analyses in International Economics, no. 5. 2d ed. Washington, D.C.: Institute for International Economics.

Williamson, John, and Marcus H. Miller. 1987. *Targets and Indicators: A Blueprint for the International Coordination of Economic Policy.* Policy Analyses in International Economics, no. 22. Washington, D.C.: Institute for International Economics, September.

About the Contributors

**Rudiger Dornbusch,** Ford International Professor of Economics at the Massachusetts Institute of Technology, was born in Germany and was trained at the University of Geneva and the Graduate Institute of International Studies in Geneva. He received a Ph.D. in economics from the University of Chicago. After teaching at the University of Rochester and the University of Chicago, Dr. Dornbusch joined the MIT Department of Economics in 1975. He is the author of *Expectations and Exchange-rate Dynamics*, a classic work in the theory of exchange rates.

**Steve Marcus,** an investment banker in Geneva, founded Norit S.A., an asset-management and financial-services firm. He is president of the Israeli International Institute for Applied Economic Policy Review, established in 1987 to provide position papers and policy-oriented research on central issues of immediate concern—primarily those likely to become important in the short and medium run. An independent, nonprofit organization, the Institute focuses analysis and research on the Israeli economy and the international economic arena. As part of its regular activities, it holds symposiums and seminars with leading members of government, the business community, and academia.

**Stanley Fischer,** on leave from the Massachusetts Institute of Technology, is vice president, development economics, and chief economist of the World Bank. Born in Lusaka, Zambia, Dr. Fischer earned both B.S. and M.S. degrees in economics at London University. He received his Ph.D. from MIT in 1969 and, before becoming a professor of economics there, was a postdoctoral fellow at the University of Chicago; taught at Hebrew University, Jerusalem; and was a visiting scholar at the Hoover Institution.

**Jacob A. Frenkel** is the economic counsellor and director of research of the International Monetary Fund. Before assuming his position with the IMF, he was David Rockefeller Professor of International Economics at the University of Chicago and had also held academic posts at Hebrew University and Tel Aviv University, Israel. Born in Israel, Dr. Frenkel earned a B.A. in economics and political science from Hebrew University and received a Ph.D. in economics in 1970 from the University of Chicago. He is the author of several books and numerous articles and is a member of the Group of Thirty.

**Morris Goldstein** is the deputy director of the Research Department of the International Monetary Fund. He has been a member of the Fund staff since 1970 and has also served as senior technical advisor in the U.S. Treasury Department, as visiting research associate at the London School of Economics, and as a research fellow at the Brookings Institution. Dr. Goldstein received a B.A. in economics from Rutgers University in 1966 and a Ph.D. in economics from New York University in 1971. He has published widely on the international monetary system, empirical trade equations, and the effects of IMF adjustment programs.

**Pierre Jacquet** is a graduate of the Ecole Polytechnique and of the Ecole Nationale des Ponts et Chaussées, Paris. He belongs to the higher civil service Corps des Ponts et Chaussées. After working as a project analyst and consultant on African energy projects with the French development bank, he joined the French Institute of International Relations (IFRI) and in 1985 became an associate director of IFRI and head of economic studies. He is currently a lecturer at the Ecole Polytechnique and has been since 1987 a professor of international economics at the Institut d'Etudes Politiques de Paris.

**Roberto Junguito** was Colombia's minister of finance in the administration of Belisario Betancur. He has had an outstanding policy career, having been his country's minister of agriculture, ambassador to the

European Economic Community, and ambassador to France, as well as finance minister. He studied at the Universidad de los Andes in Bogotá, the London School of Economics, and the Université Libre de Bruxelles and earned an advanced degree from Princeton University. He is president of the board of Banco Sudameris, Bogotá, and serves as president of the Colombian Association of Coffee Exporters.

**Anne O. Krueger** is Arts and Sciences Professor of Economics at Duke University. During the first several years of the debt crisis, she was vice president, economics and research, at the World Bank. She has also been professor of economics at the University of Minnesota, a research associate of the National Bureau of Economic Research, and director of the NBER projects on alternative trade strategies and employment and on U.S. trade relations. Dr. Krueger is the editor of *Development with Trade: LDCs and the International Economy*, published by ICEG in 1988.

**Paul R. Masson** is an advisor in the Research Department of the International Monetary Fund. Before his appointment to the IMF, he held posts at the Organization for Economic Cooperation and Development in Paris and at the Bank of Canada in Ottawa. Born in Montreal, he received a B.A. from McGill University and a Ph.D. in economics from the London School of Economics and Political Science. He has published extensively in the areas of international macroeconomic modeling, exchange rate determination, and the effects of monetary and fiscal policies.

**Thierry de Montbrial** was born in Paris and is a graduate of the Ecole Polytechnique and Ecole des Mines. He earned a Ph.D. in economics from the University of California, Berkeley. He is professor of economics and chairman of the Department of Economics at the Ecole Polytechnique. He is also a professor at the Institut d'Etudes Politiques in Paris. He has been first director of the Policy Planning Staff in the French Ministry of Foreign Affairs; and in 1979 he founded the French Institute of International Relations (IFRI), of which he is director. He is the author of several books in economics and international affairs.

**Wolfgang Rieke** is head of the International Department of the Deutsche Bundesbank. He was born in Hamburg and earned a diploma in economics from Hamburg University and a doctorate from Kiel University, where he studied in the Institute for World Economics. Dr. Rieke has also served in the Economics and Statistics Directorate of the Organization for European Economic Cooperation, in Paris, and in the European Department of the International Monetary Fund.

**Jesús Silva-Herzog** is director of the Centro de Estudios Monetarios Latinoamericanos, Mexico City. During the first years of the debt crisis, he was Mexico's minister of finance and public credit. He had earlier served as director general of the National Housing Fund Institute for Wage-Earners, general manager of the Banco de Mexico, and deputy minister of finance. He studied at the National School of Economics of the University of Mexico and holds a graduate degree from Yale University. He is the author of ICEG Occasional Paper no. 17, *Some Problems in Implementing Economic Policy*.

**Alexander K. Swoboda** is professor of international economics at the Graduate Institute of International Studies in Geneva and director of the International Center for Monetary and Banking Studies. He is also professor of economics at the University of Geneva. Dr. Swoboda received his Ph.D. from Yale University and has taught in the Graduate School of Business at the University of Chicago, the Johns Hopkins School of Advanced International Studies in Bologna, the London School of Economics and Political Science, and Harvard University. Dr. Swoboda has published widely on international financial problems.

# INDEX

Adjustment program, Colombia
　elements of, 68–77
　sequence of events in, 62, 67–68
African countries. *See* Sub-Saharan
　African (SSA) countries
Agreements for debt relief, 21
Alfonsín, Raúl, 16
Artis, Michael, 148, 180n1

Baker, James, 12, 105
Baker Plan, 12, 76, 106
Balance of payments, Colombia, 67, 70–72
Bank for International Settlements (BIS)
　bridge loan for Mexico of, 55–56
　creation and goals of, 131
　framework for central bank cooperation of, 83, 127
　role in bank cooperation of, 122, 127
Banks, central
　cooperation under Bretton Woods regime of, 83–86, 132–35
　coordination in IMF system by, 82–83
　factors influencing cooperation of, 86–87, 120–22
　historical cooperation activity of, 120, 129–32
　independence of, 124–25
　role in Mexican debt crisis of, 55–56
　swap network cooperation of, 83–84
　*See also* Cooperation, international; Policy coordination, international
Banks, commercial
　lending practices of, 12, 32–33, 37, 53
　role in debt reduction of, 22, 48–49
　role in debt servicing of, 11–12
　role in loans to Colombia of, 74–77
　role in Mexican debt crisis of, 38–40, 56–57
　use of oil revenues by, 31, 37
Basel-Nyborg Accord (1987), 110–11
Baxter, M., 6
Bayne, Nicholas, 181nn 16, 17
Bérégevoy, Pierre, 110

193

Betancur, Belasario, 62–63, 72, 75
BIS. *See* Bank for International Settlements (BIS)
Blumenthal, Michael W., 175n8
Bocklemann, H., 180n11
Bonn economic summit (1978), 87, 104, 148, 181n16
Brady Plan
 commercial debt focus of, 23
 debt relief agreements using, 20–21
 elements and focus of, 11–14
 eligibility for, 22, 26
 mechanisms created by, 19
 role of IMF and World Bank in activity of, 22
 support funds for, 21
Brainard, William C., 158–59
Brazil, 37
Bretton Woods
 capital flows under regime of, 29–31
 central bank cooperation under, 132–35
 effect of breakdown of, 101
 exchange rate fluctuations under, 5
 implicit contract under, 156
 international coordination provisions of, 82–84, 88, 101–2
 lessons of, 134–35
Bridge loans, 168n15. *See also* Bank for International Settlements (BIS)
Bryant, Ralph, 147, 180nn 3, 14, 183nn 48, 53
Buchanan, James, 128
Budget deficit
 in Colombia, 63, 74
 in the United States, 89–90
Buiter, Willem H., 181n24

Calvo, Guillermo, 181n25
Canada, 23
Capital flight. *See* Flight capital, role in Central America of
Capital flows
 effects of, 8–9
 into indebted countries, 43
 from Mexico, 21, 52–53
 perceptions of, 28–31
Carrasquilla, A., 171n1

Cartagena Group, 72
Clarke, Steven V. O., 130, 131, 176n4
Cline, William, 168n21
Colombia
 balance of payments problem of, 70
 domestic debt in, 76
 economic adjustment program of, 67–77
 economic performance of, 76–77
 economic policy of, 63–64
 fiscal adjustment in, 68–69
 *See also* Debt, external
Committee of Twenty, 133–34
Commodity Credit Corporation, U.S., 56
Commodity prices
 depressed, 43
 volatility of, 5
Concorde loan, 76
Contadora Group, 63
Cooper, Richard N., 144, 148, 165n1, 180n1, 182n31
Cooperation, international
 in 1985, 105–6
 of central banks within EMS structure, 113
 under emergency and normal conditions, 125–29
 with floating exchange rates, 101–2
 IMF requirements for, 102–3
 importance of, 115–16
 for monetary policy, 98–99, 102–5
 *See also* Bank for International Settlements (BIS); Banks, central
Coordination. *See* Policy coordination, international
Corden, W. Max, 180nn 4, 5
Currency
 devaluation in Colombia, 70–71
 devaluation in Mexico, 53–55
 *See also* Exchange rates
Current account
 deficit of United States in, 90–91
 policy coordination to balance, 88
Current account equilibrium model, 96–98
Currie, David, 162
Cyclical unevenness, international, 88

Debt, domestic. *See* Colombia
Debt, external
 of Colombia, 64, 67, 70–77
 commercial and official categories of, 23
 of countries outside existing mechanisms, 24
 of countries with official debt, 24–25
 crisis related to, 10, 14–15, 26–27, 33–38, 48–49
 of developing countries, 19–20, 31–36
 errors in diagnosing, 42–44
 factors regulating developing country, 19–20
 participants in negotiations of, 77
 reduction and forgiveness for, 20–24
 rescheduling and forgiveness of official, 23
 rescheduling of commercial bank, 46–47
 response to crisis related to, 38–44
 service by Colombia of, 72
 service by Mexico of, 37–38, 39–40
 servicing problems of, 11–15, 34, 37, 40–42
 tools for crisis in, 23–25
 *See also* Baker Plan; Brady Plan; Innovation; Mexico; Development assistance, official (ODA)
de la Rosière, Jacques, 39, 60
Delors, Jacques, 177n26
Democratic governments, Latin America, 15–16
Developing countries
 debt-servicing problems of, 40–42
 economic performance of, 43
 loans from commercial banks to, 32–33
 official lending to, 29–31
 as oil importers, 31–32
 reaction to oil price shock in, 31–32
 role of international agencies in, 44–45
Development assistance, official (ODA), 25
de Vries, Margaret 167n9, 168n15
Diaz-Alejandro, Carlos, 167n10
Dini, Laberto, 150, 181n15

Discretion. *See* Policy coordination, international
Dollar, need for stability of, 102

Economic policy
 externalities of, 144–46
 importance of United States, 102
 international cooperation in, 105
 lack of adjustment mechanism for, 8–10
 reform for Latin American, 14–15
 *See also* Columbia; Policy coordination, international; Trade policy
Economy, model of world, 96–98
Edison, Hali J., 91, 98
Eichengreen, Barry, 129, 157, 177n12
Einaudi, Luigi, 15
Einzig, Paul, 177n11
EMS. *See* European Monetary System (EMS)
European and Economic Monetary Union, 115, 135
European Currency Unit (ECU), 104
European Economic Community (EEC)
 establishment of, 135
 role in exchange rate policy of, 113
European Monetary System (EMS)
 coordinated intervention of, 113
 as coordination mechanism, 147
 currency realignments of, 110–11, 112–13, 157
 for exchange rates, 104–5
 hegemony versus symmetry in, 157
 implicit contract under, 156–57
 influence of, 112
 lessons of, 135–37
 role of, 101–2, 104, 110
 as rule-based system, 102
 *See also* Basel-Nyborg Accord (1987)
Exchange rates
 adjustments in Colombia of, 64, 67–68, 70–71
 central banks' role in system of (1920s), 129–30
 conditions for stability of, 116
 developed and developing country systems of, 33–34

Exchange rates (*continued*)
European "snake" stabilization system for, 101, 104
fixed, 8, 33–34
flexible or floating, 8–9, 134, 146
in Mexico, 52–55
misalignment of, 6–7
required management for, 121
volatility of, 4, 4–121
*See also* Real exchange rates
Exchange rate system
conditions for stability of, 114
EMS and stability of, 101–2, 104, 110
IMF provisions for, 102
U.S. intervention in, 105
Export promotion, Colombia, 71

Feldstein, Martin, 143, 146, 148, 158, 168–69n21, 180n4, 183n53
Fiscal policy
in Germany and Japan, 90
impact of United States, 89–90, 123
for international policy coordination, 98–99
*See also* Columbia; Tax system
Fischer, Stanley, 168n19, 180nn 1, 8, 181n15, 182n33
Fleming, J. Marcus, 180n3
Flight capital, role in Central America of, 13–15
Flood, Robert, 182n36
France, 23
Frankel, Jeffrey, 7, 9, 160, 161, 180n14
Frenkel, Jacob, 110, 153, 154, 180nn 3, 8, 12, 181n19, 182nn 34, 35, 37, 42
Friedman, Benjamin M., 176n2
Froot, Kenneth, 7
Funabashi, Yoichi, 137, 139, 178nn 28, 30

Garay, L., 171n1
Garber, Peter, 182n36
Gavin, Michael, 180n7
Genberg, Hans, 91, 92, 173nn 1, 2, 3
General Agreement to Borrow (GAB), 83–84, 133
Genoa conference (1922), 129, 130
Germany, 23
Ghosh, Atish, 159, 161, 183nn 47, 54

Ghosh, Swati, 159, 183n54
Giavazzi, F., 174n4, 182nn 32, 43
Giovannini, A., 174n4, 182nn 32, 43
Gold pool, 83–84, 132
Gold standard
as hegemonic system, 157
specie-flow mechanism of, 153
as stabilization mechanism, 130–32
Gold Standard Act (1925), Great Britain, 130
Goldstein, Morris, 110, 153, 154, 180n9, 182nn 37, 42
Group of Five (G5), 106
Group of Seven (G7)
coordination work of, 151–52, 156
Louvre Accord policy of, 88, 106–7
role in Plaza and Louvre agreements of, 137–40
Group of Ten (G10), 83, 127
role in international economics of, 133
Group of Thirty, 87

Hamada, Koichi, 180n1
Hegemony in coordination, 156–58
Heller, H. Robert, 180n10
Helliwell, John, 180nn 3, 14
Henning, C. Randall, 148
HICs. *See* Highly indebted countries (HICs)
Highly indebted countries (HICs), 20
effect of debt relief agreements for, 22
withdrawal of credit to, 25
Holtham, Gerald, 155, 160–61, 183n46
Hope, Nicholas, 167n1
Horne, Jocelyn, 180n1
Hughes Hallett, Andrew, 160–61
Human capital investment, Latin America, 15

IBRD. *See* International Bank for Reconstruction and Development (IBRD)
IDA. *See* International Development Association (IDA)
IFIs. *See* International financial institutions (IFIs)
IMF. *See* International Monetary Fund (IMF)

IMF–World Bank meetings (Berlin: 1988), 23–24
Import licensing, Colombia, 63
Indicators
  economic, 151
  policy, 154–56
Innovation
  in financing, 25–26, 46, 121
  institutional, 46
Inter-American Development Bank (IDB), 60
Interim Committee, IMF, 134, 149
International Bank for Reconstruction and Development (IBRD)
  and Colombian debt arrangements, 74–76
  establishment and role of, 29
  *See also* International Development Association (IDA); World Bank
International Development Association (IDA)
  concessional funds of, 23–24
  establishment and role of, 30
International financial institutions (IFIs), 22
  *See also* Multilateral institutions
International Monetary Fund (IMF)
  and adjustment program for Mexico, 52, 53
  Articles of Agreement of, 102, 114, 134
  design of system for, 82–84
  Group of Ten within, 133
  interaction with commercial banks of, 46–47
  interaction with World Bank of, 44–45
  Interim Committee of, 149
  role during 1970s of, 33–36
  role in Colombian debt crisis of, 61, 74–76
  role in debt relief of, 20–21, 34–36, 44–48
  role in Mexican debt crisis of, 39–40, 60
  rule-based cooperation required by, 102–3, 104
  Special Drawing Rights (SDRs) of, 85
  standby agreement with Colombia of, 74–76
  structural adjustment funds of, 23
  *See also* Bretton Woods
Intervention, coordinated
  effect of, 134
  within EMS, 113
Investment, foreign direct, 25
  *See also* Capital flows
Investment in human capital, 15
Ito, T., 7

Jacquet, Pierre, 177n20
Jamaica agreement (1976), 134
Japan, 21
Junguito, Roberto, 67, 74, 172n5
Jurgensen, Philippe, 182n40

Keating, Giles, 155, 183n46
Kenen, Peter B., 176n10, 180n1, 182nn 28, 32
Kindleberger, Charles, 85, 126, 130, 131, 177n19
Kraft, Joseph, 168nn 13, 15
Krueger, Anne O., 167nn 4, 7, 169n23
Krugman, Paul, 6, 169n22
Kydland, F., 181n25

Lamfalussy, Alexandre, 183n53
Levine, Paul, 162
López Portillo, José, 56
Lora, E., 64, 171n1
Louvre Accord, 88, 106–7, 149
  as example of policy coordination, 137–40

McKibbin, Warwick J., 183n52
McMurray, David, 167n1
Marjolin, Robert, 135
Marshall Plan, 29
Marston, Richard C., 181n24
Masson, Paul R., 110, 159, 161, 180n1, 183nn 47, 54
Meade, James, 91
Menem, Carlos, 16
Mexico
  debt crisis of, 37–42, 53–59, 62
  debt relief agreement of, 21–22

Mexico (*continued*)
  economic performance of, 52–53, 57–58
  effect of oil price changes on, 52–53
  Multiyear Rescheduling Agreement (MYRA) for, 46
  oil boom in, 52, 57
MIGA (Multilateral Investment Guarantee Agency). *See* World Bank
Miller, Marcus, 7, 9, 91, 98, 182nn 37, 41
Model uncertainty, 158–63
Monetary policy and international coordination, 85–88
Monetary system, proposed reform of international, 133–34
Mulford, David, 176n6
Multifibre Arrangement, 47
Multilateral institutions
  Colombia's obligations to, 61
  lending activity of, 12, 23–25
  *See also* International financial institutions (IFIs)
Multiyear Rescheduling Agreement (MYRA), 46
Mundell, Robert, 8, 85, 145, 177n25, 180n3
Mundell-Fleming condition, 92
Mussa, Michael, 180n3, 182n40
MYRA. *See* Multiyear Rescheduling Agreement (MYRA)

Nau, Henry, 178n34
Niehans, Jurg, 180n4, 182n33
Norman, Montague, 131

Ocampo, J. A., 64, 171n1
ODA. *See* Official development assistance (ODA)
Official debt. *See* Multilateral institutions
Official development assistance (ODA), 20
  availability of resources of, 25
Oil-exporting countries, 31
Oil price increase
  first, 31–36
  second, 36–38

Organization for Economic Cooperation and Development (OECD)
  Economic Policy Committee of, 133
  Working Party 3 (WP3) of, 83, 127, 133
Ostry, Sylvia, 148, 180n1
Oudiz, Gilles, 161, 183n52

Padmore, Tim, 180nn 3, 14
Padoa Schioppa, Tommaso, 136
Paris Club, 35, 37, 38
the Philippines, 21
Pinochet, Augusto, 16
Plaza agreement, 88, 105–6, 121
  as example of policy coordination, 137–40
Poehl, Karl Otto, 180n4, 181n26
Polak, Jacques J., 147, 180n1, 182nn 28, 33
Policy coordination in Colombian debt crisis, 70–77
Policy coordination, international
  adjusting scope of, 148–52
  barriers to, 146–48
  choice of single or multiple indicators for, 154
  discretion-based approach to, 152–55
  effect on central banks of, 121
  effects of uncertainty in, 158–60
  with emergency cooperation, 126–28
  EMS example of, 111–12
  hegemonic versus symmetrical approach, 156–58
  IMF provisions for, 102–3
  impact of fiscal policy and saving-investment on, 98
  importance of, 115–16
  incentives for, 111
  to internalize externalities, 144–46
  international organizations practicing, 149
  model for analysis of, 92–95
  with model uncertainty, 158–63
  Plaza and Louvre examples of, 137–40
  recommendations for, 99
  role of central banks in, 81–88

rule-based approach for, 102, 152–53
  using policy indicators in, 154–56
  *See also* Bretton Woods; Louvre Accord; Plaza agreement
Policy coordination model
  conclusions of, 93–95
  elements of, 91–93
Prescott, E., 181n25
Privatization, 14
Protectionist measures
  of Colombia, 71
  of industrialized countries, 43, 47
  *See also* Multifibre Arrangement
Public goods, 145–46
Putnam, Robert D., 148, 181nn 16, 17

Rational-speculation paradigm, 6–7
Razin, Assaf, 180n3, 181n19
Reagan, Ronald, 75
Reagan administration, 12
Real exchange rates, 4–5
Recession
  effect of, 43
Regan, Donald, 55, 105
Rockett, Katherine, 9, 160, 161, 180n14
Rogoff, Kenneth, 134, 146
Rule-based approach to policy coordination, 152–55

Sachs, Jeffrey, 161, 183n52
Schact, Hjalmar, 131
Schultze, Charles, 147, 183n53
Self-discipline, national, 113–17
Sievert, Olaf, 175n10
Smithsonian agreement (1971), 133, 150
Solomon, Robert, 132, 134, 177nn 13, 17
SPA. *See* Special Program of Assistance (SPA)
Special Program of Assistance (SPA), 23–24
Spencer, Peter, 155, 183n46
Spending, government
  austerity in Colombia for, 69
  requirement to cut, 14
SSA countries. *See* Sub-Saharan African (SSA) countries

Stallings, Barbara, 171n4 (ch.5)
State-owned enterprises, Latin America, 14
Stein, Herbert, 180n4
Stockman, A., 6
Strong, Benjamin, 130, 131
Sub-Saharan African (SSA) countries
  concessional assistance to, 31
  rescheduling official debt of, 23–24
Summers, Lawrence, 7
Swap arrangements, 54, 83–84, 104, 132
Swoboda, Alexander K., 8, 91, 173nn 1, 2, 3
Symmetry in coordination, 156–58

Tanzi, Vito, 155, 180n13, 182n40
Tariffs, Colombia, 71
Tax system
  reform of, 14
  reform in Colombia of, 68–69
Taylor, John, 183n52
Tinbergen, Jan, 91
Tinbergen-Meade principle, 91
Tobin, James, 7, 143
Toronto summit agreement, 23–24
  rescheduling options under, 166n1
Trade policy
  of Colombia, 63–64
  of developing countries, 34
  of industrialized countries, 47
  liberalization in Colombia of, 71
  liberalization in world of, 121
Treaty of Rome (1957), 135
Triffin, Robert, 156
Tripartite Agreement (1936), 131
Turkey, 37

Uncertainty in policy coordination, 158–60
United States
  cooperative efforts of, 105–6
  debt forgiveness by, 23
  impact of monetary and fiscal policy of, 85, 122–23
  role in Colombian debt arrangements of, 74–75
  role in Mexican debt crisis of, 54, 55–57, 59–60

Vaubel, Roland, 180n4, 182n27
Vidalis, Nicholas, 162
Volcker, Paul, 60, 75

Wallich, Henry C., 111, 143–44, 180n1
Williamson, John, 7, 9, 91, 98, 182nn 37, 41
Wolfensohn, James D., 175n11
World Bank, 24
  establishment of, 30
  interaction with IMF of, 35–36, 44–45
  Multilateral Investment Guarantee Agency (MIGA) of, 25
  role in debt relief of, 20–22, 35–36, 44–48
  role in developing countries of, 44
  role in Mexican debt crisis of, 60
  Special Program of Assistance (SPA) of, 23–24
World Monetary and Economic Conference (1933), 131

# ICEG Academic Advisory Board

Abel G. Aganbegyan
*Academy of Sciences of the USSR, USSR*

Michael J. Boskin*
*Stanford University, USA*

Hakchung Choo
*Asian Development Bank, Philippines*

Rudiger Dornbusch
*Massachusetts Institute of Technology, USA*

Ernesto Fontaine
*Pontificia Universidad Católica de Chile, Chile*

Herbert Giersch
*Kiel Institute of World Economics, Germany*

Francisco Gil Díaz
*Ministry of Finance, Mexico*

Malcolm Gillis
*Duke University, USA*

Arnold C. Harberger
*University of Chicago, USA*

Helen Hughes
*Australian National University, Australia*

Shinichi Ichimura
*Osaka International University, Japan*

Glenn Jenkins
*Harvard Institute for International Development, USA*

D. Gale Johnson
*University of Chicago, USA*

Roberto Junguito
*Banco Sudameris, Colombia*

Yutaka Kosai
*Japan Center for Economic Research, Japan*

Anne O. Krueger
*Duke University, USA*

Deepak Lal
*University College London, United Kingdom*

Ronald I. McKinnon
*Stanford University, USA*

Charles E. McLure, Jr.
*Hoover Institution, USA*

Gerald M. Meier
*Stanford University, USA*

Seiji Naya
*Resource Systems Institute, East-West Center, USA*

Juan Carlos de Pablo
*DEPABLOCONSULT, Argentina*

Affonso Pastore
*Universidade de São Paulo, Brazil*

Gustav Ranis
*Yale University, USA*

Michael Roemer
*Harvard Institute for International Development, USA*

Leopoldo Solís
*Instituto de Investigación Económica y Social Lucas Alamán, Mexico*

David Wall
*University of Sussex, United Kingdom*

Richard Webb
*Pontificia Universidad Católica del Perú, Peru*

James Worley
*Vanderbilt University, USA*

\* on leave